First published in Great Britain 1992 by
THE MACMILLAN PRESS LTD
Houndmills, Basingstoke, Hampshire RG21 2XS
and London
Companies and representatives
throughout the world

This book is published by Macmillan in association with the School of Slavonic and East European Studies, University of London, in their joint series *Studies in Russia and East Europe*.
Chairman of the editorial board: M. A. Branch, Director, SSEES

A catalogue record for this book is available
from the British Library

ISBN 0–333–48452–5

Printed in Great Britain by
Antony Rowe Ltd, Chippenham, Wiltshire

First published in the United States of America 1992 by
Scholarly and Reference Division,
ST. MARTIN'S PRESS, INC.,
175 Fifth Avenue,
New York, N.Y. 10010

ISBN 0–312–07580–4

Library of Congress Cataloging-in-Publication Data
Economy and society in Russia and the Soviet Union, 1860–1930: essays for Olga Crisp / edited by Linda Edmondson and Peter Waldron.
p. cm.
Papers presented at a colloquium in honour of Olga Crisp's retirement held in London at the School of Slavonic and East European Studies, in 1987.
Includes bibliographical references and index.
ISBN 0–312–07580–4
1. Soviet Union—Economic conditions—1861–1917—Congresses.
2. Soviet Union—Economic conditions—1918– —Congresses. 3. Soviet Union—Economic policy—Congresses. I. Crisp, Olga.
II. Edmondson, Linda Harriet. III. Waldron, Peter. IV. University of London. School of Slavonic and East European Studies.
HC334.5.E33 1992
330.947—dc20 91–37444
CIP

10 9 8 7 6 5 4 3 2
04 03 02 01 00 99 98 97 96

Contents

List of Figures

Preface

This collection of essays arose from a desire to pay a fitting tribute to Olga Crisp, as scholar, teacher and colleague, on the occasion of her retirement in 1986 from her chair in Russian economic history at the School of Slavonic and East European Studies in London. It was decided to organise a colloquium, which took place at the School the following year; the quality of the papers and the vigour of the ensuing discussions bore witness to the great esteem in which Olga Crisp is held by scholars around the world, and encouraged us to prepare these essays for publication as a book.

Olga Crisp was born in Poland in 1921 and grew up in the city of Lwów. After the war she came to England and made her home in London, creating a completely new life for herself in this country. She resumed the studies that she had had to abandon during the war and registered as a mature student at the School, graduating with first-class honours in 1948. Among her student colleagues was one of the contributors to the present volume, Bob Davies. After a course in librarianship and archive management at the University of London, she embarked on her PhD, again at the School. Her thesis was a study of the financial aspects of the Franco-Russian alliance from 1894–1914. While completing her thesis, she was appointed as a lecturer at the School, where she taught until her retirement.

It is true to say that Olga Crisp's scholarship is held in the very highest regard by historians of Russia from all backgrounds. An insistence on laying bare the sinews of a problem and then subjecting it to rigorous analysis is the hallmark of her work. This approach has allowed her to question some of the fundamental tenets of Russian economic history and to present interpretations based on deep knowledge of the sources and on original and vibrant thought. While her work has been focused on economic issues, her profound appreciation of the political and social history of imperial Russia and the Soviet Union has served to illuminate her writing and to give her especial insight into the way in which the economy operated.

The lasting work that Olga Crisp has done lies in her essays

Notes on the Contributors

John Channon lectures on the economic and social history of Russia and the USSR at the School of Slavonic and East European Studies, University of London, and was educated at the Universities of Leeds and Birmingham. He has published on Russian and Soviet agrarian history, and is currently working on a study of Soviet agriculture under Gorbachev.

R.W. Davies is Emeritus Professor of Soviet Economic Studies at the Centre for Russian and East European Studies, University of Birmingham, and was formerly Director of the Centre. He specialises in Soviet economic history and the contemporary economy. He is writing a series of volumes on the *Industrialisation of Soviet Russia*, the most recent of which is entitled *Soviet Economy in Turmoil, 1929–1930*. He has recently published *Soviet History in the Gorbachev Revolution*.

Linda Edmondson is ESRC Research Fellow at the Centre for Russian and East European Studies, University of Birmingham. She is the author of *Feminism in Russia, 1900–1917* and co-editor with Olga Crisp of *Civil Rights in Imperial Russia*. She is currently working on an ESRC-funded project to study women's emancipation and theories of sexual difference.

Peter Gatrell is Senior Lecturer in Economic History in the Department of History, University of Manchester. He is the author of *The Tsarist Economy, 1850–1917*. He has recently completed a monograph on armaments, industry and government in Russia, 1900–14.

Paul Gregory is Professor of Economics at the University of Houston. He is the author of *Russian National Income, 1885–1913* and *Restructuring the Soviet Economic Bureaucracy*, and co-author of *Soviet Economic Structure and Performance*.

John P. McKay is Professor of History at the University of Illinois at Urbana-Champaign. His published books and articles focus primarily on Russian and European economic history.

NOTE ON TRANSLITERATI

Transliteration of Russian foll
minor modifications. Personal
according to this system, but
diacritical marks (Kharkov, not
Anglicised form.

Roger Munting is a lecturer in economic and social history at the University of East Anglia in Norwich and was educated at the Universities of Sheffield and Birmingham. He has published several works on Russian and Soviet economic history. These include a number of articles on nineteenth-century Russian agriculture, Anglo-Russian trade, the Soviet economy in World War II and a general work, *The Economic Development of the USSR*.

Alec Nove is Emeritus Professor of Economics and was formerly Director of the Institute of Soviet and East European Studies, University of Glasgow. He is the author of books on the Soviet economy and Soviet history, including *The Soviet Economic System* and *Glasnost′ in Action: Cultural Renaissance in Russia*.

Maureen Perrie is Lecturer in Russian History at the Centre for Russian and East European Studies, University of Birmingham. She is the author of *The Agrarian Policy of the Russian Socialist-Revolutionary Party* and *The Image of Ivan the Terrible in Russian Folklore*. She has also published a number of articles on various aspects of Russian history, from the sixteenth to twentieth centuries. She is currently editing a book on pretenders in early seventeenth-century Russia.

Robert Service is Professor of Russian History and Politics at the School of Slavonic and East European Studies, University of London. He has published books on the Bolshevik party and the Russian Revolution.

Stuart Thompstone is Lecturer in Russian Economic History at the University of Nottingham and was educated at the University of London. He has published articles on Russian economic history and on contemporary Central Asia.

Peter Waldron is Senior lecturer in Modern History at the University of Sunderland. He has published articles on late Imperial Russian history and is the joint author of *The Emergence of the Modern Russian State, 1855–1881*.

Stephen G. Wheatcroft is Director of the Centre for Soviet and East European Studies, Melbourne University, and is an Honorary Research Fellow at the Centre for Russian and

East European Studies,
published extensively on
omic history.

Howard White is Lecture
School of Economics, an
London. He has publishe
Government and is worki
the Revolution of 1917.

Introduction: Olga Crisp's Contribution to the Economic History of Russia

Peter Gatrell

The enormous and singular contribution made by Olga Crisp to Russian economic history can best be appreciated by reflecting on the state in which the subject found itself nearly forty years ago, when she published her first article on the subject. At that time, most scholars were either unwilling or unable to draw upon manuscript sources. In a pioneering doctoral dissertation and her subsequent articles, Olga Crisp used material from French government and bank archives to illuminate the financial history of tsarist Russia at the end of the nineteenth century. In examining the documentary evidence thoroughly, Olga Crisp anticipated other economic historians inside and outside the Soviet Union. Her familiarity with bank archives was matched only by Iosif Gindin, the outstanding Soviet economic historian. From an historiographical point of view, her work proved no less significant. In 1950, the field was dominated by the encyclopedic work of Petr Lyashchenko, large parts of which had recently been translated into English. Lyashchenko's mammoth work had been awarded a Stalin prize (in orthodox fashion, he had painted the Russian economy in sombre colours and emphasised its subordination to foreign capital), and in its monumental size and dullness it was entirely reminiscent of Stalinist architecture. Apart from specialised works on Russian agriculture and peasant society by Pavlovsky and Robinson, the only general surveys of Russian economic history to which the English-speaking student might be referred were a well-informed but out-dated study by James Mavor and a volume by Margaret Miller, which covered the decade before the First World War, but which was essentially an extended commentary on the available statistics.

and partly because of the need to integrate production processes, in order to insure against interruptions in supply.

In an important article on French investment in Russian industry, Olga Crisp established the limits of foreign influence. Foreign interests were divided, rather than unified; the Russian government kept a watchful eye on foreign companies and syndicates; and foreign banks were keen to delegate business to Russian banks, rather than keep them on a tight rein (in any case, tsarist government support to Russian commercial banks allowed them a good deal of leverage vis-à-vis their foreign counterparts).

In seeking to account for the economic liberalism that characterised government policy during the 1860s and 1870s, Olga Crisp anticipated recent work which has stressed the financial burden placed upon the Treasury and State Bank by the great reforms. In these circumstances, the state encouraged 'autonomous' forces, until during the 1880s interventionism once more gained the upper hand, largely in response to the need to boost government revenue by means of tariff protection and to build strategically important railway lines.

Many of Olga Crisp's insights still await full and proper investigation. These include her observations about rural living standards. She has argued – in the opinion of the present writer, convincingly – that peasant purchasing power did not fall after emancipation. Redemption payments, as she points out, were frequently lower than the dues owed formerly to landlords; and incomes increased, because grain prices rose and because newly-built railways allowed grain to be marketed that hitherto lay rotting on the stalk. How, furthermore, can we speak of generalised agrarian crisis, when peasants succeeded in purchasing land? This brings us on to a related aspect of Olga Crisp's work, to which she has recently made an important contribution. In her article on peasant property rights, she argues that peasants drew a conscious distinction between private and commune allotment land, and that wherever possible they maintained a balanced portfolio of both types of land: private land, which was not subject to communal control, and communal land, which gave them security of tenure. All students of Russian economic history would do well to reflect on the implications of the fact that more than two million peasants purchased land with the assistance of the Peasant Land Bank between 1883 and 1914, not to speak of those who purchased by other means. Furthermore, in drawing attention to the provisions in the emancipation decree for the creation of private farms, she opens up a fruitful debate about government and peasant conceptions of property, and about the changes in government attitudes after the 1880s (it will be recalled that legislation in 1893 prevented former serfs from converting their allotments into hereditary holdings, even where they had discharged their redemption debt). Perhaps someone will write a comprehensive study of government economic policy during the important and fascinating years in which Bunge and Vyshnegradskii held office, when the proponents of economic liberalism and conservatism struggled to gain the upper hand, and the latter emerged victorious.

Olga Crisp's contribution has been to highlight business, peasant, landlord and government behaviour, within a high-risk natural environment and a rapidly changing international context. That is to say, in her view one cannot appreciate the motivation and behaviour of individuals or groups without first understanding the unfavourable Russian environment. Next, one must recognise that institutions, as well as the environment, affected the potential for economic activity.

From time to time, the tsarist government did affect the level of savings in Russia, by creaming off resources for military adventure. But it is the interaction between individuals and their environment, and between individuals and prevailing institutions, that is her main concern. She does not believe in environmental determinism, nor does she subscribe to a belief in the overarching role of government or other institutions in Russia.

No doubt, the next few years will see genuine scholarly collaboration between Russian and non-Russian economic historians, rather than the posturing that was designed to buttress this or that preconceived position. Such collaboration should begin by identifying the key hypotheses that are worth testing against the abundant data that exist in Russian government publications and Soviet archives. In drawing up such hypotheses, comparing (for example) the role of financial institutions during the 1890s and the 1900s, re-examining the economic importance of small-scale industry or exploring the profitability of different branches of Russian industry, Olga Crisp's thought-provoking essays will be an obvious starting-point. Although, in her typically modest fashion, Olga Crisp would strenuously deny the fact, she has put all students of the subject greatly and permanently in her debt.

1 Rents, Land Prices and Economic Theory: The Russian Agrarian Crisis

Paul Gregory

THE AGRARIAN CRISIS REVISITED

Established doctrine teaches that Russian agriculture went through an agrarian crisis following the 1861 emancipation. One finds references to the 'agrarian crisis' in the writings of Soviet and Western historians, and there appears to have been a consensus at the end of the nineteenth century that Russia was in the throes of an agrarian crisis. This agrarian crisis manifested itself in a number of forms – declining per capita rural incomes, 'land hunger', the rising incidence of rural poverty, and growing tax arrears. The agrarian crisis is said to be a prime contributor to the peasant unrest of 1902 and 1905–7. It has been argued that the failure of the tsarist regime to solve the agrarian crisis contributed mightily to its downfall. According to this view, Bolshevik revolutionaries were able to form an alliance or *smychka* with disaffected peasants, who had been denied the fruits of economic progress by a regime that had kept it confined to the traditional commune. The tsarist regime offered the peasants a viable form of agriculture too late. The Stolypin reforms of 1906 and 1910 came too late to establish a viable form of private agriculture in Russia.

Whether or not Russia experienced an agrarian crisis is therefore no small matter. This author has contributed to the 'revisionist' writings, which question whether Russian agriculture, *as a whole*, experienced the agrarian crisis described above. Revisionists claim that per capita agricultural output was growing and that peasant living standards were rising along with peasant marketings. This chapter offers some ideas to explain why scholars have come to radically different conclusions concerning the state of Russian agriculture between the emancipation and turn of the century. It also seeks to explain at a somewhat abstract level of analysis why the revisionist view that Russian agriculture *on average* was not in an agrarian crisis is correct. Basically, I argue that Russian communal agriculture operated according to a more flexible set of working arrangements than has been admitted so far, and I offer a different interpretation of the 'land hunger' phenomenon.

In a sense, this chapter offers a synthesis by showing that proponents and critics of the agrarian crisis hypothesis use different types of information, largely for different purposes. Critics of the agrarian crisis hypothesis use primarily macro performance indicators to assess Russian agriculture. These macro indicators have been reconstructed for the purpose of retrospectively evaluating Russian economic growth. Proponents of an agrarian crisis rely on anecdotal information and regional data to explain political and social history rather than reviewing retrospectively the totality of Russian economic development.

RUSSIAN AGRICULTURE AND THE FRONTIER

One basic point must be emphasised at the outset. Russian agriculture had for centuries developed in an extensive manner.[1] The opening of the Russian frontiers via military conquest, expansion into low-density areas inside the periphery, and later by the railways was a major source of growth of agricultural output. Russian agriculture had grown largely through the expansion of cultivated area, not through improvements in productivity. Even the central black-earth zones, on which students of the agrarian crisis have focused, was once a relatively empty agricultural area in which rapid population growth was even encouraged.[2] In this sense, Russian agricultural development followed the typical pattern of an economy with a vast frontier.

Neither the critics nor the proponents of the agrarian crisis suggest that there was a crisis on Russia's agricultural frontiers. The institutional impediments to rational land cultivation which were the purported source of the agrarian crisis were less prominent in the frontier areas. The agricultural development of Western Siberia, for example, appeared to proceed largely on the basis of land freeholdings much like in Western Europe. If the existence of an agrarian crisis depended upon whether frontier agriculture were included in the picture or not, there would be an easy synthesis between the two positions. This appears not to be the case. My finding of positive per capita growth of Russian agricultural output does not appear to hinge upon the inclusion or exclusion of the periphery.[3]

THE AGRARIAN CRISIS ONCE AGAIN

Lazar Volin summarises the remarkable degree of agreement among contemporary observers in the late nineteenth century that the condition of the Russian peasant had actually worsened since the peasant emancipation. Among informed observers writing during this period, the deterioration of peasant living standards over the last quarter century 'required no special demonstration'. To quote a vehement member of the Kharkov Provincial Committee:

> I suppose no one will require from me proof that our countryside is deteriorating. . . . We who live in the countryside can observe directly how, on the one hand, peasant agriculture is becoming impoverished and declining . . . and how, on the other hand, estate agriculture is also declining.[4]

The view that peasant living standards were deteriorating was echoed by prominent scholars and political thinkers of the last quarter of the nineteenth century. There appear to be few cases of social and economic writers who felt that Russian agriculture was progressing on a promising course.[5] For both Lenin and Tugan-Baranovskii, the agrarian crisis played a prominent role in their analyses of the pre-revolutionary economy. Among modern economic writers, Alexander Gerschenkron and Lazar Volin have provided the strongest theoretical and empirical support for the proposition that the condition of the Russian peasantry worsened after the emancipation.[6] Contemporary Soviet scholars of pre-revolutionary agriculture, such as Koval'chenko and Milov and Mironov, take the existence of an agrarian crisis as a confirmed fact.[7]

Relatively little consideration has been given to the fact that a long-term deterioration of peasant living standards, especially during this period of substantial agricultural progress in other countries, would have been a very rare phenomenon, requiring convincing explanation. In such a setting, the burden of proof would appear to be on those arguing for a long-term decline in peasant living standards. The proponents of the agrarian crisis hypothesis maintain that there was an actual decline in real peasant incomes over an extended period of time. They are not talking about the natural ups and downs of agricultural incomes that accompany the natural ups and downs of agricultural prices and agricultural output. Moreover, this crisis was manifesting itself at the very time when the fruits of railway development were being felt, transportation costs were being lowered, world technological progress in agriculture was rapid, and Russian agriculture was being integrated into world markets. It was during this very period that Russia and the United States emerged as the major suppliers of grain to the rest of the world.

The emancipation was necessitated in the first place by a combination of political foreboding over a restless enserfed peasantry and by the conviction that Russian serf agriculture was in a sorry state. To assert that peasant living standards deteriorated, in the long run, even further from the very low starting point of 1861 requires a convincing explanation.

THE GERSCHENKRON MODEL

The Gerschenkron model is well known.[8] I will cover only those points of the model relevant to the present discussion. The significance of the Gerschenkron model is that it supplies the theoretical explanation for the unusual case of a long-term decline in peasant living standards, which as I noted above, should be regarded as a very rare and highly suspect phenomenon.

In the Gerschenkron model, the agrarian crisis was caused by the emancipators' economic and political decision to keep communal agriculture. Land was handed over to the commune, not to peasant households. Moreover, the commune became responsible for the mortgaged value of the land that was ceded to the commune, and it was responsible for making the mortgage (redemption) payments on this land, which it had to collect from the individual peasant families. Political authorities wanted the policing and tax-collection services of the commune, and the gentry wanted cheap labour services, which were to be guaranteed by inadequate land allotments to the commune.

A heavy tax burden, by itself, would not be grounds for predicting a general decline in rural living standards. If the land allotments had gone directly to peasant families and the communal form had been dropped, those peasants having the best farming skills would eventually have bought out other peasants, and a private agriculture based upon medium-scale units would have emerged along with the more viable large estates. Labour would have naturally sought out its highest return, and for many peasant families this would have meant giving up their land and working as farm hands, in the factory, or in rural artisan activities.

The retention of communal agriculture, according to Gerschenkron, made this type of Western European agricultural development impossible. The restrictive features of the commune were too strong.

The emancipation act required that peasant families pay off fully their mortgage responsibilities before being allowed to withdraw their land from the commune. The emancipation act failed to create a capital market for peasant land purchases, which would have allowed them to pay off their redemption obligations. Even if a capital market had existed, the principal which the mortgage payments amortised exceeded prevailing land prices and the capitalised value of yields from the property. In other words, the paying off of mortgage principal was not a viable option for the peasants in the first decades after the emancipation nor would it have made much business sense.

The formal rules of the commune did not encourage productivity improvements. If a peasant family made capital improvements, its investment might benefit another family at the next periodic redistribution. Joint responsibility for debts meant a giant 'free rider' problem in that the more industrious peasant families might have to pay the debts of laggards. Key cultivation decisions, such as when to plant and when to start joint improvement projects, were left up to elected village elders, who often were elected by offering vodka to their supporters. The peasant families that sent their adult members to the city stood to lose land. Periodic redistributions were to be based upon the number of adult family members, so the loss of a family member to the city would reduce the family's claim to land. Because of natural differences in productivity and location, the equity-minded commune would not be able to consolidate land holdings. Instead, peasant family holdings would be comprised of strips of land located in different areas of the commune's land holdings.

According to Gerschenkron, the retention of a communal form of agriculture, overburdened by debt, caused the growth of agricultural output to fall short of the growth of agricultural population. The most widely cited statistic demonstrating this fact is Gerschenkron's assertion that per capita wheat and rye available for domestic consumption in the late 1890s was lower than in the early 1870s. Other aggregate indicators of the agrarian crisis are the growth in peasant tax arrears and rising land prices and rental rates. The strongest and apparently most compelling evidence of an agrarian crisis appears to be the well-documented existence of rural poverty in Russia. This rural poverty was chronicled by the Valuev Commission in the 1870s, by the numerous zemstvo studies of peasant consumption and wealth holdings. The terrible famine of the early 1890s was followed by famines in 1897 and 1901.

The 'revisionists' present a quite different picture of post emancipation Russian agriculture. Revisionist writings include studies by the present author as well as by Raymond Goldsmith, Arcadius Kahan, and Steve Wheatcroft.[9] Relying on aggregate data, they show that per capita agricultural output grew at positive rates. My studies show that per capita output growth rates were roughly comparable to Western Europe. The 'revisionists' contend that agricultural capital stock was growing on a per capita basis, and that farm consumption in kind (a common indicator of peasant living standards) was growing at a rate comparable to per capita national income. My studies show that contrary to the Gerschenkron-Lenin depiction of a 'dual Russian economy' of a backward agricultural and a capitalist industry, agricultural labour productivity grew during the 1880s and 1890s at about 75 per cent of the growth of industrial labour productivity – a ratio not unlike those of Germany and Canada. This 'revisionist' picture of Russian agriculture, it should be noted, is not really new. The most authoritative study of Russian agricultural output (published in 1907 by Lyashchenko) also found a long-term rise in per capita agricultural output and a rise in per capita peasant consumption between the 1870s and 1900.[10] Moreover, N.D. Kondrat´ev (in a 1922 publication) found substantial improvements in cereal yields between 1860 and

1910, and Varzar's output indexes published from his private papers also suggest rising per capita output.[11]

The different interpretations attached to growing agricultural marketings and agricultural exports should be noted. On the one hand, Gerschenkron and Lenin attribute rising marketings to the growing peasant tax burden, which forced marketings out of a reluctant peasantry. The revisionists, on the other hand, interpret rising marketings as an expansion of voluntary exchanges between the countryside and the rest of the world and as a sign of rising prosperity rather than of growing poverty.

ANECDOTAL EVIDENCE IN HISTORICAL ANALYSIS

Much historical analysis rests upon 'anecdotal' evidence. This is true of the study of Russian economic history. By 'anecdotal', I mean the use of what is basically microeconomic evidence for historical analysis. Anecdotal evidence varies in its level of aggregation. The lowest level of aggregation of anecdotal evidence would be travellers' accounts, accounting books from a single farm, or fictional stories relating to rural life. Examples of anecdotal evidence at its highest levels of aggregation would be the various zemstvo studies of rural economic life in different zemstvo regions. In fact, when cumulated, the zemstvo budget studies approximate non-anecdotal evidence. For example, the Valuev Commission succeeded in estimating the average aggregate ratio of redemption values to current land prices for the non-black earth and black earth regions.[12]

It is indeed true that anecdotal evidence, at both its highest and lowest levels of aggregation, captures a part of reality. Yet there are three dangers of generalising to an economy-wide level from anecdotal evidence. First, anecdotal evidence tends naturally to focus on the extreme end of the distribution. If one envisages a distribution of Russian peasant living standards, the collector of anecdotal evidence would be most attracted to either of the extremes of the distribution and not to its central tendency (the mean or mode). Second, anecdotal evidence does not capture secular time trends well. Prominent or catastrophic events (such as famine) justifiably attract the attention of the collector of anecdotal evidence. The impact of the catastrophic event on the consciousness of purveyors of anecdotal evidence is so strong that it is difficult to see secular trends which involve an averaging of periodic catastrophes.

A third source of imprecision is the confounding of relative and absolute trends. Insofar as trends in personal economic welfare tend to be judged in relative rather than absolute terms, it is not unlikely that individuals whose living standards are rising more slowly than others, consider that their living standards have declined in absolute terms. If indeed average rural living standards were rising in Russia in the 1880s and 1890s at the economy-wide average, those who were falling below the average would have assessed trends in their living standards negatively. A related point (which applies particularly to modern users of anecdotal evidence) is that the late nineteenth century was still a relatively brutal time in which to live – with its high rates of infant mortality (which affected noble and peasant alike), periodic famines, and crude transportation network. No one would deny the harshness of Russian peasant life in this period, as viewed from a modern perspective or even from the perspective of contemporary Western Europe. What counts, however, is the rate of improvement from an earlier period.

The purveyor of anecdotal evidence has a very difficult job in discerning trends in means or modes of distributions. Not only must the central tendency of the distribution be properly identified at one point in time (which is difficult because of the attraction of the extremes of the distribution), the central tendencies of the distribution at two distinct points in time must be identified and compared in meaningful units.

An indicator of the inability to perceive trends was the contemporary reception of the 1897 study of A.I. Chuprov and A.S. Posnikov, who estimated that between a quarter and a third of the grain crop was marketed, meaning that the remaining three quarters or two thirds was consumed on the farm. Contemporary observers felt that these ratios were low (and a sign of deteriorating peasant living standards); yet my own study of grain marketings shows that this ratio remained remarkably stable over the years.[13]

The fact that anecdotal evidence, ranging from observations of a single economic unit (such as a peasant family or a gentry farm) to a single regional aggregation, is an unreliable indicator of per capita trends in macrovariables does not detract from the value and weight of such evidence. What relevant decision makers thought at the time when decisions were made is much more important than what statisticians, reconstructing macro events in retrospect, say happened at the macro level. Political events, such as peasant uprisings, occur in specific locations and regions. It is therefore highly relevant that peasant living standards were declining in a region in which civil unrest occurred, even if peasant living standards, on average, were improving throughout the economy.

Despite its inherent unreliability to gauge macroeconomic trends, anecdotal evidence can form a social consensus concerning macroeconomic phenomenon. As Volin writes:

> In belles-lettres, which always reflected accurately the pulse of social thought in pre-Soviet Russia, the theme of rural distress was taken up by outstanding writers of the period, such as Gleb Uspenskii and Zlatovratskii, and later Chekhov. Perhaps the best portrayal came from the pen of A.N. Engelhardt . . . who in the late seventies depicted rural poverty in his celebrated *Iz derevni* (From the Countryside).[14]

Volin writes further about the remarkable social consensus that existed among numerous observers of rural conditions of the growing destitution of the village. Volin cites numerous other sources of evidence to support the view of deteriorating living conditions in the countryside. One is the valuable census of livestock in the Kromskoi district of Orel province in central Russia taken in both 1887 and 1901. The censuses show a decline in livestock holdings per family between the two census dates. Zemstvo commissions documented the prevalence of epidemics and unsanitary conditions under which peasants lived. They have also documented the malnutrition of the peasant diet in many districts and the high rates of infant mortality among peasant families.

As these accounts show, there were appalling cases of rural poverty in Russia at the turn of the century. The existence of rural poverty in a particular time and place, however, does not necessarily yield accurate evidence about its trend over time or about its spatial distribution. The evidence cited by Peter Gatrell, for example, shows that agricultural decline was especially prominent in the central black earth region, whereas agriculture was expanding in other regions, especially on the periphery.[15] In the natural course of economic events, there will be rising and declining regional economic fortunes. As Gatrell points out, the declining agricultural fortunes of the central black earth region were being offset by the rising fortunes of Western Siberia and the Baltic provinces.

The best available data on agricultural output, marketings and population (compiled by myself, Goldsmith and Wheatcroft) yield a picture quite different from that presented by the anecdotal or regional data. For agriculture as a whole, output per capita was rising, marketings were rising in absolute terms and were relatively stable as a share of output, and retained farm consumption was rising (and also stable as a share of output).

Aggregate data reveal mean performance. The mean smooths out differences on the tails of the distributions. Belles lettres naturally focus on the lower tail of the distribution. Government commissions are usually organised to study problems, not to record successes. They focus on the lower tail of the distribution as well.

WHY WAS AVERAGE AGRICULTURAL PERFORMANCE IMPROVING?

If one accepts the aggregate data on Russian agricultural performance, one must ask why per capita agricultural output, marketings and living standards were rising *on average*? The case made by Gerschenkron, Lenin, Tugan-Baranovskii that conditions were not favourable for agricultural improvements really consists of two points related to communal agriculture and the emancipation. The first point is that the village commune was a severe obstacle standing in the way of productivity improvements. The second point (and apparently there was a social consensus on this issue) was that the heavy debt burden placed on the peasantry by the redemption debt and by the small allotments of land made it impossible for the peasant to accumulate the reserves required to raise agricultural productivity.

The Flexibility of the Commune

In its formal legal form, the Russian commune, both before and after the emancipation, could not have been set up in a worse form for raising productivity. Periodic redistribution, strong equity notions, and collective responsibility, *if strictly observed*, should have offered strong impediments to productivity improvements. The real issue, however, is not the formal rules of the commune, but its actual operating arrangements. Those scholars who take the position that the commune actually operated according to its legal rules are implicitly accepting the populist arguments of Chayanov that Russian peasants did not act as rational economic agents, but rather operated according to an unusual set of rules that caused them to satisfy and to give priority to equity considerations.[16]

The alternative approach would be to assume that Russian peasants generally observed the rules of neoclassical behaviour. They sought out profit opportunities, and acted as utility maximisers. If this assumption is correct, then the neoclassical model would predict that many of the formal rules of the commune would have been overridden by economic considerations.

If the commune indeed distributed land in a manner uncorrelated with peasant farming skills (such as the initial emancipation distribution), there would have been a number of incentives for a redistribution to occur among peasant households on the basis of informal agreements and side payments. The more able farmers would have offered the less able farmers incentives to cultivate the latter's land on terms that would increase the welfare of both parties. A mutually-beneficial exchange of this sort would have given the less able farmer the opportunity to employ his labour elsewhere more productively. Side payments could have varied from the use of draught-animals, to a share of the crop, to a money payment. With a profit-minded peasantry, it would be difficult to envisage Russian agriculture not operating on this basis. The initial distribution of land, therefore, would have had a much stronger effect on the distribution of income within peasant agriculture than on the productivity of peasant agriculture. In effect, an equal distribution of land would have resulted in the eventual redistribution of income from the more able to the less able peasant farming population.

I am not an expert on the Russian commune, but I would expect that a close analysis of actual behaviour within the commune would show a strong pattern of informal land and wealth redistributions based upon mutually-beneficial side payments. A land distribution based upon equity rather than productivity need not detract significantly from long-run productivity as long as a system of informal side payments exists to redistribute land to its most productive use.

The restrictive feature of the commune emphasised strongly in the Gerschenkron model was the inability (and unwillingness) of adult members of the commune to leave their land for alternative employment. The argument was that a permanent departure of an adult family member would have reduced the family's claim to land at the next redistribution. The neoclassical model, however, would predict that the decision to leave the commune permanently would involve a comparison of lifetime family earnings (assuming the maximising unit is the peasant family) with or without the permanent departure of an adult family member from the commune. This decision to leave would depend positively upon the discounted value of the lifetime earnings outside the commune and negatively on the discounted value of the extra earnings from an eventual higher land allotment and on the marginal productivity of having an additional family member on the family plot. If earnings outside the commune were relatively high, the time between redistributions long, or the link between adult family size and the redistribution weak, then the hold of the commune on departing family members would be limited.

Most studies agree that the commune's hold on departing family members was quite weak. In this regard, I refer to studies of internal passports, the weak rural ties of the urban labour force, the rapid growth of the industrial labour force, and the vast internal migration of the Russian population after 1861.[17] The surprising feature of the commune's limited hold on departing members was that this weakness was already apparent in the eighteenth century.[18] As Gatrell concludes, the notion of a permanent attachment to the commune by those who had left was more romanticised than real.

If indeed a peasant family's long-run land holdings depended upon family size, then fertility might be higher in those areas in which land was periodically redistributed. Gatrell has reviewed the evidence for and against this proposition and finds that strong conclusions cannot be drawn from the available evidence.[19] This question would have to be studied empirically by relating regional fertility and marital rates to chronicled land redistribution practices rather than to rural land density. The empirical evidence is mixed because the direction of causation between per capita land holdings and marriage and fertility is uncertain (there is usually a positive correlation) and because the pattern may be dictated by longstanding customs and practices that vary by region of the country (for example, the more 'Western' pattern of demographic behaviour of the Baltic provinces).

In a neoclassical framework, the relationship between completed family size and land redistribution practices is complex. The rearing of a child would have its costs and the payoff in terms of a larger family allotment would be delayed until the child came of age. It is also unclear whether the peasant family would opt to maximise per capita family output from the family plot or *total* output. If the desire were to maximise per capita output, the calculation would become very complex because the family would have to determine whether the eventual marginal product of the new family member would be greater than the average product, hence raising per capita family output.

Another open question is the extent to which the post emancipation Russian commune actually implemented its formal egalitarian principles. If indeed a peasant family could be deprived of its improved land (either allotted by an initial distribution or acquired via a side payment), this would have placed a real damper on productivity improvements. I repeat that I am not an authority on the Russian commune, but neoclassical theory would predict that redistributions would be spaced far apart (giving the proprietor a long-term lease) and that, when they took place, they would not seriously disrupt the existing distribution of land wealth. If the existing distribution were based upon side payments, then the informal side payment could be continued. Presumably, the elected village elders would be chosen from the more experienced and successful farmers (or their representatives), and these elders would be unlikely to penalise a family that had done well and carried a disproportional burden of the commune's tax obligations. A rational commune government, pressured to meet its tax obligations, would recognise the long-run 'free rider' problem fostered by egalitarian redistributions.

Analysis of these issues requires the ability to look inside the governance of the commune to see exactly how these matters were dealt with in reality. One indirect indicator of the commune's adherence to a purely egalitarian policy is the extent to which the tax burden was distributed equally among commune members. I believe that the existing evidence points in the direction of a distribution of the tax burden according to ability to pay.[20] The acceptance of this principle would have made it difficult to pursue a purely egalitarian periodic redistribution policy, at least unmitigated by a well-established system of side payments.

I anticipate that the Russian commune was much more flexible in its actual working arrangements than its formal rules suggest. Throughout its history, Russian serf and communal agriculture proved to be a relatively flexible institution. In the eighteenth century, it was flexible enough to allow serf-owning serfs and serf industrialists, and it did not prevent the settlement of a vast frontier. The emancipation's removal of feudal obligations should have increased rather than reduced this natural flexibility. In fact, Lenin emphasised the vast array of institutional arrangements in Russian peasant agriculture in the second half of the nineteenth century, many of which circumvented the formal rules of the Russian commune.[21]

The Tax Burden

The inflexibility of Russian communal agriculture is not the only source of the purported agrarian crisis. A second argument is that the tax burden placed by the state on the peasant population was so large that incentives were destroyed and peasants were deprived of the opportunity to accumulate capital. The origin of this unmanageable tax burden was the overvaluation at the time of the emancipation of peasant land values relative to the capitalised value of net income, resulting in a mortgage debt burden that strapped the tax-paying capacity of the peasantry. Left with less land than before the emancipation, peasants scrambled to acquire additional land. This scramble for land drove up land prices (creating a 'land hunger'), which made it even more difficult for peasants to meet their tax obligations. How valid are these arguments?

The first point to note is that long-run land prices should equal the present value of the anticipated perpetual net earnings stream *net of taxes* from the land. Thus for land prices to rise, either prices received for farm output would have to rise or the productivity of land would have to rise, yielding rising present values of income from land after payment of tax obligations.

Typically, rising land prices are not taken as a sign of declining farm income but of rising farm income. At a microeconomic level, rising land prices and rents would of course be perceived by individual peasants as an unpleasant rise in the cost of doing business, and peasants with fewer farming skills and less accumulated capital would find themselves priced out of land markets. Yet on average, rising land values mean a rising effective demand for farm land that was being exercised by one segment of the peasant population. The statistics suggest that the distribution of land between peasant and gentry shifted in favour of peasants during this period.[22] Therefore, a considerable portion of the effective demand for land was being exercised by the peasant population.

The massive research of Koval'chenko and Milov confirms the theoretically-expected relationship among agricultural prices, land prices, and land rents during the 1861 to 1900 period.[23] The Koval'chenko-Milov study is itself an example of the pitfalls of generalising from isolated regional data because of the enormous regional disparities in output prices, land prices, and rents throughout this period. One can draw virtually any picture of post emancipation agriculture one wants simply by selecting a particular region that confirms the desired picture. Koval'chenko and Milov avoid these pitfalls by examining the functional relationships that emerge from the regional data. They do confirm that land prices depended positively on agricultural prices and that land rents were correlated with land prices. Thus land prices rose rapidly when agricultural prices were rising rapidly, and land prices fell (or failed to rise rapidly) when agricultural prices were falling (or not rising rapidly). The Koval'chenko-Milov study is based primarily on retail and wholesale prices (which include transportation costs), rather than on prices received at the farm level. Nevertheless, despite this inexactitude, the neoclassical functional relationships come through strongly.

The Koval'chenko-Milov study also reveals that land prices had risen by 1879 to a level generally higher than the above-market prices upon which the redemption payments were based. Although Russian peasants entered the emancipation era saddled with debt based upon overvalued land prices, this disadvantage was wiped out within less than twenty years.

According to Anfimov's study, direct taxes took about 6 per

cent of peasant income in 1901 with indirect taxes taking another 7 per cent.[24] It would be hard to argue that direct taxes averaging 6 per cent of peasant income represented ruinous taxation. Data from the state bank also show that peasant tax arrears rose substantially between 1866 and 1881.[25] It appears that peasants tended to adjust their tax payments to trends in grain prices, increasing their arrears during periods of falling prices and being more conscientious debtors during periods of rising prices. This is not an unexpected pattern in a world in which debt payments were fixed in nominal terms and there were radical fluctuations in prices.

The most important fact arguing against the ruinous taxation argument is that the secular trend in land prices was upwards. As long as land prices represent the present discounted value of the earnings stream from the land, rising prices indicate that rising productivity and expected future prices more than compensate for the tax burden. Another important point to emphasise is that land taxes should not affect agricultural output and productivity. As Henry George taught, land taxes affect only the distribution of income by redistributing land rents from land owners to the state. In this sense, land taxes should not affect agricultural output and productivity.

CONCLUSIONS

This chapter makes theoretical counter-arguments to Gerschenkron's theoretical arguments for the existence of an agrarian crisis. It shows that, if peasants were indeed utility maximisers, the commune would have been much more flexible than its formal rules suggest. Empirical evidence for the greater flexibility of the communal form is the creation of a growing and seemingly permanent industrial labour force, the geographical mobility of the peasantry, and the distribution of tax burdens according to ability to pay. I would argue that much more research on the actual operating arrangements of the Russian commune in the late nineteenth century is required. The chapter also argues that the 'irrational' rules of the commune would be more likely to affect income distribution than agricultural productivity. The macro evidence of rising per capita output and retained farm products and the evidence of rising land prices support this position. Rising land prices are theoretically inconsistent with the notion of a ruinous tax burden, and the percentage tax burden of the Russian peasant was probably not large by international standards. Finally this chapter points out that anecdotal evidence and macroeconomic evidence serve two different functions. Growth of macro variables does not deny the existence of massive rural poverty.

NOTES

1. Arcadius Kahan, *The Plow, the Hammer and the Knout: An Economic History of 18th Century Russia* (Chicago, 1985) ch. 2.
2. Peter Gatrell, *The Tsarist Economy 1850–1917* (London, 1986) p. 56.
3. Paul Gregory, *Russian National Income 1885–1913* (Cambridge, 1982) Appendix D.
4. Lazar Volin, *A Century of Russian Agriculture* (Cambridge, Mass., 1970) p. 58.
5. For an exception, see the study of P.I. Lyashchenko, *Ocherki agrarnoi evolyutsii Rossii* (St Petersburg, 1908) pp. 278–301.
6. L. Volin, *A Century of Russian Agriculture*; Alexander Gerschenkron, 'Agrarian Policies and Industrialization: Russia 1861–1917', *Cambridge Economic History of Europe*, vol. V, part 2 (Cambridge, 1965).
7. I.D. Koval'chenko and L.V. Milov, *Vserossiiskii agrarnyi rynok XVIII – nachalo XX veka* (Moscow, 1974); B.I. Mironov, *Khlebnye tseny v Rossii* (Leningrad, 1985).
8. See Gerschenkron, 'Agrarian Policies and Industrialization', and Gerschenkron, *Economic Backwardness in Historical Perspective* (Cambridge, Mass., 1962).
9. For this bibliography, see Paul Gregory, 'The Agrarian Crisis Revisited', Robert Stuart (ed.), *The Soviet Rural Economy* (Totowa, NJ, 1984) pp. 21–31.
10. P.I. Lyashchenko, *Ocherki agrarnoi evolyutsii Rossii*, pp. 278–301.
11. P. Gatrell, *The Tsarist Economy*, p. 122.
12. L. Volin, *A Century of Russian Agriculture.*
13. P. Gregory, 'Grain Marketings and Peasant Consumption, Russia 1885–1913', *Explorations in Economic History*, 17 (Mar. 1974) 135–64.
14. L. Volin, *A Century of Russian Agriculture*, p. 57.
15. P. Gatrell, *The Tsarist Economy*, ch. 4.
16. Daniel Thorner, B. Kerblay and R.E.F. Smith (eds.), *A.V. Chayanov on The Theory of Peasant Economy* (Homewood, Illinois, 1966).
17. P. Gatrell, *The Tsarist Economy*, ch. 3.
18. A. Kahan, *The Plow, the Hammer and the Knout*, ch. 2.
19. P. Gatrell, *The Tsarist Economy*, chs. 3 and 4.

20. Olga Crisp, *Studies in the Russian Economy Before 1914* (London, 1976) ch. 3.
21. V.I. Lenin, *The Development of Capitalism in Russia* (Moscow, 1977) ch. 2.
22. P. Gatrell, *The Tsarist Economy*, pp. 105–18.
23. Koval´chenko and Milov, *Vserossiiskii agrarnyi rynok*, pp. 257–82.
24. Anfimov's study is cited in P. Gatrell, *The Tsarist Economy*, p. 201.
25. P. Gatrell, *The Tsarist Economy*, p. 197.

2 Economic Change and the Russian Gentry, 1861–1914

Roger Munting

'So here you are, you've returned to Russia – what precisely do you intend to do?'
'To plough the land,' answered Lavretsky, 'and to strive to plough it as well as possible.'

I. Turgenev, *Home of the Gentry*

The main emphasis in the English language historiography on the Russian gentry after emancipation has been on their economic weakness and their social and political impotence.[1] The peasant emancipation changed the social and economic basis of the Russian countryside – the basis on which the landed gentry had rested (sometimes literally!) for so long. The removal of serf property, the prime source of wealth and income, was without question profound and arguably traumatic. In Terence Emmons' terms the act 'dealt the gentry class an economic blow from which it never recovered';[2] to quote another the act 'was nothing short of a social cataclysm'.[3] It left the gentry as a 'losing social class baffled and bewildered by the crashing of the old order'.[4]

A revision to the negative emphasis has been made by Olga Crisp in her analysis of the Meyendorf estates.[5] Other writers have also been evident in this regard, including Roberta Manning, Peter Gatrell and more particularly Seymour Becker.[6] It was, after all, only between emancipation and the revolutions of 1917 that the commercialisation of agriculture, agrarian 'capitalism', could properly exist; a number of Soviet writers have sought to demonstrate the development of these capitalist forms of production.[7] However, the notable scholars Anfimov and Minarik have, more recently, shown the slow development of capitalism on the largest gentry estates.[8] Similarly, Koval'chenko adduces cautious conclusions on the extent of gentry capitalist production on the eve of revolution.[9]

Obviously and immediately the initial outcome of emancipation was the loss of land. Although landed property had been inadequately measured in Russia (prior to 1861 wealth was measured in serfs owned; land holding was not formally recorded) the overwhelming private landowners under serfdom were the serf-owning gentry. Land allotments made to the former serfs can only have come from gentry landed property. Svyatlovskii estimated a loss of some 21 million desyatins upon emancipation.[10] On the other hand the marginally dispossessed gentry were financially overcompensated for such losses because of the overvaluation of the land for redemption purposes. Between 1863 and 1872 the total redemption price of 867 million rubles compares with a free market price of 648 million rubles, an effective 119 million ruble state handout.[11] To balance the equation, however, it must be remembered that outstanding debts accounted for the greater part of this redemption payment. Hause puts the accrued debts by landowners as high as 647.7 million rubles in 1860, nearly 75 per cent of redemption payments.[12] In addition, 80 per cent of the redemption payment was made in interest bearing government bonds which, when sold, lost 30 per cent of their face value,[13] thus compounding the capital loss to the gentry.

A further, and qualitatively more important, point is that, with few exceptions, gentry landowners had never been farmers before. Rather, the very purpose of serfdom had been to provide them with income, in kind or in money, as effective rentiers, absentee or otherwise. Thus it was only with the ending of serfdom that the landed gentry (*pomeshchiki*) were faced with the tasks of estate management, agricultural production, even book-keeping. The common view is that these demands proved too much for the generality of gentry landowner. 'The process of decay of large-scale farming . . . continued unabated after the reform.'[14]

The loss of real resources of capital and labour were further exacerbated by disadvantageous movements in the terms of trade, especially marked from the late 1870s to the 1890s. Falling agricultural prices (world wheat prices fell by half between 1875 and 1895) produced a ruinous commercial environment for most agricultural producers in Europe. As prime grain producers and exporters Russia's farmers were not excluded from this. Protective tariffs were almost universally introduced in Continental

Europe.[15] Objective economic determinants were compounded by, to quote a recent observer, 'profligacy, the fatal attractions of city life, feckless inability to successfully employ wage labour . . . and loss of nerve', as a result of which, he goes on, 'Russia's former landowners were relinquishing their estates and hence their residual control of Russia's countryside.'[16]

In 47 provinces of European Russia (excluding the Baltic) total gentry landholding declined from 85 093 200 desyatins in 1863 to 49 768 200 in 1905 and 38 989 000 in 1915.[17] The main land buyers were the peasantry, though other social estates (*sosloviya*), such as merchants, also showed significant gains. While total landholding fell dramatically, the number of gentry properties fell much less, from 128 500 in 1858 to 107 200 in 1905.[18] Aggregate figures conceal much variation and qualification to the general picture of decline. These points have been more fully explored elsewhere[19] and need only be summarised here.

The contraction of gentry ownership was by no means uniform regionally. The greatest real decline was in Central Russia and the mid-Volga. Gentry landholding was most resilient in the Baltic (excluded from the figures above), Belorussia and Lithuania and the Urals. There was also some social variation. Data from 44 provinces show that there was an increase in the number of holdings below 100 desyatins in size while the number of larger groups declined [Table 2.1]. There was certainly a volatile land market and the gentry themselves were amongst the major buyers of land. Indeed, a landowner was more likely to have sold land to another member of the gentry than to another social group. This was no new development. The long established family holding was far less evident in Russia than in much of Western Europe. As is well known there was no necessary connection at all between gentry status and title and land holding. By 1905 less than 40 per cent of the gentry class (*dvoryanstvo*) were land owners compared with over 80 per cent in 1861. But this was more a function of bureaucratic growth than a decline in the absolute numbers of gentry landowners.[20] Some of the gentry land buyers may have been office holders seeking land to accompany their status, but it is as likely that land changed hands amongst the gentry as it had done for centuries.

Even many of the largest family holdings at the end of the nineteenth century (sometimes extending over a number of

TABLE 2.1 *Distribution of gentry landholdings in 44 provinces of European Russia* (in thousand desyatins)*

Size	*1877* Holdings	*1877* Land	*1895* Holdings	*1895* Land	*1905* Holdings	*1905* Land
<100 des.	56 411	1 916.8	66 389	1 851.5	59 748	1 600.9
%	50.2	2.8	57.8	3.2	58.9	3.4
101–500	33 361	8 316.1	29 230	7 208.0	25 557	6 396.5
%	29.6	12.1	25.4	13.4	25.3	13.3
501–1000	10 636	7 520.4	9 589	6 650.2	8 006	5 633.8
%	9.4	10.9	8.4	12.4	7.9	11.8
1001–5000	10 401	21 121.2	8 334	16 435.1	6 882	13 600.1
%	9.2	30.7	7.3	30.5	6.8	28.3
over 5000	1 819	29 889.7	1 239	21 799.3	1 131	20 699.1
%	1.6	43.5	1.1	40.5	1.1	43.2
Total	112 628	68 774.2	114 781	53 944.1	101 324	47 930.4

* excluding Arkhangelsk, Bessarabia, Don *oblast'* and Baltic provinces.

SOURCE A.P. Korelin, *Dvoryanstvo v poreformennoi Rossii, 1861–1904 gg.* (Moscow, 1979) p. 62.

estates) had been relatively recently acquired. Prince S.S. Abamaleek-Lazarev owned over 800 000 desyatins; his forebears had bought much of this land from Stroganov earlier in the nineteenth century. The Kleinmikhel family bought land in Kursk, Kharkov and Chernigov between 1830 and 1850, which was to become the basis of family holdings of 64 000 desyatins by the end of the century.[21] In the years between the peasant emancipation and the end of the nineteenth century, overall gentry land purchases (excluding the Baltic) were equivalent to 50 to 60 per cent of gross land sales by the gentry [Table 2.2], though the proportion declined after 1905. This does not reduce the real decline but does suggest that some members of the gentry were investing in land rather than facing irretrievable ruin.

The leasing of land was far more extensive than sale, though less perfectly recorded. Official records suggest that, at the turn of the century, about a third of gentry owned land was rented out to peasants.[22] Koval'chenko and others put the figure much higher, at between a half and two-thirds of all gentry arable

TABLE 2.2 *Sales and purchases of land by gentry 1863–1909: 44 provinces** *(in thousand desyatins)*

	Sold	*Bought*
1863–72	16 120	9 673
1873–82	23 431	13 940
1883–92	17 996	9 688
1893–1902	21 016	10 979
1903–9†	12 087	4 520

* excluding Baltic, Astrakhan, Arkhangelsk.
† 1903–9 figures refer to 47 provinces, excluding the three Baltic provinces.

SOURCES A.P. Korelin, *Dvoryanstvo v poreformennoi Rossii, 1861–1904 gg.* (Moscow, 1979) p. 57.
Materialy po statistike dvizheniya zemlevladeniya v Rossii (St Petersburg, 1904–15) passim.

land.[23] Data from the Gentry Land Bank can throw some light on this, though do not reflect the full picture. In the period from 1886 to 1890, 32 per cent of the estates mortgaged to the Bank were farmed directly, and a similar figure were let out for rent in entirety. The residual (38 per cent) were partly let and partly farmed by their owners. With the recovery in grain prices from the mid-1890s one would expect there to have been a decline in the proportion let out but the opposite was the case. Between 1896 and 1900 some 47 per cent were let out in entirety; only 21 per cent farmed directly. However, there appears to have been a recovery thereafter. In 1905 47.5 per cent of the land mortgaged to the Gentry Land Bank was farmed 'directly', suggesting that a little over half was let out in whole or in part.[24] These latter figures refer to land rather than estates so are not strictly comparable. Quite simply it was often more profitable to let land than cultivate it directly. Even the most go-ahead of estates rented out part of their land. Rent was an important source of income, if not always higher then often more stable and secure than that from farming proper. It was, in other words, a rational use of a capital asset. Sales, on the other hand, liquidated an asset. In Kaluga province, in 1896–7, when grain prices were recovering, a sample of 1217 gentry estates produced an average net income of 1838 rubles (per estate); of this 812 rubles came from farming, 1026 from rent.[25]

Anfimov has shown that land leasing tended to increase with the size of the estate, though variations over time are more difficult to ascertain. Anfimov cautiously deduced an increase in renting to peasants between 1885 and 1900.[26] After the turn of the century, with grain prices increasing, the amount of land rented out decreased. By 1914 the figure was down to less than a third of gentry land (a reversal of the position around 1900) though of a smaller total.[27]

Data from the Gentry Land Bank indicate a huge recourse to borrowing, a continuation of the pattern of debt familiar from earlier in the nineteenth century. Nor is this the whole story, for loans were raised with other institutions as well. It would be a mistake, however, to interpret all such borrowing as indicative of poverty and feebleness; debt does not in itself reflect irresponsibility. The highest proportions of land were mortgaged to the Bank in the richest agricultural regions – New Russia and the south west Ukraine.[28] For an exceptional minority loans were raised to finance investment. Prince Meshcherskii for example borrowed 60 000 rubles from the Gentry Land Bank in 1898, towards the cost (120 000 rubles) of an estate in Smolensk.[29] This can hardly be taken as typical; most loans were used for consumption.

But this should come as no surprise; the very purpose of the estate had been to maintain a style of life, in Russia as elsewhere in Europe. The English aristocracy, long held in historical regard as economic and commercial leaders of their European social peers, effectively diverted huge sums from productive investment to current consumption.[30] Few of their class were practising farmers or innovators: 'commercial innovation and entrepreneurial dynamism were usually the work of commoners . . . while fully appreciative of the profitability of commercial activity, the aristocracy shunned direct involvement.'[31]

Of course, the social structure of the Russian countryside bears little resemblance to that in England; detailed comparisons would be fruitless. In Russia, technical and commercial superiority usually lay with the privately owned estate, predominantly in gentry hands, though the relative superiority evidently declined in the years immediately preceding 1917. Chelintsev

TABLE 2.3 *Yield ratios in Tula Province (1883–1909 average)*

Crops	*Private Land*	*Peasant Land**
Winter rye	5.38	4.33
Winter wheat	6.25	5.83
Oats	4.60	3.07
Potatoes	5.03	4.84
Buckwheat	3.77	3.40
Barley†	4.47	4.01

* It is unclear whether this refers exclusively to allotment land.
† There were few peasant records for barley.

SOURCE *Urozhai khlebov v Tul'skoi gubernii za 1883–1909 gg* (Tula 1913) passim. Data from Central Statistical Committee.

noted that in the 1880s private holdings produced yields 15 to 20 per cent higher than on peasant land.[32] Data assembled in 1882, from sample surveys, revealed that yields of the major crops – rye, wheat and oats – were higher on private land than on peasant land in all parts of the country.[33] Yield ratios were also higher (Table 2.3).

Further, private holdings displayed much lower variations in yield from year to year than peasant farms, and had a more varied crop pattern. Such crops as millet, peas, spring wheat and flax were rarely grown on peasant land.

Material from a single province, as this is, does not fully reflect circumstances in the country as a whole; more partial evidence may be even more suspect. Koval´chenko, Selunskaya and Litvakov have expressed scepticism about the value of certain evidence. Material from individual estates, they note, may not be used as a basis for general conclusions (though Anfimov and Minarik have done precisely that); archive sources (not easily available anyway) tend to be about the better estates.[34] The valuable survey of estates made in the mid 1890s and published in thirteen volumes, is limited in scope, both in time and geography, to a sample from the Baltic and central provinces. They also tend to be concerned with the 'above average' estates. Despite these limitations the 'accounts' (*opisaniya*) offer detail and insight which are arguably more real than aggregate generalities.

The examples considered here provide information for the mid-1890s from different provinces, Saratov, Orel and Kazan, together with some archive evidence for Saratov.[35] The estates vary in size, though none is typically small; landholding below 100 or even 500 desyatins would be more representative but data are not available.

In Saratov, the Sokur estate of Baroness Sofia Egorovna von Benkendorf-Hindenburg provides an example of a by no means poor, but relatively inefficient estate. The estate was located in the north-west part of Saratov district (*uezd*), 60 versts from the town of Saratov (the major market) and 45 versts from the railway. Total landholding was 14 121 desyatins, of which 8338 were arable. There were large areas of forest (2379 des) and of long fallow (*zalezh*) (2211 des). The land was located in one place but farmed as five units (*khutora*) presumably for organisational convenience. It was by no means uncommon for larger estates to be physically fragmented, which was a further incentive to let separated sections to peasants. The estate was relatively large, employing 18 'salaried' staff (including a manager (*upravlyayushchii*), assistants, cashiers, forest guards and various clerks), between 15 (winter) and 70 (summer) regular workers and anything up to 500 casual labourers for the harvest. There was no difficulty in recruiting labour because of the proximity of nearby settlements (two large villages, six smaller hamlets). But the labour market was essentially local; other estates in Saratov did have difficulty recruiting labour for the summer season.[36] Significant local variations in the labour market are evident also in other parts of the country.

Livestock consisted of 150 oxen, which did most of the heavy draft work, and 30 horses; equipment comprised 45 ploughs (or similar tillage implements) and a variety of machinery, including one steam-powered threshing machine. The fields were cultivated using both a four-field system (a relatively unsophisticated advance on three-field with a reduced fallow period) and, more generally, the traditional three-field system. In the latter cases the spring-sown summer season fields were usually rented out to peasants. Such rent income was apparently quite important, though records do not allow a detailed breakdown. Other income was derived from milling charges (the estate had eight water mills, but charges are unknown), from grain sales in Saratov and, particularly, from wool. The estate had 7000 head of Merino which produced roughly 12 000 rubles gross income 1894–5.[37] Other livestock did not contribute directly to money

TABLE 2.4 *Income from the Sokur Estate*

	Gross		*Net*	
1890	60 132		29 665	
1891	55 574		23 431	
1892	94 192		58 479	
1893	82 043		44 377	
1894	78 127		39 941	
		average	39 179	or 4.70 rubles per desyatin arable (2.83 per des. total)

income. Dairy cattle provided for direct, household consumption and manure for the farm. Recorded income was as shown in Table 2.4.

The estate was by no means unprofitable but the accounts were poor (a point made by the authors of the *opisaniya*); sources of income were inadequately recorded. But this example does indicate both the importance of rent income, even where labour was available, and of non-arable sources – in this case wool. There was also an important element of 'natural economy' or direct consumption.

Another example in Saratov province allows some comparison. The estate of Princess Gagarina, Andreevskoe village had a total landholding of 11 976 desyatins in 1895, of which 4151 were arable. Material on this estate has been taken from archive sources[38] and has the advantage of revealing, a little more, some of the changes experienced after emancipation, though the years of price depression are not covered.

In this estate costs were higher in relation to gross income than Benkendorf's, and net income much lower. The impact of emancipation can be seen with the evident intrusion of market relations. In 1865 a complex and lengthy contract was drawn up to let a flour mill for local use.[39] The year following, 1014 desyatins of fertile land were let to peasants in the village of Zhurnoe.[40] Income from rent was probably quite a high proportion of the whole, judging by the amount of land that was leased out.[41] The 1866 figure was about a quarter of all arable. In 1895 a rental agreement for 171 desyatins to a hundred local peasants for one year (on individual terms, not collectively) shows rents to vary from an exceptionally low 2.75 rubles per desyatin to a more usual 6.25 rubles.[42] In 1895 total land rented to peasants was 1099 desyatins on a crop share (*ispol'nyi*) basis; 905 desyatins for cash.[43] The total was equivalent to 48 per cent of the estate's arable land. It may be that renting increased substantially between 1866 and 1895 or that the earlier figures excluded crop-share renting. Accounts for one month, September 1895, show that rent income from the water mill alone yielded 1920 rubles (obviously a period of peak demand following the harvest) from a monthly total of 9831 rubles gross. Incomes from rent were, therefore, particularly significant.

The estate was farmed primarily on a 'traditional' three-field rotational system – in three units (*khutora*). The winter crop was exclusively rye with wheat and oats as spring crops. Occasionally there were variations of millet, sunflower or sown grasses in small areas. The remainder of the estate was made up of meadows, pasture, gardens, forest and long fallow. There is little sign of any innovation in the estate, though it did invest in a Clayton and Shuttleworth steam threshing set in 1871.[44] There was no evidence of adjustment to conventional rotations – clearly it was more worthwhile to lease land to the peasants. Incomplete records give an imperfect picture but as far as may be judged, the only notable variation on arable farming was in sheep rearing and, presumably, wool sales. The estate employed 37 workers to care for the sheep, (including 11 shepherds) in 1895. This implies a fairly large herd. Other full time employees were a manager with a further 19 others in a managerial, clerical capacity or as household estate servants. Twenty-six were employed for field work, three for livestock, two for gardens and eight for forestry; a grand total of 96.[45] No mention is made of casual labour.

Costs were relatively high, though as a proportion of gross income they declined over the period for which data are available.[46]

	1866–7 (Sept – August)	1895–6 (Oct – Sept)
	Rubles	
Gross income	22 617.12	62 552.24
Expenditure	19 976.36	49 890.10
Net income	2 640.76	12 662.14

Income per desyatin of arable land, in 1895, was 3.05 rubles. This appears to be a small return on capital, though capital figures are not available. Like Benkendorf the estate owner in this case was clearly an absentee. One might speculate that this added to the relatively high costs.

Contrasting style and scale can be found in the estate of F.E. Romer, Orel Province. From a total landholding of 866 desyatins[47] 140 desyatins were let out to peasants, apparently on a long term basis (separate income is not specified). Of the remainder, 510 desyatins were arable, 154 meadow, 26 under garden and orchards (of which the greater part was also leased out), 22 forest (the rest being pasture, dwellings etc.). Unusually, the owner managed the farm himself with the help of two stewards, a gardener and cowman (as 'salaried' staff) and 25 workers, together with casual and seasonal labour. Local circumstances enabled easy recruitment of workers.

The arable land was fragmented and apparently mingled with others, which may well have been one reason why some was rented out on long lease. In other respects this was an 'innovating' estate. Romer used a six-field rotation, incorporating clover to reduce fallow (wheat was the normal winter crop, rather than rye), quantities of manure were applied to the fields and up to date equipment was employed (including threshing machines, winnowers, seed drills, potato and grain sorters, horse drawn rakes etc.) – to a value of 7500 rubles. This was a high figure for an estate of this size. Working livestock was made up of 80 horses and 15 pairs of oxen. Money income came substantially from non-arable production. Fourteen desyatins of garden were leased to peasants, from a recorded total of 22 desyatins, for a rent of two to three thousand rubles annually. Up to 5000 trees were sold each year (as trees not as cut timber) plus varieties of apples and pears. Further, Romer bred horses for work and for sale; 15 to 20 foals annually, a minority of which were sold at prices ranging from 180 to 400 rubles. Other livestock income came from pigs and sheep. Although the estate had from 150 to 200 head of cattle, which it bred itself, they produced no cash income, but were rather kept for the manure they produced and, presumably, milk.

Over the ten years before the data were recorded (1895) net income averaged between 10 000 and 11 000 rubles per annum. It is noteworthy that fairly detailed costs were recorded for many branches of the farm but there is no disaggregation of income data in the record. It does reflect the care and attention paid to costing on this estate – a relatively unusual phenomenon. In general, animal products produced a better return than field crops. This finding is also borne out by information from Kaluga province, where grain sales were the least profitable of farm activities.[48] The figure from Romer's estate was much higher, at 12.2 rubles per desyatin total, than the other, more extensive estates considered.

The estate of Vladimir Petrovich Rodionov was in Kazan province, near Bezdon, 20 versts from Spasskii. Total land area was 4084 desyatins, of which 2580 were arable, 180 meadow, 84 pasture, 761 forest, 426 waste, marsh etc. and 53 for dwellings. The Rodionov family had bought most of this land, from neighbours, between 1872 and 1882. On the basis of the purchase price (presumably) the authors were able to record a land valuation of 353 000 rubles. Buildings (65 000), machinery (12 000) and livestock (11 000) brought the total valuation to 441 000 rubles. The estate was above average size, but smaller than the examples in Saratov. It fell within the category adduced by Roberta Manning as the most likely to innovate.[49] It appears to have been managed with a great deal of commercial acumen. Rodionov managed the estate himself with the help of a steward (*prikazchik*) and assistant, a cashier, two guards and three others (referred to as *starosty*). There were 40 permanent workers and various numbers of day workers. There were also specialised workers to handle machinery.

The major source of income was the arable, yet the rotation had not been varied from the three field system. Substantial inputs of manure were made (2400 puds per desyatin). Other capital was machinery, including a steam powered thresher (Ruston and Hornsby, with a straw burning engine), harvesting machines and several Ransomes ploughs. It is striking how carefully costing had been calculated.

Each working day for the threshing machine cost 48.43 rubles for 2000 puds of grain (for fuel, maintenance and labour) plus 25 per cent of capital cost per annum for amortisation and repair. Clearly the use of such equipment was carefully scrutinised. It was not thought economical, for instance, to use a harvesting machine for peas and millet, but cheaper to employ peasant labour for payment in kind. Machines and tools were valued at 12 000 rubles or 4.65 per desyatin of arable (or less than half the level on Romer's estate in Orel). In addition, there were 103 working horses, bred on the estate stud, though, surprisingly, costs and returns on this were not made clear.

A herd of 91 dairy cattle produced a loss, on milk, of 378 rubles; the real value being in the provision of manure. This was probably common – few took the trouble to calculate costs so exactly. Even the Moscow estate of Orlov-Davydov produced a loss on milk production despite careful selection of the herd.[50] Total income was high, at 28 783 rubles or 11.16 rubles per desyatin arable (7.33 rubles net for the whole estate). A further 1550 rubles were made from the sale of hay.

This was an unusually well run and carefully costed estate. It was unusual in the precision of its capital valuation. The high income per desyatin was achieved not from radical restructuring but by efficient use of land, careful use of natural fertiliser and scrutiny of investment in capital equipment – especially useful in rapid threshing and distribution after the harvest. Grain was sold exclusively in Spasskii, transport costs reckoned at 2 to 2.5 kopeks per pud. No chance was lost to make a kopek. Straw was sold to local peasants for 40 to 45 kopeks per square sazhen.

This estate, and that of Romer, were evidently exceptional in their efficiency and commercial success. Other examples can be found of enterprising estates exploring particular market opportunities or commodities (timber, fruit, draught horses or whatever). But commercially, the generality of estates were adversely affected by low grain prices and careless management. Poor accounting is the most frequent criticism made by the authors of the *opisaniya*. In particular, there are strong indications (as a general observation it can be put no stronger than that) of very low returns on capital (rarely were capital valuations available), even though large estates produced large absolute incomes. Further, most estates produced a substantial proportion of consumption goods (animal and human food in particular but frequently timber and building materials as well) directly within the estate.

These particular examples in themselves can tell us little about the general picture of the gentry in the economy. However they, and many others, suggest that the more successful producers were often those who were able to diversify. Beyond the geographical scope of these particular cases are the sugar producers of the Ukraine, for instance. Sugar beet was a well-established crop, dating from the early nineteenth century, but falling grain prices provided an extra incentive to produce this cash crop in the last quarter of the century. Until the twentieth century sugar beet was almost exclusively grown on gentry estates and some factory owned 'plantations'.

There is no doubt that the landowning gentry significantly reduced their share in total agricultural production. In the 1850s gentry farms produced about a quarter of the total crop production and more than half the amount sold.[51] According to Nifontov between 82 and 85 per cent of grain sales came from gentry farms.[52] By 1916 gentry estates account for 11.3 per cent of sown land and 20.6 per cent of marketed crops, with rather lower figures for livestock products.[53] In his extensive and detailed analyses of grain production data, Wheatcroft presents different estimates of the proportion of grain produced on gentry estates in the early twentieth century. They vary from 12 per cent (Kondrat´ev, 1909–13) to 24 per cent (Lyashchenko, 1901–5) of grain production. The higher figure implies that 22.7 per cent of total marketed product came from gentry estates,[54] (a figure very close to Koval´chenko's estimates for 1916). The gentry estates were commercially more significant than their relative landholding might suggest.

This was more striking in the case of exports. In the last quarter of the nineteenth century grain exports more than doubled: in 1881 202.8 million puds; 1893–7 522.8 million puds.[55] At the same time there was a shift to the southern ports as major trading outlets, aided by the development of the railway system. From 1895 to 99 and 1906 to 10 there was a 42 per cent increase in general grain haulage, but an 80 per cent increase in haulage to the southern ports. The major export outlets were Odessa, Novorossiisk, Nikolaev and Rostov, with the most rapid growth experienced in the smaller ports of Berdyansk, Mariupol and Taganrog.[56]

The major regions producing for export were in the southern steppe and right bank Ukraine, as well as the Baltic provinces – areas where gentry landholding and farming remained relatively resilient. Indeed Wheatcroft notes that the largest share of gentry landholding was in the 'Southern Producing Region', which had higher than average yields and produced more traded surpluses than elsewhere.[57]

Early in the twentieth century, and more especially after 1905, social and political changes naturally affected the gentry estate economy. Sales of gentry land accelerated (and purchases by them fell) though the trend was reversed, 1911 to 1914. Roberta Manning notes a parallel, if contradictory, commercial strengthening within the estate sector, pointing out that by 1914 68.3 per cent of gentry owned arable was being cultivated directly. '[I]n the early twentieth century,' she writes 'gentry entrepreneurship *for the first time* became a significant factor in Russian agriculture'[58] (my emphasis). This appears to be an exaggeration. The evidence adduced above, together with the extensive findings of Becker,[59] suggest that such entrepreneurship, qualitative changes in estate management, had been developing since well before the end of the nineteenth century.

After 1905 the government made capital investments easier for large-scale landowners. The State Bank gave short term credits for the purchase of machinery. Further, the Gentry Land Bank, after 1907, allowed mortgaged land to be re-mortgaged for further loans, though the credits were specified to be for productive purposes.[60] However, such generosity in the provision of credit could, and did, have a double effect. Gentry indebtedness increased further. Such was the demand for loans (often based on a deliberate overvaluation of the mortgaged land) that the Bank loaned, in 1910–13, more than it received in payment. It would be naive and mistaken to associate all such borrowing with capital investment. Hause has calculated that in each year from 1911 to 1914 the Gentry Land Bank lent more in re-mortgages than new loans. As a result gentry debts in 1915, at over two thousand million rubles, were nearly double peasant debts.[61] Similarly, when a tax reform in 1906 introduced a small property tax for the gentry, arrears quickly mounted, though the government took no action. Arguments have been brought forward elsewhere, though not without dispute, that peasant tax (redemption payment) arrears of the late nineteenth century, were more the function of a refusal or reluctance to pay than inability to pay resulting from extreme poverty.[62] What are we to make of gentry tax arrears?

It could not be maintained that this resulted entirely from poverty or profligacy. The important point to note is that mortgage debt as a proportion of land values showed no general increase, but rather diminished after 1905. On the other hand one would not maintain that the gentry *as a whole* made up a class of dynamic and far sighted entrepreneurs. All such generalisation is misleading. Arguably, differences and differentiation were at least as extreme as amongst the peasantry, and probably more so. Thus it would be difficult to accept uncritically Becker's contention that the landowning gentry became *a class*.[63] He is, however, persuasive in the suggestion that the gentry displayed commercial acumen more reflective of business classes than of the traditional social estate (*soslovie*).

In the eastern fringes of Europe the aristocracy clung to power and influence through the nineteenth century while their influence in the west was being eroded by revolution and reform. The emergence of industrial capitalism and commercial farming is associated (and not simply in Marxist conception) with the economic and social advance of a bourgeoisie or 'middle class'.

Further east (the Elbe is conventionally taken as the margin) aristocratic landowners and peasant farmers continued to dominate society and much of the economy until the eve of the First World War. They were not swamped by the march of capitalism. Unlike the Prussian or Hungarian aristocracy the Russian nobles or gentry had long lost independent political force by the mid-nineteenth century. With peasant emancipation they were to lose their major economic support. The story of their subsequent decline can all too easily be attributed to ruin in the face of capitalist development. But the story is more complex than that. It was only during this period that there was real freedom of commercial enterprise, and many members of the gentry made the most of the opportunity. It was not so much capitalist development which ruined the gentry as the ever expanding demand from the peasantry. Many members of the gentry became capitalists (and not just in farming), sometimes despite serious deterioration in market conditions.

Over the two decades from the mid-1890s to the eve of war in 1914 there were marked fluctuations in agricultural fortunes in Russia, but nonetheless a secular improvement in grain prices and terms of trade. Many gentry landowners shared in this improvement in fortune. Yet there were greater fortunes to be made in other spheres. Apart from industrial and commercial ventures, government stock often paid a higher return than farming proper. Rates of interest on state bonds were typically 4.5 to 6 per cent – uniquely high by European standards. As far as may be judged from limited data even the most go ahead estates could rarely exceed this rate of return. Thus the rational landowner would have fruitfully employed his assets by renting out land to peasants, retaining a home farm for direct consumption and as a summer retreat, while investing spare capital in government bonds. The 'typical' landowner, in living from rent and dividends, was little different from social peers in much of Europe. (In the Russian case government service was often also a vital source of income.) They were less concerned with maximising profits than with minimising social or personal disruption.

However, it is equally evident that investments were made in estates. A problem with making any assessment of the returns on such investments is the paucity of real accounting on estates. Further, overall capital valuation is affected by marked increases in land values. Few landowners undertook such valuation. The crucial determining factor was not so much the average return on capital, but the marginal return on new investments, in working capital or buildings. It is reasonable therefore to accept the 'revisionist' ideas of Becker that the landowning gentry, rather than simply 'declining', adapted rationally and successfully to changing economic circumstances. Thus in 'backward' Russia we find gentry estates well developed and profitably organised whose contribution to total product and to the dynamics of the Russian economy was disproportionate to their ownership of resources.

NOTES

1. A classic example is R. Pipes, *Russia Under the Old Regime* (London, 1974). It contains a section entitled 'Catastrophic Decline of the Dvoriane after 1861'. See also J. Blum, 'Russia', in D. Spring (ed.), *European Landed Elites in the Nineteenth Century* (London, 1977).
2. T. Emmons, *The Russian Gentry and Emancipation* (London, 1968) p. 421.
3. L. Pavlovsky, *Agricultural Russia on the Eve of Revolution* (London, 1925) p. 99.
4. A. Mazour, quoted in E. Beyerley, *The Europe Centric Historiography of Russia* (Paris, 1974) p. 25.
5. Olga Crisp, 'Horses and Management of a Large Agricultural Estate in Russia at the end of the Nineteenth Century' in F.M.L. Thompson, *Horses in European Economic History* (Reading, 1983) pp. 156–76.
6. Roberta Manning, *The Crisis of the Old Order in Russia, Government and Gentry* (Princeton, 1982); P. Gatrell, *The Tsarist Economy 1850–1917* (London,

1986); S. Becker, *Nobility and Privilege in Late Imperial Russia* (DeKalb, Illinois, 1985). See also A. Kahan, 'Capital Formation during the Period of Early Industrialisation in Russia, 1890–1913' in *Cambridge Economic History of Europe*, vol. VII (Cambridge, 1978) pp. 299–300, which shows the rapid increase in capital stock, particularly in machinery and equipment, in the agricultural sector.

7. Most obviously Lenin in *Development of Capitalism in Russia*; notably also in P.I. Lyashchenko, *Istoriya narodnogo khozyaistva Rossii*, 2 vols, (Leningrad, 1947–8).
8. A.M. Anfimov, *Krupnoe pomeshchich'e khozyaistvo Evropeiskoi Rossii kontsa xix – nachalo xx vv.* (Moscow, 1969); L.P. Minarik, 'Ob urovne razvitiya kapitalisticheskogo zemledeliya v krupnom pomeshchich'em khozyaistve Evropeiskoi Rossii'. *Ezhegodnik po agrarnoi istorii vostochnoi Evropy, 1964* (Kishinev, 1966) pp. 616–26.
9. I.D. Koval'chenko, N.B. Selunskaya, B.M. Litvakov, *Sotsial'no-ekonomicheskii stroi pomeshchichego khozyaistva Evropeiskoi Rossii v epokhu kapitalizma* (Moscow, 1982).
10. V.V. Svyatlovskii, *Mobilizatsiya zemlevladeniya v Rossii* (Moscow, 1907).
11. T.S. Hause, 'State and Gentry in Russia 1861–1917' (PhD, Stanford University, 1973) p. 46.
12. Ibid, p. 49. This figure is higher than in many other sources.
13. Manning, *Crisis of the Old Order*, p. 9.
14. M. Florinsky, *Russia, a History and an Interpretation* (New York, 1970) p. 928.
15. In Germany grain duties were raised in 1879; in France they reached even higher levels. For Russian figures see Olga Crisp, *Studies in the Russian Economy before 1914* (London, 1976) p. 30.
16. R. Bideleux, *Communism and Development*, (London, 1985) p. 21.
17. A.M. Anfimov and I.F. Makarov, 'Novye dannye o zemlevladeniya Evropeiskoi Rossii', *Istoriya SSSR*, 1 (1974) p. 87.
18. A.P. Korelin, 'Dvoryanstvo v poreformennoi Rossii (1861–1904)' *Istoricheskie zapiski*, 87 (1971) p. 146.
19. For example, Anfimov and Makarov, 'Novye dannye', Manning, *Crisis of the Old Order*, ch. 1, R. Munting, 'Gentry Landownership in European Russia', *New Zealand Slavonic Journal*, 1 (1978).
20. Korelin, 'Dvoryanstvo v poreformennoi Rossii', Becker, *Nobility and Privilege*, pp. 29, 187–8.
21. L.P. Minarik, 'Proizkhozhdenie i sostav zemel'nykh vladenii krupneishikh pomeshchikov Rossii' in *Materialy po istorii sel'skogo khozyaistva i krest'yanstva SSSR*, vol. V. (Moscow, 1962).
22. *Materialy vysochaishe uchrezhdennoi 16 noyabra 1901g. kommissii*, (St Petersburg, 1903).
23. Koval'chenko et al., *Sotsial'no-ekonomicheskii stroi.*
24. N.I. Vorob'ev, 'Chastnovladel'cheskoe polevoe khozyaistvo' *Vestnik sel'skogo khozyaistva*, 12, (1906) p. 4
25. V.I. Pronin, 'Dokhodnost'l pomeshchich'ego zemledel'cheskogo khozyaistva Kaluzhskoi gubernii na rubezhe xix i xx vekov', *Ezhegodnik po agrarnoi istorii vostochnoi Evropy 1970* (Riga, 1971) p. 202.
26. A.M. Anfimov, *Krupnoe pomeshchich'e khozyaistvo* (Moscow, 1969) p. 85.
27. Manning, *Crisis of the Old Order*, p. 20. She puts the figure at 68.3 per cent

farmed directly implying a 31.7 per cent share being rented out.

28. G. Hamburg, 'Land, Economy and Society in Tsarist Russia' (PhD, Stanford University, 1975) p. 96.
29. A. Meshcherskii, 'Pis'ma kul'turnogo khozyaina', *Zemledel'cheskaya gazeta*, 2 (1904) 66.
30. K. Bush, *The English Aristocracy* (Manchester, 1984) p. 173.
31. Ibid.
32. A.N. Chelintsev, *Russkoe sel'skoe khozyaistvo pered revolyutsiei* (Moscow, 1928) p. 192. Data refer to 1887.
33. These were average net yields collected from 2000 correspondents, published in *Sel'skokhozyaistvennye i statisticheskie svedeniya po materialam poluchenym ot khozyaev*, vol. I (1884) pp. 2–17.
34. Koval'chenko et al, *Sotsial'no-ekonomicheskii stroi*, pp. 32–3.
35. The major source is *Opisaniya otdel'nykh russkikh khozyaistv* (St. Petersburg, 1897–8), 13 vols. together with some material from *Tsentral'nyi gosudarstvennyi arkhiv drevnei aktov* (TsGADA), fond 1262, Gagarinykh, opis 1, d.4448–4464. The *opisaniya* material is limited in space (to 13 provinces) and time (to a single survey in the mid-1890s) as well as in the representative nature of the estates considered. These accounts are, however, amongst the most useful of sources in presenting a picture of estate economy and organisation. The three examples selected here are deliberately of different size, with varying product specialism and from different provinces.
36. The Mende estate is one example, *Opisaniya*, vol. IX, p. 7.
37. This has been calculated from average wool yields and prices; it is not stated as such in the source.
38. *TsGADA*, f.1262, op.1. Records were available for the 1860s and 1895–6 only.
39. Ibid. d.4462, 1–3. Presumably it had been informally available before.
40. Ibid. d.4463.
41. Details of aggregate receipts from rent were not available.
42. *TsGADA*, d.4463, 1.
43. Ibid, d.4504.
44. 29 Oct. 1871 at a cost of 4130 rubles, plus 23.50 r. delivery; credit to January 1872. *TsGADA*, f.1262 op. 1 d.4492.
45. Ibid, d.4502, 108–9.
46. Ibid, d.4464, d.4502, passim.
47. There is some discrepancy in the source. The total is given as 860 des. but the parts add up to 866.
48. Pronin, 'Dokhodnost' pomeshchich'ego zemledel'cheskogo khozyaistva', p. 201.
49. Manning, *Crisis of the Old Order*, p. 20.
50. K.N. Khodnev, 'Iz praktiki molochnogo khozyaistva', *Vestnik Russkogo sel'skogo khozyaistva*, 11 (1903) pp. 6–7.
51. Koval'chenko, et al, *Sotsial'no-ekonomicheskii stroi*, p. 116.
52. A.S. Nifontov, *Zernovoe proizvodstvo Rossii vo vtoroi polovine xix veka*, (Moscow, 1974).
53. Koval'chenko, et al., *Sotsial'no-ekonomicheskii stroi.*
54. S.G. Wheatcroft, 'Grain Production and Utilization in Russia and the

USSR before Collectivization' (Ph.D., University of Birmingham, 1980) pp. 275–9.
55. T.M. Kitanina, *Khlebnaya torgovlya Rossii v 1875–1914 gg.* (Moscow, 1979) p. 69.
56. Ibid, p. 127.
57. Wheatcroft, 'Grain Production and Utilization', pp. 291–2.
58. Manning, *Crisis of the Old Order*, pp. 18, 20–1.
59. Becker, *Nobility and Privilege*, ch. 2.
60. Hause, 'State and Gentry', pp. 205–8.
61. Data from Hause, ibid, pp. 212–3.
62. J. Simms, 'The Crisis in Russian Agriculture at the end of the Nineteenth Century: A Different View', *Slavic Review*, XXXVII (1978) p. 483.
63. Becker, *Nobility and Privilege*, pp. 172–3.

3 The 1891–92 Famine in Russia:

Towards a More Detailed Analysis of its Scale and Demographic Significance[1]

S.G. Wheatcroft

This paper is part of a larger study of Russian and Soviet famines in the nineteenth and twentieth centuries. It incorporates a detailed study of food supply, the crisis in peasant living standards, food aid and some of the demographic consequences of the famine. Each of these elements is considered in some detail concerning its chronology and regional dimension. Following a review of each of these components an attempt is made briefly to compare the relationship between these factors in regional and temporal terms.

Food Supply

The main foodstuff was grain which supplied over 75 per cent of the calorific value of the diet, with livestock produce (meat, milk and cheese) providing about 11 per cent, potatoes about 8 per cent and fish, vegetables and fruit the remaining 6 per cent.[2] Short term variations in the level of grain production were predominantly the consequences of fluctuations in grain yields caused by the weather; the area sown stayed relatively stable from year to year. Bad weather years tended to predominate over good; the famine of 1891 was primarily the result of a decline in grain yield resulting from a drought, but following a series of poor yield years: 1890 and especially 1889.

Russia was already a major grain exporter at this time and was regularly exporting 15 to 20 per cent of its crop by the late 1880s (that is, between six and nine million tons of grain per year). There had been only a very slight decline in exports in 1889 and 1890, although there was a far more substantial decline

TABLE 3.1 *Grain production, exports and domestic residual per head of the population in the 50 provinces of European Russia, 1883–1914 (in million tons and tons per head per year)*

	Production	*Export*	*Net*	*Population*	*Per capita production in tons* Gross	*Net of exports*
1883	33.95	5.24	28.71	76.85	0.44	0.37
1884	37.32	5.63	31.69	77.81	0.48	0.41
1885	31.67	4.55	27.12	79.11	0.40	0.34
1886	35.87	6.44	29.43	80.21	0.45	0.37
1887	41.69	8.98	32.71	81.47	0.51	0.40
1888	40.15	7.63	32.52	82.72	0.49	0.39
1889	30.48	6.85	23.63	84.18	0.36	0.28
1890	36.86	6.40	30.46	85.28	0.43	0.36
1891	28.76	3.21	25.55	86.48	0.33	0.30
1892	34.46	6.62	27.84	87.68	0.39	0.32
1893	48.03	10.48	37.55	88.10	0.55	0.43
1894	48.65	9.42	39.23	89.34	0.54	0.44
1895	43.79	8.30	35.49	90.65	0.48	0.39
1896	44.66	8.01	36.65	91.94	0.49	0.40
1897	37.07	7.52	29.55	93.78	0.40	0.32
1898	43.07	5.67	37.40	95.16	0.45	0.39
1899	49.54	6.88	42.66	96.63	0.51	0.44
1900	48.32	7.64	40.68	98.38	0.49	0.41

SOURCES Grain production 1883–1914: V.M. Obukhov, 'Dvizhenie urozhaev v evrop. Rossii v period 1883–1915gg.' in V.G. Groman (ed.) *Vliyanie neurozhaev na narodnoe khozyaistvo Rossii* (Moscow, 1927) part 1, p. 2.
Exports: V.I. Pokrovskii (ed.) *Sbornik svedenii po istorii i statistike vneshnei torgovli* (St Petersburg, 1902).
Population: 1867–1914 as given in A.G. Rashin, *Naselenie Rossii za 100 let* (Moscow, 1956) p. 46.

after the famine year of 1891, when grain exports were temporarily halted. (See Table 3.1)

The growth of grain production in the last twenty years of the nineteenth century was sufficiently rapid to provide for the large growth in population and in grain exports. In terms of the scale of population, grain production was rising from 0.45 tons per head in 1883–7 to 0.48 tons per head in 1896–1900; and even in terms of net grain retentions in the country (i.e. production net of exports) the level was still rising slightly: 0.38 tons per head in 1883–7 and 0.39 tons per head in 1896–1900.[3] (See Table 3.1)

However in individual years, and also in clusters of years the levels did fall quite sharply.

The per capita data net of grain exports also reveal the interesting fact that the level in the famine year of 1891 was higher than in 1889. The reason why the famine came in 1891 and not 1889 is fairly complex. To some extent it could be explained in terms of the peasants having more reserves in 1889 which were exhausted by 1891; but it was also likely to be related to two other factors: the sharp decline in living standards of part of the peasant population in 1891, with the deterioration in rural wage rates and the increase in peasant indebtedness (see below); and the regional incidence of the harvest failure.

Grain production in 1889 was particularly low in the relatively wealthier southern region (the Ukraine and North Caucasus), but was high in the more problematical central producer regions (the central agricultural region and the Volga regions). In 1891 the drought affected the Volga and central agricultural regions, where production levels plummeted. However, grain production remained fairly high in the south. The wealthier southern provinces were able to withstand their poor harvests of 1889 with only a limited reduction in exports, but the decline in the struggling central provinces was much more serious. Table 3.2 provides an indication of the levels of grain production in the major regions of Russia in these years.[4]

TABLE 3.2 *Russian grain production by region in million tons*

Year	*Northern Consumer Region*	*Southern Consumer Region*	*Southern Producer Region*	*Central Producer Region*	*Eastern Producer Region*	*Russia*
1883	8.32	1.55	10.34	12.63	5.0	37.84
1884	7.11	1.55	12.51	13.79	5.11	40.07
1885	6.74	1.56	8.41	12.02	5.26	33.99
1886	9.03	1.56	7.97	14.43	5.41	38.40
1887	9.04	1.57	15.41	14.12	5.56	45.69
1889	8.43	1.57	7.59	14.33	5.85	37.78
1890	8.23	1.58	13.50	12.30	6.00	41.63
1891	7.48	1.58	11.30	6.64	6.15	33.15
1892	7.18	1.58	13.04	10.04	6.30	38.14
1893	8.37	1.59	21.61	14.72	6.45	52.73
1894	8.97	1.59	18.84	17.32	6.59	53.32
1895	8.05	1.60	15.25	15.43	6.74	47.06

TABLE 3.3 *Provinces in which the 1891 grain yields was at least 25% below the normal level. (Grain yields in hundred kg per hectare; norms from 1883–1915 trend)*

Province	*1891* *Rank*	*Yield*	*% of norm*	*1890* *% of norm*	*1889* *% of norm*	*1889–91* *% of norm*	*Rank*
50 provinces		4.15	–29	–7.3	–18.2	–18.17	
25 black-earth		3.66	–36.5	–7.4	–24.9	–22.93	
25 non black-earth		5.38	–11.4	–7.2	–1.5	–6.70	
Voronezh	1	1.40	–75.5	38.8	–37.5	–24.73	11
Orenburg	2	1.60	–70.1	–51.3	30.1	–30.43	4
Kazan	3	1.90	–64.9	–30.2	–9.7	–34.93	2
Samara	4	1.50	–64.2	–31.6	–21.6	–39.13	1
Simbirsk	5	2.50	–58.1	–27.5	–9.2	–31.60	3
Tambov	6	3.10	–56.5	2.1	–33.3	–29.23	5
Saratov	7	2.50	–54	–18.7	–11.2	–27.97	7
Penza	8	3.00	–52.2	–33	–.2	–28.47	6
Ryazan	9	3.30	–51.5	–2.7	11.2	–14.33	19
Arkhangelsk	10	3.40	–45	22.3	17.2	–1.83	22
Kursk	11	3.70	–40.7	4.1	–36.1	–24.23	14
Vyatka	12	3.30	–39.1	–22.4	–12.7	–24.73	11
Ufa	13	3.60	–38.8	–40.9	–.5	–26.73	8
N. Novgorod	14	3.80	–35	–27.3	–7.5	–23.27	16
Kherson	15	3.20	–34.9	13.8	–51.6	–24.23	14
Pers	16	4.60	–31.9	–33.9	–10.8	–25.53	9
Tula	17	4.70	–30.5	4.9	7	–6.20	21
Taur da	18	3.50	–30.4	6.1	–37.6	–20.63	17
Orel	19	4.50	–26.7	12.4	–10.2	–8.17	20
Don Oblast'	20	3.50	–26	13.6	–30.7	–14.37	18
Kharkov	21	4.00	–25.6	–17.1	–32.6	–25.10	10
Astrakhan	22	2.00	–24.4	–22.4	–27.3	–24.70	12

SOURCE Calculated from V.M. Obukhov, 'Dvizhenie urozhaev v evrop, Rossii v period 1883–1915gg.' in V.G. Groman (ed.) *Vliyanie neurozhaev na narodnoe khozyaistvo Rossii*, part 1 (Moscow, 1927) pp. 33, 59–108.

The drought of 1891 and the subsequent famine were most intense in the Volga and central agricultural region as can be seen from Table 3.3 above, which presents a listing of the 22 worst affected provinces ranked according to the extent in which the 1891 yield was below the 1883–1915 norm and also the extent to which the average 1889–91 yield was below the norm.

The central grain surplus areas, which were the main victims of the 1891 drought, had been the traditional suppliers of grain surpluses to the northern cities. In more recent times, these old traditional grain surplus areas in the centre had been superseded by the Ukraine and the North Caucasus as the major grain surplus producing provinces. These Southern surplus producer areas tended to export most of their grain surpluses through the Black Sea, and they were the source of the large grain exports of this period. The famine was primarily located in these central grain surplus areas which were already undergoing a decline in comparison with the newer and more prosperous southern surplus-producing area. The growth in production in the south tended to obscure the serious crisis that was occurring in the traditional farming areas in the centre.

The Crisis in Peasant Living Standards

Although a fall in grain production and grain reserves was the main cause of the overall crisis, the specific position of any individual peasant depended upon a complex of factors which included alternative sources of income, dependence on the market for food supplies, incidence of taxation and availability of relief measures.

A decline in grain production would not necessarily lead to a decline in all peasant living standards; when grain prices rose those peasants who were able to maintain control over their grain surpluses could end up with greater incomes. Those peasants who had no surpluses and who depended on the market for their own food would be the most affected by the grain shortages and the rising prices. In the northern areas the poor peasants who produced insufficient grain for their own households had greater prospects of industrial, urban or forestry employment to supplement their incomes. In the south the predominant means of supplementing incomes was to seek employment as seasonal labour in agriculture; and here the problem was particularly severe because the drought not only caused grain prices to rise, but it also tended to lead to a fall in rural wages and a reduction of rural work prospects, since less labour was required to bring in the smaller harvests. It was within this group of rural wage labourers that the effect of the drought and the famine was most severe.

Table 3.4 and Figures 3.1–3.3 provide a clear indication of the

TABLE 3.4 *Rural daily wage labour in rye equivalents Sowing (S), haymaking (H) and threshing (T)*

Year	Average daily wage in kopecks			Price of rye	Real wages in kg of rye per day		
	S	*H*	*T*	kopecks per kg	*S*	*H*	*T*
1882	37.4	52.6	56.4	3.88	9.64	13.56	14.54
1883	38.3	59.1	61	3.96	9.65	14.93	15.41
1884	38.2	53	60.2	3.56	10.72	14.88	16.90
1885	37	48.4	51.6	3.01	12.30	16.09	17.15
1886	35.9	43.1	51.4	2.77	12.96	15.65	18.55
1887	34.7	47.6	51.5	2.38	14.61	20.04	21.68
1888	36.3	50.1	69.1	2.53	14.33	19.78	27.28
1889	37.3	45.9	50.3	3.01	12.40	15.26	16.72
1890	35.3	45.5	51.6	2.85	12.39	15.96	18.11
1891	33.8	42.8	46.5	5.86	5.77	7.31	7.94
1892	33.2	44	49.3	4.12	8.06	10.69	11.98
1893	34	49.3	63.7	2.77	12.27	17.79	22.99
1894	37.1	48.7	58.3	1.98	18.75	24.61	29.46
1895	37.6	47	52.2	2.14	17.59	21.99	24.42
1896	37.5	48.3	50.7	2.14	17.54	22.60	23.72
1897	38.2	49.9	51.3	2.93	13.04	17.04	17.51
1898	40	52.2	56.8	3.40	11.75	15.33	16.69
1899	40.5	52.6	54.9	3.17	12.79	16.61	17.34
1900	43.8	55	59.1	3.00	14.60	18.33	19.70

SOURCES Wage rates from S.G. Strumilin, 'Dinamika podennoi platy za 1882–1916gg.' in S.G. Strumilin, *Izbrannye proizvedeniya*, vol. III (Moscow, 1964) p. 277.
Note these data have been reworked by Strumilin and corrected for faulty weighting.
Rye prices 1882–1900 for 50 provinces of European Russia from *Svod statisticheskikh svedenii po sel'skomu khozyaistvu Rossii k kontsu XIX veka*, vol. II (St Petersburg, 1903) pp. 24–5.
Rye prices 1890–1915 for domestic market from *Svod tovarnykh tsen na glavnykh russkikh i inostrannykh rynkakh za 1915g.*. (Petrograd, 1917) p. 11.
Other figures calculated from the above.

famine. The sharp rise in rye prices in 1891–2 (Table 3.4 col. 5 and Figure 3.2) was accompanied by a decline in rural wages (Table 3.4, cols 2–4 and Figure 3.1) which resulted in the sharp fall in real rural wage levels (Table 3.4 cols 6–8, and Figure 3.3).

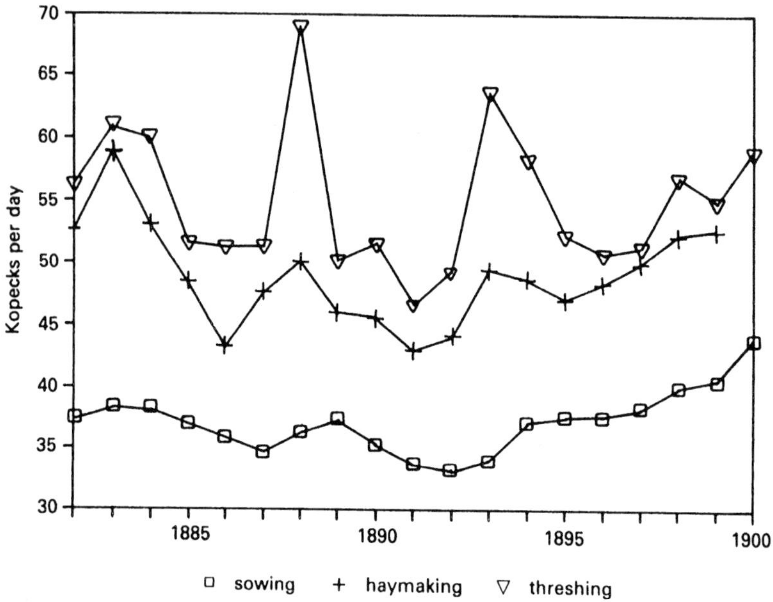

Figure 3.1 Average daily wage in kopecks per day

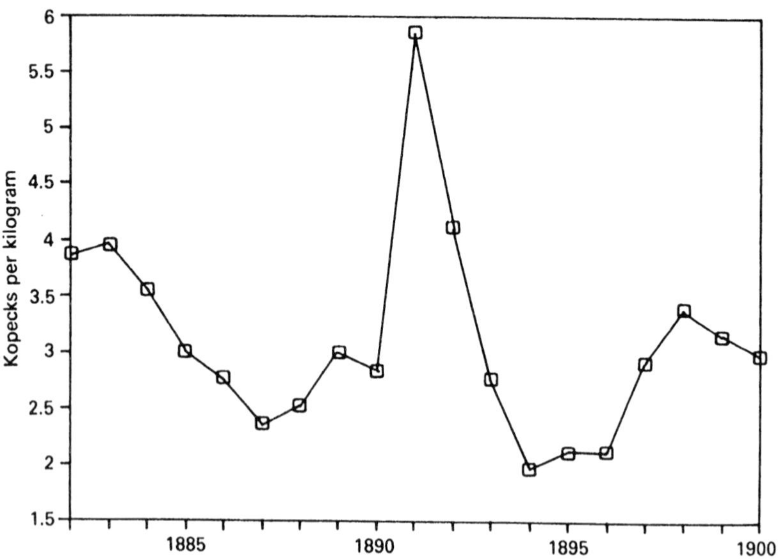

Figure 3.2 Price of rye in kopecks per kilogram.

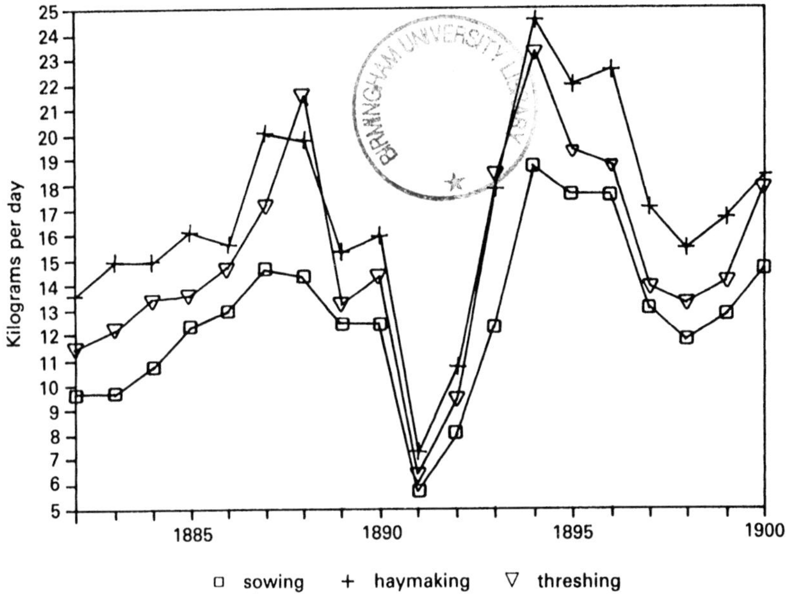

Figure 3.3 Rural daily wage labour in rye equivalents

Detailed figures for different regions indicate that the crisis was far more serious in the Volga and the Ukraine than in the northern areas closer to the industrial zone.[5]

Data on peasant indebtedness and on indirect tax payments also demonstrate the serious nature of the peasant crisis. This point needs to be emphasised because of the very misleading accounts of these phenomena that have recently been propagated by the American historian James Y. Simms.

Simms has argued that the major authorities (Wallace, Robinson, Von Laue, Volin and Milyukov) were wrong in considering that the growth in arrears of annual tax assessment payments was an indication of the peasant's inability to pay his taxes and 'prima facie evidence of distress within the countryside'.[6] Simms cites the aggregated data series given by Robinson to show that peasant arrears in redemption payments rose from 27 per cent of their annual assessment in 1880 to 119 per cent by 1898–1900, despite the reduction, deferment and cancellation of the debt that occurred in 1881, 1884, 1896 and 1899.[7] But he then proceeds to argue that these figures could not indicate peasant

TABLE 3.5 *Tax receipts for the Russian Empire in million rubles for different categories of taxation*

Year	*Alcohol receipts*	*Indirect taxes*	*Redemption receipts*
1886	237.0	35.3	48.8
1887	257.6	47.3	89.0
1888	265.1	54.5	92.3
1889	274.9	59.9	91.7
1890	268.4	64.7	88.2
1891	247.4	64.3	69.0
1892	269.0	75.3	77.1
1893	260.8	85.1	98.0
1894	297.4	100.2	92.8
1895	298.2	109.5	101.3
1896	294.3	106.0	96.9
1897	280.1	120.7	88.5
1898	289.6	126.4	86.2
1899	310.3	139.4	95.5

distress since the peasants were quite prepared to make their voluntary contributions to indirect taxes and the alcohol taxes, which tended to rise over this period. To support his case he quotes the well-known series of data (Table 3.5) on alcohol receipts and indirect tax payments that originated in the Ministry of Finances' centenary volumes and have been reproduced by one of the major Soviet economic historians.[8]

Simms concludes that rising peasant tax indebtedness should be interpreted as tax avoidance rather than as a sign of real desperation, and he denies that there was an overall crisis in Russian agriculture at this time.

However, on closer inspection it can be seen that these data on alcohol receipts show an overall decline in the famine years between 1889 and 1893. Furthermore, Simms' arguments totally collapse when we go behind his aggregated series and look at the regional picture. The use of the simplest of regional divisions, for example, the northern regions, the central regions (including the Volga and the central black-earth regions) and the southern regions (Ukraine and North Caucasus) indicate again that the crisis in the central regions were being masked by the favourable developments in the north and the south. Figure 3.4 indicates that although indirect taxation receipts increased in the north and the south during the famine, they did decline quite significantly in the Volga and central black-earth region. The blocks in the diagrams indicate that rural tax indebtedness was particularly high in the central regions, and contrary to Simms' suggestion, was actually rising during the famine when indirect taxation payments were falling.

Demographic Consequences of the Famine

The famine year of 1891–2 was marked by a distinct elevation in mortality that has normally been attributed exclusively to the famine. Richard G. Robbins, in his brief account of famine mortality, was aware that part of the extra mortality of 1892 was associated with the cholera epidemic of that year, but he nevertheless decided to include these cholera deaths as part of the famine-induced extra mortality. Relying on Pokrovskii's (1897) data, Professor Robbins calculated that:

> the average death rate in the sixteen provinces of European Russia most severely affected by the famine, rose from 3.76 percent (the norm for the period 1881–90) to 4.81 percent in 1892. In absolute figures, the number of deaths in the famine-stricken *gubernii* during 1892 was about 406,000 above normal. If the number of cholera deaths – 103,364 for the area in question – is subtracted from abnormal mortality, the estimate can be reduced to around 303,000 deaths. Since a sizeable portion of cholera mortality was undoubtedly famine-linked, however, this lower figure should not be accepted. An estimate that between 375,000 and 400,000 deaths occurred as a direct consequence of the disaster seems most reasonable.[9]

There are clearly two problems that need to be investigated here: 1) the scale and distribution of excess mortality; and 2) the relationship between cholera mortality and famine mortality. Neither of these problems is particularly simple.

The scale and distribution of excess mortality clearly depends on what is accepted as the normal level of mortality. In a footnote Robbins did admit that Pokrovskii's data raised some difficulties, and elsewhere he complained that 'because of the many factors which influenced the death rate in 1892, estimates of mortality varied.'[10] Below we will consider the different possible

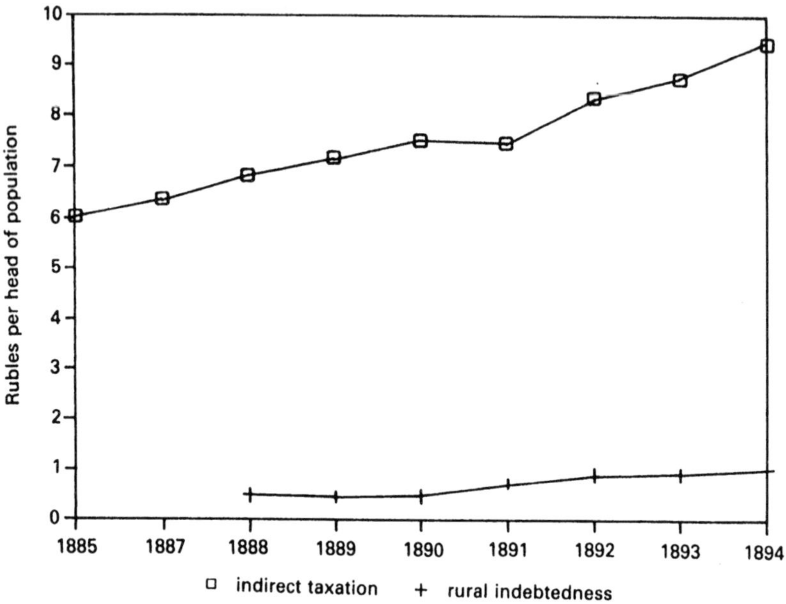
Rubles per head of population
10
9
8
7
6
5
4
3
2
1
0
1885
1887
1888
1889
1890
1891
1892
1893
1894
□ indirect taxation
+ rural indebtedness

(a)

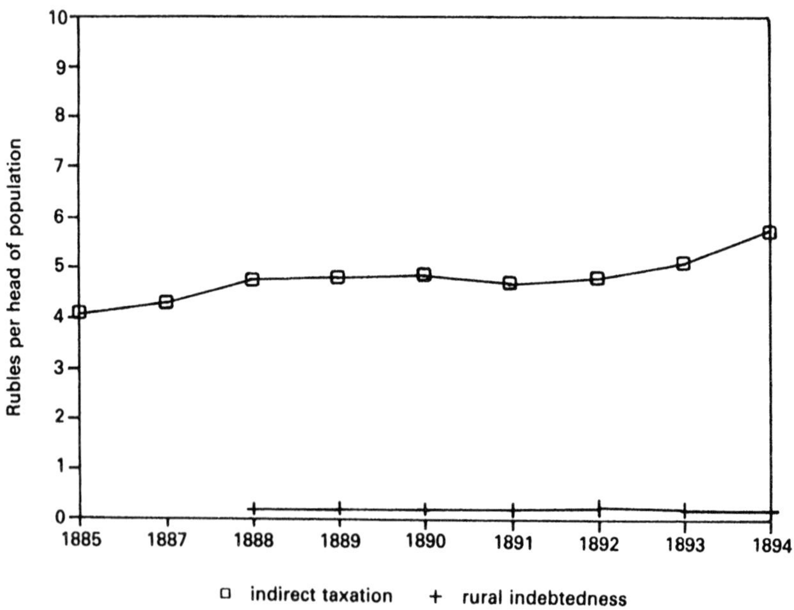
Rubles per head of population
10
9
8
7
6
5
4
3
2
1
0
1885
1887
1888
1889
1890
1891
1892
1893
1894
□ indirect taxation
+ rural indebtedness

(b)

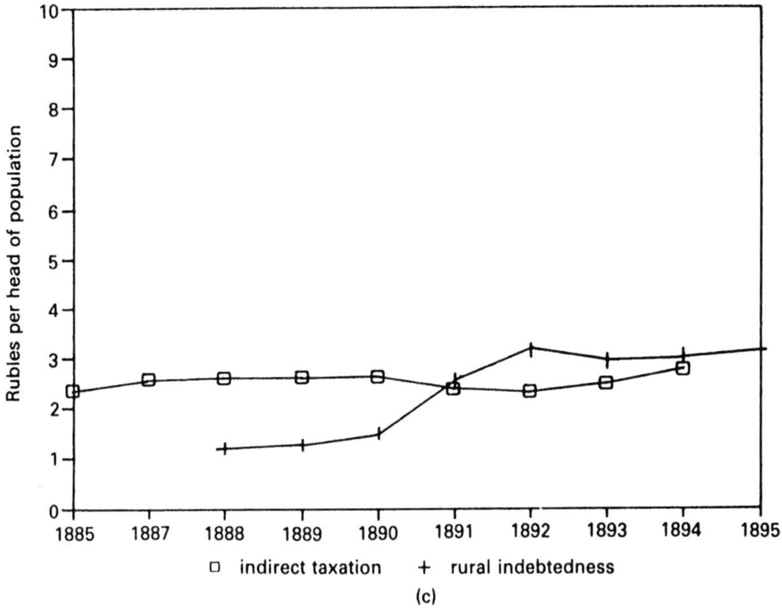

Figure 3.4 Comparative rural indebtedness on direct compared with indirect taxation per head of population by regions, 1885–95
(a) Northern consumer region
(b) Southern producer region
(c) Central producer region

indicators of the extent of the crisis in mortality and also the question of the relationship between famine mortality and cholera.

There are several possible indicators of crisis mortality; we will consider four [see Table 3.6]. The first indicator is simply the growth index of the population of the given province for 1892, calculated as the difference between the crude birth rate and the crude death rate. A minus figure indicates that births are not replacing deaths and indicates a decline in population measured per thousand of the population. Most of the Volga provinces experienced a surplus of deaths over births in these years.

The second method of calculating the level of excess mortality is the one used by V.I. Pokrovskii, who contributed the chapter on population movements to Chuprov and Posnikov's well-known book on the influence of harvests and grain prices on the Russian economy.[11] Pokrovskii compared the 1892 death rate

TABLE 3.6 *Different indicators of excess mortality in Russia in 1892*

		Total population, million	Demographic indicators				
			1	2	3	4	5
Main Volga Area			CBR*–CDR†	CDR 1892/ 1881–90	Deaths 1892/ 1890–1 & 1893–4	Deaths 1892/ 1888–90 & 1893–4	(Robbins)
(a) Central Volga							
provinces	Samara	2.65	−18.1	+56%	+56%	+59%	+67%
	Saratov	2.31	−13.8	+55%	+49%	+58%	+58%
	Kazan	2.08	−8.6	+36%	+30%	+33%	+36%
	Simbirsk	1.47	−8.5	+37%	+25%	+31%	+34%
	Penza	1.41	−3.9	+30%	+19%	+27%	+29%
(a) All C. Volga		9.92	−12.5	+44%	+39%	+45%	+48%
(b) East Volga							
provinces	Ufa	2.03	−5.2	+49%	+49%	+54%	+54%
	Orenburg	1.51	−10.9	+40%	+48%	+54%	+54%
(b) All E. Volga		3.54	−7.5	+45%	+49%	+54%	+54%
(c) West Volga							
provinces	Voronezh	2.42	−12.7	+49%	+42%	+50%	+50%
	Tambov	2.56	−0.2	+29%	+13%	+21%	+21%
	Tula	1.35	+2.4	+21%	+9%	+15%	+15%
	Ryazan	1.68	+2.4	+19%	+16%	+24%	+24%
(c) All W. Volga		8.01	−3.5	+28%	+22%	+29%	+29%

All Main Volga	21.47	−8.3	+38%	+33%	+40%	+42%
South East Volga						
Astrakhan province	0.98	−16.6	+96%	+81%	+91%	
Voinsko Don *oblast´*	2.36	(−4.4)				
Uralsk *oblast´*						
All S. E. Volga	(4.3)	−6.2				
North & West of Main Volga Area						
provinces: Vyatka	2.84	+2.4	+8%	+12%	+13%	
Orel	1.89	+6.0	+7%	+6%	+13%	
Kursk	2.25	+4.8	+7%	+6%	+11%	
N. Novgorod	1.50	(+0.5)	+4%			
Perm	2.83	−1.7	+2%	+9%	+10%	
N. & W. of Volga	11.31	+2.2	+6%			
Regions indirectly affected						
provinces: Tobolsk						
Arkhangelsk	0.33	(+10)				
Olonets	0.35	(+3)				
Kherson	2.47	(+16)		+10	+13%	
Taurida	1.30	(+14)		+16	+21%	
Kharkov						
All regions	(5.45)	(+11)		[+11]	[+16]	
All regions	(42.6)					
All 50 provinces	87.9	+5.0	+26%	+16%	+19%	

* CBR = Crude birthrate
† CDR = Crude deathrate

with his calculation of the 1881–90 death rate for the 16 provinces that were most seriously affected by the famine. According to Pokrovskii, mortality rose in these provinces from 37.6 per thousand in 1881–90 to 48.1 per thousand in 1892. This was equivalent to a level of 375,000 excess mortality.

However, Pokrovskii's data present problems, because his population figures were estimated before the results of the 1897 census were available. Consequently, they (like the official figures of the Central Statistical Committee (TsSK) of the time), were based on the results of the last 1857 *revizii* which had been updated by the current accounts of birth and death registrations. Unfortunately this procedure did not adequately take account of migrationary movements out of these regions. By 1892, according to later calculations, Pokrovskii and official statisticians were over-estimating the population of the 50 provinces of European Russia by 3.7 per cent. This has the effect of somewhat under-estimating the mortality rates.

Pokrovskii's methodology is also unsatisfactory because it fails to account for any long-term trend in the movement of mortality. It would be better to take as a norm a series of figures before and a series after the year of study. The Soviet demographer B. Ts. Urlanis compared the number of deaths in 1892 with those for the average of 1890, 1891, 1893 and 1894. Using this method Urlanis compared 3.6 million deaths in 1892 with 3.1 million in these four years, and consequently estimated a level of 500,000 excess mortality.[12] Table 3.6, column 3, uses the same method for each of the famine affected provinces.

Finally we have the slight modification on the third method used by Robbins in his book. In this method the number of deaths in 1892 are compared with the average for the five years 1888, 1889, 1890, 1893, 1894 except in those cases where Robbins considered the 1893 figures to be high; then the average of the other four figures was used. Since this seems a little arbitrary I have included a comparison with the five years in column 4, and the figures produced by Robbins in column 5. Whichever of these methods is used, they all clearly indicate that the level of excess mortality was significant and that it was concentrated in the Volga and the central agricultural regions.

The second major question in calculating famine mortality is the relationship between cholera mortality and famine mortality.

Cholera was not endemic in Russia. Each of the four epidemics which visited Russia in the nineteenth century originated in India and travelled across Asia Minor before entering Russia from the Caspian and progressing along the Volga. The approach of the epidemic from India to Persia, before it reached Russia, can easily be charted and clearly cannot be attributed to domestic developments within Russia.

Secondly, the level of case fatalities amongst cholera victims in the nineteenth century was uniformly high between 70 and 90 per cent, and there is no evidence to suggest that improved nourishment would significantly change this level.

The sole element in the incidence of cholera mortality that can be attributed to the famine was the number of individuals infected with cholera once the epidemic had reached Russia in July 1892. This element was indeed connected to famine events, but in a less direct way than is often assumed. People were catching cholera not because they were poorly fed, but because they were located in emergency insanitary locations along the Volga communications network where cholera was also prevalent. It was not so much malnutrition as the social disturbances (refugee movements, etc.) which contributed to the high incidence of cholera. The monthly chronology of mortality and its regional location clearly indicate this, as will be seen below.

The Scale of Food Aid

Robbins pointed out long ago, that the tsarist famine relief measures were remarkably good:

> Our survey of the impact of state aid programs in 1891–92 produces a surprisingly positive impression. Food supply operations were far from perfect, but they achieved the primary aims of any relief campaign. Government assistance averted the very real threat of mass starvation, held the death rate within acceptable limits, and prevented a total economic collapse in the stricken region. Admiration for official efforts increases, moreover, when we recall that they were undertaken in the face of serious institutional and political obstacles.[13]

The scale of the relief effort was indeed most impressive. The number of persons receiving food loans rose above one million in

TABLE 3.7 *Number of persons receiving food loans, by month, and excess mortality in 1891–92*[14]

1891 Harvest	*Food loans in million persons*	*Death compared with annual norms*		
		actual	*norm*	*% variation*
July	0.573	46.7	43.5	+7.4
August	0.200	40.0	41.3	−3.1
September	0.495	31.1	31.0	+0.3
October	1.331	33.3	29.7	+12.1
November	3.147	37.9	33.5	+13.1
December	5.464	33.4	34.4	−2.9
January	7.706	40.1	38.0	+5.5
February	9.669	39.5	36.1	+9.4
March	11.520	40.5	35.0	+15.7
April	11.852	38.3	33.5	+14.3
May	11.742	33.1	30.2	+9.6
June	11.141	41.4	34.9	+18.6
1892 Harvest				
July	5.070	58.8	43.5	+35.2
August	0.146	54.3	41.3	+31.5
September	0	38.5	31.0	+24.2
October	0	33.3	29.7	+12.1
November	0	35.2	33.5	+5.1
December	0	36.3	34.4	+5.5
January	0	40.4	38.0	+6.3
February	0	35.5	36.1	−1.7

October 1891, was over five million by December 1891 and was well over 11 million throughout March to June 1892. However, on examination it becomes clear that the scale of famine relief began to fall precisely at the time when mortality (primarily from cholera and other water-borne diseases) was increasing. Food relief began falling from 11 million in the first half of 1892 to five million in July and just over 140 000 in August 1892. (See Table 3.7)

The tsarist government began winding down the relief measures as soon as the more abundant supplies of the 1892 harvest started to become available, despite the fact that mortality was only beginning to rise to a level of more than 30 per cent above the seasonal norm.

A comparison of the regional incidence of grain failure, excess mortality rates and relief measures clearly indicates that the food relief was directed to the grain failure areas in the central Volga and the central black-earth districts, and that the excess mortality did coincide with some of these Volga areas but not with all of them. The highest level of mortality was in Astrakhan at the mouth of the Volga, where cholera was particularly intense, but no famine relief was directed to that location.

TABLE 3.8 *A comparison of the regional incidence of harvest failures, price rises, food-aid distribution and excess mortality*

	Food supply		*Demographic*	*Aid*
	Grain yield 1890 & 91 /norm in %	*Grain prices 1892/ 1889 in %*	*Deaths 1892/1890–1 & 1893–4 in %*	*% of population receiving food loans*
Main Volga Area				
(a) Central Volga				
Samara provinces	−48	+102	+56	39
Saratov provinces	−36	+94	+49	41
Kazan provinces	−48	+98	+30	53
Simbirsk provinces	−43	+102	+25	61
Penza provinces	−43	+119	+19	60
			+39	48
(b) East Volga				
Ufa provinces	−41	+110	+49	20
Orenburg provinces	−61	+202	+48	33
			+49	26
(c) West Volga				
Voronezh provinces	−18	+164	+42	41
Tambov provinces	−27	+110	+13	40
Tula provinces	−13	+130	+9	34
Ryazan provinces	−27	+122	+16	42
			+22	39
All Main Volga			+33	41

continued on page 62

Table 3.8 continued

	Food supply		Demographic	Aid
	Grain yield 1890 & 91 /norm in %	*Grain prices 1892/ 1889 in %*	*Deaths 1892/1890–1 & 1893–4 in %*	*% of population receiving food loans*
Other Volga areas and areas neighbouring on the Volga				
(a) South of Main Volga Area				
Astrakhan province	−23	+78	+81	0
Don *oblast′*	−6	+82		0
(b) North and West of Main Volga Area				
Vyatka provinces	−31	+98	+12	31
Orel provinces	−7	+89	+6	27
Kursk provinces	−18	+87	+4	20
N. Norgorod provinces	−31	+84	.	44
Perm provinces	−33	+78	+9	13
				25
All Other Volga Areas				20
Other regions affected				
Tobolsk provinces				(34)
Arkhangelsk provinces	−11	+63		27
Olonets provinces	+3	+66		9
Kherson provinces	−11	+75	+10	25
Taurida provinces	−12	+66	+16	14
Kharkov provinces	−21	+110	+11	0
				16
All above areas				27
All 50 provinces	−18	+78	+16	13

Conclusions

While fluctuations in overall food supply (that is, production less net exports) were undoubtedly the major cause of the famine, it is important to emphasise its regional and social incidence. Some areas were clearly much worse affected than others and the disaster was not borne equally by all sectors of the population. A study of the real wage rates of the rural labourers and the growth in indebtedness of the peasantry has helped to identify the incidence of the famine. The direct demographic consequences of the famine were probably greatly ameliorated by the extensive famine relief operations which were carried out. However, these relief measures stopped at a time when mortality was rising as a consequence of the cholera epidemic, the importance of which could only indirectly be attributed to the famine. The whole demographic position was greatly complicated by the coincidental outbreak of cholera, and the direct demographic consequences of the famine were far less than is commonly supposed.

NOTES

1. Many of the main arguments in this paper were prepared for a seminar with Maureen Perrie at the Centre for Russian and East European Studies, Birmingham, in 1980. However, they have gained greatly from discussions with Esther Kingston Mann, Timothy Mixter and Stephen Frank at a conference on the pre-revolutionary Russian peasantry, which was held in Boston in 1986. For a more detailed analysis of the agrarian crises and peasant living standards in late imperial Russia, comparing the crisis of the 1890s with that of 1904–6, see 'Crises and the Condition of the Peasantry in Late Imperial Russia', in Esther Kingston Mann and Timothy Mixter (eds) *Peasant Economy, Culture, and the Politics of European Russia, 1800–1921* (Princeton, 1991).
2. See food consumption data surveyed by S.G. Wheatcroft, *Soviet Industrialisation Project Seminar Working Paper*, no. 2, pp. 85–97, esp. p. 94.
3. Note that the growth rates are dependent to some extent on the periodisation used.
4. The following and several of the subsequent figures are based on the calculations made in S.G. Wheatcroft, 'Grain Production and Utilisation in Russia and the USSR before Collectivisation' (PhD, University of Birmingham, 1980) vol. III.
5. See S.G. Wheatcroft, 'Crises and the Condition of the Peasantry'.
6. James Y. Simms, Jr, 'The Crisis in Russian Agriculture at the End of the Nineteenth Century: A Different View', *Slavic Review*, XXXVI (1977) pp. 379–80.
7. Ibid., p. 380, citing G.T. Robinson, *Rural Russia Under the Old Regime* (London, 1932) pp. 95–6.
8. *Ministerstvo Finansov, 1802–1902*, part 2 (St Petersburg, 1902) pp. 640–47, cited by Simms, 'Crisis in Russian Agriculture', p. 382, from P.A. Khromov, *Ekonomicheskoe razvitie Rossii v XIX-XX vekakh* (Moscow, 1950) pp. 498–503. The originals were given with no regional breakdown and with no explanatory notes. The figures differ somewhat from the more detailed figures available in the ministry's publications of the time.

9. R.G. Robbins, Jr, *Famine in Russia, 1891–1892: The Imperial Government Responds to a Crisis* (New York, 1975) p. 171.
10. Ibid. In n. 17, p. 171, Robbins states that 'Pokrovskii's data are not without flaw, but they are extremely useful and accessible.'
11. V.I. Pokrovskii, 'Vliyanie kolebanii urozhaya i khlebnikh tsen na estestvennoe dvizhenie naseleniya', in A.I. Chuprov and A.S. Posnikov (eds) *Vliyanie urozhaev i khlebnikh tsen na nekotorye storony russkogo narodnogo khozyaistva* (St Petersburg, 1897).
12. See B.Ts. Urlanis, *Rozhdaemost′ i prodolzhitel′nost′ zhizni v SSSR* (Moscow, 1963) p. 83.
13. Robbins, *Famine in Russia*, p. 173.
14. These figures on food aid were presented by Robbins, ibid., pp. 186–7, citing *Statisticheskie dannye po vydache ssud na obsemenenie i prodovol′stvie naseleniyu postradavshemu ot neurozhaya v 1891–1892 gg.* in *Vremennik Tsentral′nogo statisticheskogo komiteta*, vol. XXVIII (St Petersburg, 1894) pp. 42–3. The figures on mortality were calculated from a number of issues of this publication. The norm was accepted as the average number of deaths for 1887–96.

4 'A Worker in Disguise': A.V. Peshekhonov's Contribution to the Debate on the Peasant at the Turn of the Century

Maureen Perrie

A.V. Peshekhonov is best known for his political activity as a leader of the Popular Socialist Party in 1906–18 and Minister of Food Supply in the Provisional Government in the summer of 1917. Yet some of his most important work was accomplished before the 1905 Revolution, in the form of a series of articles in the 'legal populist' journal *Russkoe bogatstvo*. Here he developed an analysis of the nature of the peasant economy which was to influence the agrarian policies of both the Popular Socialist and the Socialist-Revolutionary parties, and which also foreshadowed in many respects the views of the 'Organisation and Production' school of rural economists, headed by A.V. Chayanov, which have recently been influential in the West.[1] Peshekhonov's writings on the peasantry, therefore, not only constitute an undeservedly little-known contribution to neo-populist thought,[2] but also have relevance to a debate which continues to reverberate in academic circles to the present day, and which, if Teodor Shanin is to be believed, may also have significance for contemporary 'developing societies'.[3]

Peshekhonov himself was very familiar with the Russian countryside. The son of a village priest, he worked first as a village teacher, and then as a zemstvo statistician. In 1896–8 he headed the statistical bureau of the Kaluga provincial zemstvo, and in 1898–1901 that of Poltava province. After his arrest in 1901 for participating in a political demonstration, he was forbidden further zemstvo service, and thereafter he was involved primarily in journalistic and political activity.[4] Unlike the writings of many of his more theoretically minded contemporaries, Peshekhonov's contribution to the debate on the peasantry was firmly based on zemstvo statistical materials, and reflected his practical professional experience of peasant life.

THE 'LAND GATHERERS'

The earliest articles which Peshekhonov contributed to *Russkoe bogatstvo* were devoted to the differentiation of the peasantry. In the first of these, 'On the Question of the Role of the "Land Gatherers" in Russian Agricultural Production', he was concerned primarily with the issue of whether a class of capitalist farmers was emerging from the peasantry.[5] In this article, Peshekhonov raised the issue of the development of capitalism in Russian agriculture. In a polemic directed as much against the Ministry of Finance as against the Marxist revolutionaries, he pointed out that as the prospects of a class of large-scale agricultural capitalists emerging from the nobility or other social groups were fading, greater hopes were being placed on the development of a category of 'thrifty peasants' (*khozyaistvennye muzhichki*) who would perform the functions of 'land gatherers' by purchasing land from their destitute neighbours and from the spendthrift squires. Belief in the existence of such thrifty peasants was based on zemstvo statistics which showed the heterogeneity of the peasantry: it was thought that this inequality was the result of a process of inevitable economic differentiation which would, on the one hand, 'liberate' the worker from the means of production and, on the other, concentrate the means of production in the hands of capitalist elements. Even Count Witte in his report to the Tsar for 1896 had referred to the emergence of a 'prosperous section of the rural population' which would contribute to the national prosperity as a result of capitalist development. It was assumed that on the large (*mnogozemel'nye*) peasant farms, labour was more productive than on smaller farms, that techniques were better, and that there was greater capital investment.[6]

Unfortunately, Peshekhonov pointed out, there was no evidence that the impoverishment of the mass of the peasantry was being accompanied by a process of capital accumulation and the enrichment of a minority. There was not even any evidence that the 'thrifty peasants' were a new phenomenon: it was just as likely that they were the survivors of an earlier more prosperous peasantry, who had not yet been affected by impoverishment, or had been less affected by it than others.[7] There was even less evidence that the largest farmers were the best producers: on the contrary, the data which the author was going to adduce in his article suggested the opposite to be the case.[8]

On the basis of statistical data from Zadonskii *uezd* (district), Voronezh province, for 1886, and from Orel *uezd*, Orel province, for 1894, Peshekhonov argued that the proportion of peasant farms which could be regarded as 'land gatherers' was insignificant: in Zadonskii *uezd* 2.5 per cent of farms had more than 25 desyatins of allotment land, while in Orel *uezd* only 1.3 per cent had more than 20 desyatins. Admittedly, the proportions of land which they held were higher than this (8.2 and 5.4 per cent respectively of allotment land, and 9.3 and 6.5 per cent of all land, including purchased and rented land). But when land per head was considered, the 'excess' of allotment land held by these largest farms was only 3.0 and 3.1 per cent respectively; and of all land, 4.2 per cent in both cases. Characteristically, these largest farms also had the largest households; and this, Peshekhonov suggested, supported his hypothesis that far from representing a new economic phenomenon, these households might represent the survivors of older 'family communes' or extended-family farms which had not yet undergone division.[9]

It was often asserted, Peshekhonov continued, that the largest farms had a greater amount of capital than the smaller ones. Statistics certainly demonstrated that the amount of livestock per household or per head of population was higher in larger than in smaller farms. But in relation to land, his data showed, the larger farms in both *uezdy* actually had a smaller number of work-horses and cows than the average. Data from other districts, he asserted, would confirm his conclusions that the group of land-rich peasants was numerically insignificant; that the amount of land it had 'gathered' was negligible; that in its family composition it did not resemble a capitalist enterprise; and that it had a relatively smaller amount of livestock than the farms with less land.[10]

Peshekhonov then went on to examine more recent statistical data for Kaluga province, which he himself had edited for publication.[11] A sample survey of 8626 peasant farms showed a similar pattern to the two districts of Voronezh and Orel provinces: a small percentage of large farms (3 per cent, with 10.6

per cent of the sown area); a small amount of 'excess' land (5.2 per cent); a larger family size (11.8) than the average (6.6); and a smaller number of work-horses per 100 desyatins of sown area (24) than the average of 35.[12] On the basis of a detailed analysis of the mix of crops on the sample group of farms, and their yields and gross income, Peshekhonov concluded that the productivity of the land was higher on the smaller farms than on the large ones.[13] This therefore contradicted the hopes which certain economists placed on the development of large farms: if indeed a process of concentration of land was taking place, it did not 'promise an increase in the productivity of labour and an increase in national wealth'.[14]

Finally, Peshekhonov dealt with the question of commodity production by the peasantry. He noted that even the largest farms in Kaluga province produced less food per capita than was regarded as the minimum required for subsistence, and were therefore net purchasers rather than sellers of produce. The smaller farms, in fact, in order to raise essential cash, devoted a greater proportion of their land to industrial crops (mainly flax and hemp) for the market than did the larger farms.[15] The larger farms used their greater amount of land not to extend commodity production, but to improve the quality of the family's diet by increasing its ratio of grain to potatoes. The 'thrifty peasants', therefore, far from being 'exploiters', were the only elements in the Kaluga countryside who had anything like enough to eat.[16]

In conclusion, the author admitted that his somewhat limited evidence from one province in one year could not be regarded as definitive, and that further research was required, particularly by zemstvo statisticians. He had simply wanted to question the frequently made assumption that:

> large peasant farms are the forerunners of the capitalist development of agriculture, that they bring with them an increase in the productivity of labour and of national wealth, and that the 'land gatherers' have a mission to save our agricultural production.[17]

PEASANTS AND WORKERS IN THEIR MUTUAL RELATIONSHIPS

Peshekhonov's next major article for *Russkoe bogatstvo* was concerned with the opposite end of the differentiation debate: the issue of the proletarianisation of the peasantry.[18] 'Peasants and Workers in their Mutual Relationships' was based on the recently published results of the zemstvo statistical survey he had conducted in Kozelsk *uezd*, Kaluga province in 1896. This involved a brief census of all peasant households, plus detailed budget studies of 1313 farms.[19]

In producing a journalistic account of his specialist professional work, Peshekhonov was pursuing primarily publicistic and polemical aims. Two recent developments, one literary and the other political, had made the issue of the relationship between peasants and workers a topical one. Chekhov's short story 'Peasants' (*Muzhiki*), which gave an unflattering picture of the countryside, had been hailed by P.B. Struve as demonstrating what Marx had once notoriously called the 'idiocy of rural life'. In response, the Populist writer Mikhailovskii had condemned Struve for seeking to divide the workers and the peasants.[20] Secondly, the 'Manifesto' of the newly formed Russian Social Democratic Labour Party, written by the same P.B. Struve, had stressed the exclusive revolutionary role of the urban industrial proletariat.[21] Peshekhonov sought to enter the fray against the Marxists by stressing the common interests of the peasants and workers.

Those who contrasted the peasants (as 'petty-bourgeois') to the urban workers, he began, were influenced solely by 'theoretical constructions' which could not be justified by real life. The workers were not the only Russian representatives of 'labour ideals'; the majority of them were not even proletarians, but peasants on side earnings (*promyslovyi otkhod*); peasant and worker were combined, not so much in the same individual, as in the same family and household. 'Many people' tended to see *otkhod* as no more than a stage in the process of proletarianisation and urban relocation of the peasantry; but there was evidence that the link between peasant and worker in the same household was based on real economic interests, and was likely to be durable. The interests of workers and peasants were therefore not only not in conflict, but identical: the worker had a stake in peasant agriculture because of the contribution which the farm made to his household income; and the peasant in turn was interested in the level of industrial wages because of the part they played in his family budget.[22]

Peshekhonov's data from Kozelsk *uezd* grouped the peasant farms into six categories based on their sown area. For the purposes of his article, however, he reduced these to three groups: small (less than 3 desyatins), 33.1 per cent of farms; medium (3–9 desyatins), 56.5 per cent; and large (over 9 desyatins), 10.4 per cent.[23] He stressed, however, as he had in his earlier article on the 'land gatherers', that the fact of the heterogeneity of the peasantry was not in itself evidence of the operation of any process of stratification or differentiation within the village.[24]

In all groups of peasant farms in Kozelsk *uezd*, the overwhelming majority (about 85 per cent) were involved to a greater or lesser extent in *promysly*. Cottage industry (*kustarnye promysly*) was insignificant in the *uezd*, and the great majority of off-farm earnings came in the form of wage-work on the national industrial and, to a lesser extent, agricultural labour markets.[25] The degree of involvement of the three groups of farms in *promysly* was however different. The smaller the farm, the less was the proportion of the household's productive labour which was utilised in its own agricultural production, and the greater the proportion which was utilised on *promysly*.[26] But when the return was calculated for each day's productive labour, the situation of the three groups varied in a surprising manner. The smaller the farm, the higher the income derived per day's work devoted to agriculture, and the lower the income derived per day's work on *promysly*.[27] Although the farms utilised slightly less than half their productive labour on *promysly*, they derived considerably more than half their income from this source.[28] Overall, the peasants made a profit (a surplus of income over expenditure) from *promysly*, and a loss from their own farming, and this was also true of the large and medium-sized farms. The small farms, however, made a profit from their own farms and a loss from *promysly*.[29]

In terms of economic theory, as Peshekhonov pointed out, these conclusions were improbable. On his own farm, the peasant was a proprietor who owned his means of production, and could be expected to obtain surplus product. On side earnings, he was a freely hired worker who could be expected to obtain, in the form of a wage, only the cost of his labour. His rate of return from farming should therefore be higher than that from *promysly*; and there ought not to be any relationship between his agricultural income and his industrial wage.[30] Peshekhonov therefore concluded the first part of his article with a series of questions.

(1) Why was the peasants' utilisation of their labour on their own farms less profitable than its utilisation elsewhere as hired labour? And if this was indeed the case, why did they not abandon farming and devote themselves entirely to wage-labour?

(2) How could the peasants derive a profit from hired labour, thus apparently obtaining surplus value from wages?

(3) Why, contrary to widespread assumptions about the greater productivity of large peasant farms, was labour more productive on smaller farms? Conversely, since all were supposed to be equal on the hired-labour market, why was the labour from large farms better paid on *promysly* than that from small farms? And if this was the case, why did the larger households devote the greater proportion of their labour to farming on their own account, while the smaller households expended more of their labour on *promysly*? Why was it that the smaller the farm, the better paid was the labour expended on it, and the worse paid the labour which it sold elsewhere? And why, in that case, did the small farms not abandon their loss-making *promysly* and concentrate their resources on their own farming? Conversely, why did the large farms not reduce their loss-making agricultural production and maximise their resources in the more profitable field of *promysly*?[31] The answers to all of these questions, Peshekhonov assured his readers, could be found in the nature of the peasant economy, and, in particular, in the relationship between peasants and workers in the same household.[32]

The data from Kozelsk *uezd* provided more detailed confirmation of many of the conclusions which Peshekhonov had drawn in his earlier article on the 'land gatherers'. Small farms were more intensive than large ones: they expended more labour per unit of land; they obtained a higher income per desyatin, for the same amount of fixed and circulating capital; and their labour was better paid.[33] In a situation where farming was geared to satisfying the consumption needs of the household, rather than to production for the market,[34] the greater intensity of agriculture on the small farms was determined by their higher proportion of consumers to land. The smaller households had a higher ratio of *promyshlenniki* to agricultural producers than the larger farms; and since the *promyshlenniki* and their dependents were also consumers of the household's produce, the ratio of consumers to agricultural producers was higher on the smaller farms.[35] Because of their greater consumption needs, the smaller farms had a higher proportion of consumption animals (cattle, sheep and pigs) to work-animals (horses) than the larger farms. Overall, the smaller households had a higher ratio of livestock to land than the larger households, and this provided them with more manure per desyatin, thereby contributing to the greater productivity of their land. The smaller farms also had a higher ratio of human to animal consumers than the larger farms, and thus they devoted a greater proportion of their land to crops for human consumption rather than animal fodder. For these reasons, the smaller farms were able to grow relatively more of such valuable consumption crops as barley, potatoes, flax and millet, which required well-manured soil, while the larger farms had to devote proportionately more of their sown area both to fodder crops such as oats, and to cheaper food crops such as buck-wheat which could grow on poorer soil.[36]

Having thus explained the greater productivity of agricultural labour in the small households, Peshekhonov went on to explain the higher wages earned by workers from large farms. The large farms sent proportionately more of their workers away on distant wage-work, where wages were higher, than did the small farms. A higher proportion of small farms than large farms had only one male worker, which was the minimum required for agricultural viability. Such a worker could find only local employment, which was less remunerative than distant wage-work, and this explained the lower rates of return for *promysly* on small farms.[37]

In comparing the farms' incomes from wage-work with that from their own farming, Peshekhonov had evaluated the farm produce at local market prices. As he now recognised, however, this was not a valid procedure, since within the household, produce was exchanged not for market prices but for a share of the worker's wages; conversely, the amount of produce received by the worker in return for his wage was proportional to the household's production. Small farms produced proportionately more and better produce than large farms, but because their workers earned lower wages, their real return for their effort was the same as on large farms, where higher wages corresponded to lower agricultural productivity.[38]

In all three groups of farms, Peshekhonov calculated, the reward for a day's labour was more or less identical. This meant that the income of the peasant population was determined entirely by its labour, rather than by its land or capital, and therefore that its budget was 'the budget of a worker and not of a *rentier*'.[39] This, he added, was one form of the 'capitalisation of the income of agricultural production' (i.e. the capitalist appropriation of the income of peasant farmers) to which the populist economist Nikolai-on had previously drawn attention, except that in this case the peasant's income was being appropriated 'not just by merchant capital but also by industrial capital and by all those who buy peasant labour at a price which is only a supplement, as it is called in arithmetic, to his earnings from his own farming.'[40] The peasant's own farming, therefore, Peshekhonov argued, his land and his 'capital' was 'only a disguise (*maska*) which conceals a worker, a man of labour, a man whose income is proportional to the expenditure of his labour. The peasant is a true worker, although he works not in the town but in the countryside, not in someone else's but in his own economic enterprise.'[41]

What were the implications of this for the prospects of the expropriation of the peasantry? The Kozelsk peasants, Peshekhonov reminded his readers, already spent almost half their labour on wage-work, and therefore might seem likely candidates for proletarianisation. In practice, however, the existing situation operated to the peasants' advantage. The earnings of those on *promysly* exceeded their expenditure on their consumption needs. This was particularly true of the peasant-workers on more distant employment, where wage-levels were higher because of the presence of permanent urban workers who had to support their wives and children at urban market prices for food and clothing. The peasant-worker, by contrast, could meet the consumption needs of his family more cheaply in the village. Moreover, since the demand for urban wage-work was mostly for adult males, the permanent urban worker had to regard his wife and children primarily as dependents, while the peasant-worker's wife and children could be employed productively on the family farm.

The peasant who decided to abandon his farm and move to the town would thereby deprive himself of the two advantages of his existing situation: the cheapness of rural life and the earnings of his wife and children. In addition, the separation of worker from peasant, in the case of small farms, would mean abandoning the more profitable part of the enterprise. Conversely, if the large farms were to abandon outside earnings and concentrate on farming, they too would be sacrificing the more profitable part of their economy. It was not surprising that both groups preferred to maintain the status quo.[42]

From the point of view of the employer, too, the status quo was advantageous, Peshekhonov continued. Because the peasant-workers regarded their wage-earnings simply as a supplement to their farm income, the capitalist entrepreneur was able to purchase their labour for less than its cost, thereby 'capitalising' the income from peasant farming.[43]

In spite of his argument that the separation of worker from peasant was contrary to the interests of both workers and employers, Peshekhonov nevertheless came to the conclusion that the expropriation of the peasantry was indeed taking place in contemporary Russian society.[44] Although his data had shown that the average return for a day's work on *promysly* or on their own farms was more or less identical for all groups of farms, the annual income per head on small farms was lower than that on large farms, because small farms were able to make productive use of a smaller part of their labour time than large farms.[45] The standard of living on small farms was therefore lower than on large farms: they consumed less food per head than on large farms, and suffered higher mortality and sickness. It was not only the smallest farms which made a loss, however; after paying taxes, only a tiny minority of the large farms were in profit, and their profits were too small even to serve as a basis for their abandonment of outside wage-work, let alone for the reorganisation of their agricultural production on capitalist lines. In order to survive, the mass of the peasants would either have to cut back further on their consumption, or dispose of their means of production, and there was evidence that the smallest farms were already having to do both.[46]

The expropriation of the peasantry was therefore taking place, Peshekhonov concluded, but it was occurring not as a result of differentiation, i.e. the separation of worker from peasant, affecting only one part of the rural population, but as a result of mass destitution. Because of the advantages of retaining their farms, the peasants would resist expropriation for as long as possible, making proletarianisation a prolonged and painful process. The effects would be harmful not only for the peasantry but for the economy as a whole, as demand would be reduced, and mortality would increase. The working class too would suffer, since the influx on to the labour market of pauperised small farmers would lower the wage levels and standard of living of the urban proletariat. This unorganised mass of destitute and unemployed ex-peasants, Peshekhonov warned obliquely, could endanger the prospects of the 'promised land' of socialism which the Marxists expected proletarianisation to bring about.[47]

THE THEORY AND PRACTICE OF PEASANT ECONOMY

Peshekhonov's next major article in *Russkoe bogatstvo* was published in 1902, and dealt with the 'theory and practice of peasant economy'.[48] In his earlier articles, Peshekhonov had noted that the heterogeneity of the peasantry was not in itself evidence of the existence of a process of differentiation, and he had complained about the absence of data which would help resolve this issue.[49] In recent years, however, a number of surveys had been repeated, and it was now possible to draw some conclusions about differentiation as a dynamic process.[50]

These repeated surveys showed that the number of peasant households had increased in all the eight localities for which published data existed. The net increase in the number of households was the result of various processes. The return of families from the towns, offsetting to some extent the rural-urban migration of whole households, played a part in this increase; but the most important processes were family divisions, which outnumbered the extinction or amalgamation of households.[51] These processes tended to affect households at the extremes of the size scale: large households were most likely to divide; while small households were more likely to die out or amalgamate. The size of peasant households therefore tended towards the average rather than towards the extremes; and this process in turn derived from the very nature of the peasant household.[52]

As Peshekhonov had shown in his earlier article on 'Peasants and Workers', the organisation of the peasant farm was determined by the combination of consumption needs and forces of production within the household.[53] The size of the farm increased with that of the family, and there was a complex interaction between the two. Small households would reduce their farming, and large households would increase it, until an equilibrium was reached between the size of the family and the scale of its economic enterprise. But this tendency towards the extremes had natural limits, in the form of the 'perturbational' processes previously discussed: the tendency of large farms to split as the sons grew up and married; and of small farms to disappear through the death of older members and the marriage of young girls and widows. As a result of these processes, the tendency towards the average household size would be restored.[54]

An equilibrium between the consumption needs and productive forces of a peasant household could, Peshekhonov noted, be achieved only in ideal conditions, with the free availability of land. External circumstances, however, meant that in practice this did not happen. In the contemporary situation of land shortage, the average family size on a peasant farm was increasing while landholding was decreasing, and the equilibrium between the family's needs and its resources was being destroyed.[55] In the absence of the means of extending peasant landholding, intensification offered an opportunity to restore the equilibrium of peasant farming; but intensification required capital investment, which the peasants could not afford. The repeated surveys showed a general decline in the ratio of livestock to land, contributing further to the destruction of the equilibrium of the peasant farm.[56]

In a situation where they had little opportunity either to extend or to intensify their own farming, therefore, the peasantry were increasingly resorting to outside earnings (*promysly*), which, with the increasing capitalisation of industrial activity in the post-emancipation period, increasingly meant wage-labour. The industrial part of the population was unable to separate itself from the agricultural part, for the reasons Peshekhonov had outlined in his earlier article.[57] The peasants' weak economic position meant that their surplus product was now being appropriated not only by the landowners, through high rents, and by the merchants, through low prices for produce, but also by industrial capitalists through exploitative wages, and by taxes which served the interests of the ruling classes as well as those of the state.[58] The peasant question was thus now becoming increasingly equated with the worker question, and both could be solved only by government policies which would enable the peasant to retain enough of his surplus product to provide the capital investment which would enable him to intensify his farming. The improvement of the peasants' position would benefit the workers, whose wage-levels would no longer be undermined by impoverished peasants. And higher industrial wages would in turn benefit the peasants, both directly and indirectly.[59]

In the concluding summary of his article, Peshekhonov stressed the family character of the peasant household as the main distinguishing feature of the peasant economy. The tendency of households to revert to an average size prevented the formation of distinct classes within the peasantry. External factors could not overcome this tendency; but they were forcing the peasants into wage-work without creating a separate class of workers.[60] The peasants were ceasing to obtain surplus product, and so 'The peasantry, in the true sense of that word, as a class of working proprietors, has ceased to exist. The peasant is now no more nor less than a disguised worker.'[61] Destitution was now affecting the great mass of the peasantry, as the 'disguised workers' now bore the main burden of agricultural production in the country as a whole. Their inability to invest in the intensification of their farming was leading to agricultural decline, and threatened the entire economy with disruption. Mere palliatives could not solve the peasant question: broad socio-economic reforms were required, which would make the peasant the proprietor of his own produce, by guaranteeing him both the means and the instruments of production.[62]

THE AGRARIAN PROBLEM AND ITS SOLUTION

In his articles of 1897–1902, Peshekhonov had been mainly concerned with the debate with the Marxists about the differentiation of the peasantry, the expropriation of the peasant-worker from the means of production, and the capitalist rationality or otherwise of the peasant economy. In the period 1903–5, however, when the agrarian question was raised more sharply by the peasant disturbances of 1902 in the Ukraine and on the Volga, and by the peasant movement in the 1905 Revolution, the author devoted more attention to relations between the peasants and the gentry landlords, and to the advocacy of a solution to the agrarian question.

In 1903 and 1904 Peshekhonov published a series of articles in *Russkoe bogatstvo* which were devoted to the evidence and recommendations of the local committees on the needs of agriculture which had been established by Witte in 1902.[63] Peshekhonov argued that the origins of Russia's current agrarian problem lay in the emancipation settlement of 1861, which had deliberately given the peasants less land than they were capable of working, in order to guarantee a labour supply on the *pomeshchik* estates. Nor was the average allotment sufficient to maintain the household's consumption needs at the level it had been able to satisfy under serfdom.[64] The peasant was therefore obliged to appear on the exchange market as a worker; and with population growth this necessity became even stronger:

> In whatever role the peasant appears on the market – whether as seller or buyer, as agricultural or industrial producer, as wage-labourer or leaser of land – the other side always has the possibility of relating to him as a worker, as an object designed for exploitation.[65]

Merchants exploited the peasants by offering them low prices when they were selling produce, and high prices when they were buying it; industrial employers exploited them by paying them wages which barely covered their consumption costs; and landowners exploited them through low agricultural wages and high rents. Even as a renter of land, where the peasant might seem to be operating as an independent entrepreneur, he was often compelled by land-shortage to rent land at a price which gave him a lower return than the average agricultural wage. Because of the appropriation of his surplus product by other classes, the peasant was unable to improve or intensify his farming.[66]

The peasant thus could survive only by lowering his income to that of a wage, or even dropping below that level by selling off his property or reducing his personal consumption. In this situation the large landowner had no incentive to introduce capitalist farming methods. High land rents, pushed up by the pressures of peasant land-shortage, made it more profitable for the landlord to rent his land to the peasantry than to work it himself; nor was there any incentive for outsiders to invest their capital in agriculture, since land rents and prices were too high for farming to yield an acceptable return. Large-scale farming was therefore economic only on the basis of mass exploitation of the peasantry: there was thus no more prospect of technical progress in private agriculture than there was in peasant farming.[67] Under existing conditions, therefore, there was no possibility of improvement in either sector of Russian agriculture, Peshekhonov concluded: the peasants had no resources, and the large landowners had no incentive, to invest in intensification. The coexistence of peasant and landlord farming had negative consequences not only for Russian agriculture, but for the economy as a whole, as the impoverishment of the peasantry destroyed the domestic market for industrial goods and kept down the wages of urban workers. The only way forward was to cut the Gordian knot which bound peasant and landowner together – by abolishing private landownership, nationalising the land, and making it available for rent to the working peasantry.[68]

* * *

Peshekhonov's views fall clearly within the populist tradition of economic analysis which stressed the negative effects of capitalism on the Russian economy. While acknowledging the development of capitalism in industry and commerce, he contended that it could not develop in agriculture, because of the nature of the relationship between peasant and gentry farming which had been created by the emancipation settlement. The capitalism which had developed in other sectors of the economy, moreover, was itself helping to prevent the growth of agrarian capitalism. The capitalist appropriation of the peasants' surplus product contributed to their reduction to the status of hired workers, and prevented the intensification of either peasant or gentry farming on capitalist lines. The vicious circle which had thus been created was in its turn serving to undermine capitalism elsewhere in the economy, as the impoverishment of the peasantry reduced the internal market for industrial goods.

Viewed with the benefit of hindsight, Peshekhonov's analysis of the nature of the crisis in Russian agriculture at the turn of the century may seem excessively pessimistic and 'catastrophist', being perhaps overly influenced by populist dogma about the impossibility of agrarian capitalism in Russia. Developments between 1905 and 1914 suggest that the Russian economy was more capable of breaking out of its vicious circle than Peshekhonov had predicted. In the period in which he was writing, however, his views appeared very plausible, and his analysis of the crisis of the turn of the century is still not without interest.[69]

Not all of Peshekhonov's views, of course, are entirely convincing. He may well have exaggerated the extent to which the peasant-worker relationship impeded the proletarianisation of peasant households (as opposed to that of individuals), by contributing to the mass destitution of the peasantry as a whole, rather than the expropriation of its poorest elements. Leaving aside the question of how far Kozelsk *uezd* could be regarded as 'typical' of the Russian countryside, his own evidence had shown that the smallest farms were the worst affected by the crisis, and were the first to sell off their means of production.

His argument that the peasant was no more than a 'disguised worker' is also less than persuasive. The peasants' budget might well resemble that of the workers, in so far as their income was proportional to the amount of labour they expended, rather than to the amount of capital they owned; but to equate peasants and workers on this basis alone was to overlook the many social, cultural and economic differences between the two categories. Perhaps it is most charitable to view Peshekhonov's conclusion primarily as a debating point against the Marxists, whose own equation of the peasant with a capitalist, solely on the grounds that both owned their means of production, was equally absurd. Certainly Peshekhonov's more general argument, that the mass of the contemporary Russian peasantry were the victims of capitalist exploitation, and to that extent had a common interest with the workers in the overthrow of capitalism, was in line with mainstream neo-populist thinking in the early twentieth century.[70]

Peshekhonov's position differed significantly from that of other populists, however, in the lack of emphasis which he placed on the peasant commune. This divided him from the Socialist Revolutionaries: where the latter's agrarian programme demanded 'socialisation' of the land, the Popular Socialists called for its 'nationalisation'. Peshekhonov attributed the search within the peasant household for an equilibrium between its consumption needs and its labour resources not to the operations of the repartitional commune, but to the internal economic rationality of the family farm. He explained the persistence of the link between peasant and worker within the household not in terms of the commune 'tying' the worker to the land, but again in terms of the economic logic of the family farm. By shifting the attention of populist economics away from the commune to the household, Peshekhonov was pointing the way for the Organisation and Production School of the post-1905 period.

Peshekhonov's analysis retains its greatest interest in these areas where he most strikingly anticipates the views of Chayanov and his followers. Peshekhonov showed that statistical data revealing the heterogeneity and inequality of the peasantry did not in themselves constitute evidence of the operation of a process of differentiation in the countryside. He demonstrated that rural socio-economic mobility took the form not of polarisation, but of a 'levelling' tendency towards a mean, which impeded the formation of classes within the peasantry. And he was aware of the political and ideological implications of these findings.

In the last twenty years or so, these insights, in their Chayanovite or neo-Chayanovite form at least, have become increasingly accepted in the West. The failures of Soviet policy towards the peasantry, from the *Kombedy* of 1918 to the forced collectivisation of 1929–30, have been explained in terms of the party leadership's adherence to an inappropriate Marxist conceptualisation of the dynamics of Russian rural society.[71] The recent 'rehabilitation' of Chayanov in Russia promises a welcome re-evaluation of his ideas in their homeland. It is to be hoped that any such reassessment will give due credit to the contribution of Peshekhonov, and will acknowledge his role as a link between the older populism of the late nineteenth century and the Organisation and Production School.

NOTES

The author is grateful to R.E.F. Smith and Teodor Shanin, as well as to participants in the colloquium, for comments on the original version of this article.

1. For an English translation of Chayanov's major works, see D. Thorner, B. Kerblay and R.E.F. Smith (eds) *A.V. Chayanov on the Theory of Peasant Economy* (Homewood, Ill., 1966). Teodor Shanin acknowledges a similarity between Peshekhonov's views and Chayanov's, without exploring it in any detail: *The Awkward Class* (Oxford, 1972) pp. 102, 105.
2. There is some discussion of Peshekhonov's ideas in V.G. Khoros, *Narodnicheskaya ideologiya i marksizm* (Moscow, 1972); N.D. Erofeev, *Narodnye sotsialisty v pervoi russkoi revolyutsii* (Moscow, 1979); and V.N. Ginev, *Bor'ba za krest'yanstvo i krizis russkogo neonarodnichestva, 1902–1914 gg.* (Leningrad, 1983).
3. Teodor Shanin, *Russia as a 'Developing Society'* (London, 1985).
4. For biographical information on Peshekhonov, see the entries in the Granat *Entsiklopedicheskii slovar'*, the *Sovetskaya istoricheskaya entsiklopediya* (by D.A. Kolesnichenko) and the *Modern Encyclopedia of Russian and Soviet History* (by M. Perrie).
5. A.V. Peshekhonov, 'K voprosu o roli "sobiratelei zemli" v russkom zemledel'cheskom proizvodstve', *Russkoe bogatstvo*, 7 (1897) part 2, pp. 34–50.
6. Ibid., pp. 34–7.
7. Ibid., p. 37. Peshekhonov did not use the term 'kulak' for these 'thrifty peasants'; he did not deny the existence of the 'rural rich' (*derevenskie bogatei*), but suggested that they derived their wealth from usury, trade and non-agricultural activities, rather than from agricultural production (ibid., p. 38n).
8. Ibid., pp. 37–8.
9. Ibid., pp. 38–9.
10. Ibid., pp. 39–40.
11. *Statisticheskii obzor Kaluzhskoi gubernii za 1896 g.* (Kaluga, 1897).
12. Peshekhonov, 'K voprosu o roli "sobiratelei zemli"', p. 41.
13. Ibid., pp. 42–8.
14. Ibid., p. 48.
15. Ibid., pp. 48–9; cf. pp. 42–5.
16. Ibid., pp. 48–50.
17. Ibid., p. 50.
18. A.V. Peshekhonov, 'Krest'yane i rabochie v ikh vzaimnykh otnosheniyakh', *Russkoe bogatstvo*, 8 (1898) part 1, pp. 173–95; 9 (1898) part 1, pp. 54–82.
19. Ibid., p. 179. The survey was published as *Statisticheskoe opisanie Kaluzhskoi gubernii.* vol. I. *Kozel'skii uezd.* 2 vyp. (Kaluga, 1897–8). Chayanov was later to praise this study of Peshekhonov's for being years ahead of its time in its concentration on the production processes of the peasant farm: A. Chayanov, *Byudzhetnye issledovaniya; istoriya i metody*, (Moscow, 1929) pp. 192, 281–4. See B. Kerblay (ed.) *Oeuvres choisies de A.V. Cajanov*, vol. VII (Paris, 1967) pp. 206, 296–9.
20. Peshekhonov, 'Krest'yane i rabochie', p. 173.
21. For Peshekhonov's necessarily guarded reference (in the legal press) to the Social Democrats' 'Manifesto', see ibid., p. 179.
22. Ibid., pp. 173–9.
23. Ibid., p. 181.
24. Ibid., pp. 179–80.

25. Ibid., p. 182.
26. Ibid., pp. 186–8.
27. Ibid., p. 189.
28. Ibid., p. 191.
29. Ibid., pp. 191–3.
30. Ibid., p. 189.
31. Ibid., pp. 193–5.
32. Ibid., p. 195.
33. Ibid., pp. 56–9.
34. Ibid., pp. 54–6.
35. Ibid., pp. 65–6.
36. Ibid., pp. 59–65. Some of the evidence here appears inconsistent with the finding of Peshekhonov's earlier article that larger farms grew proportionately more grain than smaller ones. Cf. 'K voprosu o roli "sobiratelei zemli"' pp. 44, 49, with 'Krest'yane i rabochie', pp. 56–7.
37. 'Krest´yane i rabochie', 66–8.
38. Ibid., pp. 68–70.
39. Ibid., p. 70.
40. Ibid., pp. 70–71.
41. Ibid., p. 71.
42. Ibid., pp. 71–4.
43. Ibid., pp. 75–7.
44. Ibid., p. 77.
45. Ibid., p. 78. The main reason for this was the under-utilisation of women's labour on small farms – they had to spend proportionately more time on domestic work (which was not counted as productive labour), and had less opportunity to engage in agricultural work or on outside earnings (Ibid., pp. 184–6).
46. Ibid., pp. 78–81.
47. Ibid., pp. 81–2.
48. A. Peshekhonov, 'Iz teorii i praktiki krest'yanskogo khozyaistva', *Russkoe bogatstvo*, 9 (1902) part 1, 160–93; 10 (1902) part 1, pp. 71–119.
49. Peshekhonov 'K voprosu o roli "sobiratelei zemli"', p. 37; id., 'Krest´yane i rabochie', p. 180.
50. Peshekhonov 'Iz teorii i praktiki', pp. 164–5.
51. Ibid., pp. 166–73.
52. Ibid., pp. 174–9.
53. Ibid., p. 187
54. Ibid., pp. 188–93.
55. Ibid., pp. 71–80.
56. Ibid., pp. 80–9.
57. Ibid., pp. 92–4.
58. Ibid., pp. 94–5.
59. Ibid., pp. 95–6.
60. Ibid., pp. 116–7.
61. Ibid., p. 118.
62. Ibid., pp. 118–9.
63. A.V. Peshekhonov, 'Zemel´nye nuzhdy derevni (Po rabotam sel´sko-khozyaistvennykh komitetov)', *Russkoe bogatstvo*, 9 (1903) part 1, pp. 55–92;

11 (1903) part 1, pp. 110–30; 12 (1903) part 1, pp. 113–30; id., 'Krest'yanskoe malozemel'e, kak problema ekonomicheskoi politiki. (Po rabotam sel'sko-khozyaistvennykh komitetov)', *Russkoe bogatstvo*, 7 (1904) part 2, pp. 84–122. These articles were re-published as a separate pamphlet in 1905, together with an article entitled 'Osnovnye zadachi agrarnoi reformy', first published in *Russkie vedomosti* in April 1905: *Zemel'nye nuzhdy derevni i osnovnye zadachi agrarnoi reformy* (St Petersburg, 1905).

64. Peshekhonov, *Zemel'nye nuzhdy derevni* (1905), pp. 39–42.
65. Ibid., p. 43.
66. Ibid., pp. 43–8.
67. Ibid., pp. 49–52. The same argument is also put forward in Peshekhonov's 'Osnovnye zadachi agrarnoi reformy', in ibid., pp. 146–7; and in his *Agrarnaya problema v svyazi s krest'yanskim dvizheniem* (St Petersburg, 1906), pp. 79–80.
68. Peshekhonov, *Zemel'nye nuzhdy derevni*, pp. 51–2, 147. For Peshekhonov's arguments in favour of land nationalisation as the only solution to the agrarian problem, see Ibid., pp. 150–8; *Agrarnaya problema*, pp. 81–93.
69. Compare, for example, the analysis offered by Teodor Shanin in *Russia as a 'Developing Society'*.
70. See for example Maureen Perrie, *The Agrarian Policy of the Socialist-Revolutionary Party, from its Origins through the Revolution of 1905-1907* (Cambridge, 1976).
71. Cf. Shanin, *The Awkward Class*.

5 Restructuring the Russian Petroleum Industry in the 1890s: Government Policy and Market Forces

John P. McKay

In recent years some economic historians have been rethinking the problem of Russian economic development before 1914. One of the most influential contributions to this rethinking has been Olga Crisp's study entitled 'The Pattern of Industrialization in Russia, 1700–1914', first published in 1972 as part of a collected work on European industrialisation in the nineteenth century.[1] At a time when Western writing on tsarist industrial development consisted mainly of variations on Alexander Gerschenkron's brilliantly constructed theme of state-induced industrialisation under conditions of extreme backwardness,[2] Olga Crisp's stimulating re-examination insisted on the continuity of development and on the considerable vitality of an 'autonomous growth stream'.

Moreover, Olga Crisp was keenly aware of the ambiguities in government economic policy. She noted that 'the finance ministry became something of a ministry of economic development', but that 'narrowly financial matters were still its primary concern and . . . took the upper hand over general economic interests.'[3] Government action remained the critical causal factor in her explanation of Russia's late-nineteenth-century surge, but the state's impact appeared more complex and less systematically positive than generally believed. She implied that more focus on 'the *interaction* of government policy and market forces' could lead to a better understanding of Russian industrialisation.[4]

It is within this context that I wish to examine one such interaction in the late nineteenth-century Russian petroleum industry. My first task is to assess the relative contributions of government policy and market forces, including action by private entrepreneurs, to the petroleum industry's development. To the extent that the government's contribution was ambiguous at best, as I shall try to show, this study should suggest that the long-accepted stress on Russia's 'state-induced industrialisation' is in need of revision. Whatever the ultimate macroeconomic assessment may be, I intend to show that the interaction of government policy and market forces in this particular industry was more complex and reciprocal than would normally be supposed.

THE EMERGENCE OF THE BAKU PETROLEUM INDUSTRY

This chapter will concentrate on the interaction of state policies and market forces in the late 1880s and the 1890s. However, that interaction was itself structured by previous public and private initiatives and responses. A brief examination of the industry's rapid emergence to the early 1880s must therefore serve as our point of departure.

The pre-revolutionary Russian petroleum industry was located on the southern fringe of the tsar's enormous multinational empire, in and near the ancient city of Baku in modern Azerbaijan. The Russian state inherited regalian rights to the ancient petroleum deposits when it absorbed the Baku khanate in 1813. For the next sixty years the Russian state alternated between an *otkup* – a typical tax-farming or monopoly contract system – and direct state exploitation of Baku's oil wells. Results were poor in either case, since lease payments were small and state enterprise produced nothing but losses. Production and markets failed to develop. Crude oil from Baku continued to smell when used as fuel, and smoke when used for lighting – a product of last resort in the homes of the poor on the arid, deforested shores of the Caspian Sea.[5]

Of critical importance, Baku's ancient petroleum industry fell far behind its American counterpart, which burst upon the scene after Edwin Drake struck oil by drilling in 1859 and refined kerosene began to replace vegetable and mineral oils as a good cheap source of household lighting. By the late 1860s, foreign demand for American kerosene was also growing rapidly. Russia participated fully and by 1872 it had become the largest national importer of American kerosene.[6] In spite of a high Russian tariff, the United States was supplying 80–90 per cent of the Russian demand for kerosene between 1869 and 1872, a demand that almost doubled in those years. The 'autonomous growth stream' that Olga Crisp found for consumer products in the post-reform era was very much in evidence in the enthusiastic acceptance of the new lighting oil.

Baku tried to respond to the new opportunity in the late 1860s, but without great success. By 1869, 23 factories had appeared in Baku to produce lighting oil. These factories were really tiny workshops, where artisan manufacturers and their workers 'cooked' crude oil in open stills and produced kerosene of poor quality. The refined oil was then shipped in barrels across the Caspian Sea and thence up the Volga River to compete with American kerosene imported through St Petersburg. Production of the raw material remained in the hands of the monopoly leaseholder, who continued to obtain all crude oil by bailing the seepage from shallow wells and who sold it at the high monopoly price authorised by the state.

It was against this background of successful American development and in response to pressures from disgruntled businessmen and technical experts, ably led by the Moscow entrepreneur V.A. Kokorev and the famous chemist Dmitrii Mendeleev, that the government launched a comprehensive re-examination of its petroleum policy. In due course the commissions and interministerial conferences concluded that the state-sponsored monopoly of crude oil production was the primary cause of the industry's arrested development. Embracing Mendeleev's liberal assumption that free competition was the source of economic and technical progress, the government decided to relinquish control of Baku's known oil deposits. In December 1872, it auctioned them off as semi-permanent leaseholds to private entrepreneurs in small plots of ten desyatins. The new owners immediately introduced the American technique of drilling for oil in the main producing area, located ten to fifteen versts from Baku. In July 1873, the first of many powerful gushers blew in. The old monopoly price for crude oil quickly fell by 95 per cent. Within a year the number of kerosene refiners in Baku had surged to about eighty as new entrants raced to capitalise on the cheap and abundant raw material.[7]

Although the embryonic industry faced a host of challenges which cannot be considered here, state policy continued to rely almost exclusively on economic liberalism and autonomous private enterprise for their successful resolution. In the face of renewed pressure from businessmen and technical experts, the Ministry of Finance reluctantly admitted in 1877 that it had been a mistake to impose a tax on kerosene to compensate for the revenue that was lost by abolishing the *otkup*. Inappropriately modelled after the vodka tax and requiring refiners to pay on the basis of still size and hours of operation, the kerosene tax had resulted in poor quality lighting oil, disregard of potentially valuable by-products, and limited tax revenue. In order to permit technological innovation and sound development, the State Council therefore freed the petroleum industry from any special taxation in July 1877, as the Ministry of Finance had belatedly recommended.[8]

Moreover, the government subsequently remained true to the policy of unfettered private enterprise as the Nobel Brothers Petroleum Company rose swiftly to revolutionise and dominate the industry between 1877 and 1883. The state permitted Swedish-born Ludwig Nobel and his company to create an integrated big business that threatened many firms with destruction. For example, Nobel Brothers Petroleum was permitted to build the first cost-cutting pipeline to carry crude oil from its wells to its Baku refinery, in spite of intense opposition from local Azerbaijani hauliers who feared with reason for their livelihoods. The company also received government permission to ship kerosene across the Caspian Sea in the world's first tankers and to place its own tank wagons on state-controlled railways, despite strong protests from competing refiners.[9]

The ten years following the abolition of the *otkup* in late 1872 marked the emergence of the Russian petroleum industry. In 1883, production of crude oil was more than twenty times what it had been in 1872. Baku refiners, led by Nobel, who accounted for fully 55 per cent of all kerosene output in 1883, had just succeeded in driving all American imports from the Russian market. With domestic consumption growing at about 14 per cent per year and with the first Russian exports of kerosene beginning to trickle abroad, prospects for continued growth were excellent.

The rise of the Baku petroleum industry provides an instructive commentary on the problem of autonomous market forces and state economic action. First, the basic consumer market for lighting oil was quite comparable to those of the United States and of Western Europe, as witnessed by the rapid acceptance of American kerosene. Second, state action played a critical role in the industry's emergence, but in the opposite sense to that posited by the state-led-industrialisation thesis. As the government came to appreciate, state-sponsored monopoly and pervasive tutelage had resulted in stagnation and relative retrogression. The government's use of market forces to promote growth was remarkably successful. The industry's development was a notable vindication of those 'notions of economic liberalism' that Professor Crisp highlighted in her study and the government's 'genuine if short-lived attempt to allow autonomous forces free sway.'[10]

GOVERNMENT INITIATIVES IN THE 1880s

The 1880s saw a reorientation of government petroleum policy in a more interventionist direction, a reorientation that paralleled the abandonment or sharp curtailment of liberal economic policies in this era. One factor in the reorientation was pressure from the petroleum industry itself. The majority of Baku's 150 refiners – largely Armenian and Russian but including some Azerbaijanis, Jews, and foreigners – had suffered from Ludwig Nobel's rapid ascendancy and the concurrent 'crisis of overproduction' that had sent petroleum prices plunging by 60 to 70 per cent from 1880 to 1883. They charged that Nobel Brothers Petroleum was creating a monopoly and they looked to the state for protection and countervailing measures.[11]

Most of Baku's industrialists realised that Nobel Brothers had used its capital-intensive system of bulk transport and distribution to gain a commanding position in the domestic market, and they saw little potential in marketing almost worthless *ostatki* as liquid fuel. They believed that their salvation lay in foreign markets, provided of course that Nobel (or some other firm) did not gain a stranglehold over kerosene exports as well. Growing at about 8 per cent per year, the world market was taking at least six times as much kerosene as Russia was producing in 1883. Virtually all product came from the United States and John D. Rockefeller's Standard Oil Trust. Yet properly refined Russian kerosene equalled its American counterpart in quality, and the crude oil necessary for a given unit of kerosene cost less than a quarter as much in the Baku region as in Pennsylvania. The prospect of exports was very enticing.

However, there was a critical problem – transportation. Baku's incredibly productive oil fields lay on the wrong side of the Caucasian land mass as far as easy exports were concerned. In May 1883, the Tiflis to Baku portion of the 846-verst railway from the Caspian to the Black Sea had finally opened to provide Baku with an outlet to the Black Sea. Yet the railway extension had been built primarily in response to military needs highlighted during the Russo-Turkish War of 1877–8, and the railway proved capable of carrying only a trickle of petroleum products.[12] Baku's industrialists complained bitterly to the state, which had guaranteed the railway company's increased capital, and they lobbied for additional investment in locomotives and rolling stock to realise the railway's export potential. The Ministries of Transportation and Finance were directly concerned, but it was a reorganised Ministry of State Property that sought to respond to the challenge.

In April 1883, the administration of Caucasian mines and the petroleum industry was transferred from the Ministry of Finance to the Ministry of State Property, headed from 1881 to 1893 by an energetic Mikhail Ostrovskii, brother of the famous playwright. According to Finance Minister Bunge (1881–6), the reorganisation was intended to encourage a 'broad state view' and more expeditious interministerial agreement, which '[could] take years'.[13] Forming an unfavourable impression of Baku and strongly influenced by Dmitrii Mendeleev's critical analysis, Ostrovskii concluded that bold initiatives were necessary to restructure the petroleum industry and assure its success.

Drawing upon American practice, indisputable technical realities, and numerous proposals from would-be pipeline entrepreneurs, Ostrovskii's ministry argued in 1884 that the Transcaucasian railway could not be expanded to a point where kerosene exports would attain 'any real significance'. Therefore the Ministry of State Property proposed 'a more radical measure, namely, the construction of a pipeline carrying crude oil from Baku to Batum and the building of refineries there.'[14] Carrying oil in great quantity and much more economically, as in the United States, the pipeline would permit the creation of new refineries on the Black Sea. These refineries would process

Baku's heavy crude more rationally and would not leave two-thirds of the raw material as low-value liquid fuel. To promote best the general interest and forestall the dangers of private monopoly, the ministry proposed a crude oil pipeline owned and operated by the state.

Ostrovskii's project raised a storm of controversy.[15] Crude oil producers generally supported the proposal. Petroleum refiners, led by Ludwig Nobel, were adamantly opposed. They favoured instead one or more kerosene pipelines. But they were split as to whether such pipelines should be common carriers open to all, or whether they might be built by individual companies, notably Nobel Brothers. The railway engineers in the Ministry of Transportation were also opposed to Ostrovskii's plan. They pressed for credits to purchase kerosene tank wagons and to construct an expensive tunnel through the mountains at the Suram Pass, the railway's most serious bottleneck. But Ostrovskii pushed ahead, recasting the original pipeline project as a regulated private company in order to find the capital the government could not provide. In March 1887, the Council of Ministers approved a revised proposal. Here, indeed, was a bold developmental initiative by the state.

In fact, Ostrovskii's project was not realised. Continued strong opposition from Baku's refiners and widespread fears that the crude oil pipeline would only facilitate the migration of the industry abroad were clearly important factors. But the key from our point of view was that the pipeline concession gradually lost out to the rival state policy of railway expansion and to general financial considerations. Critical interrelated government decisions – to build the tunnel through the Suram Pass and to permit refiners to purchase their own tank wagons for use on the railway – were made by late 1886. These decisions promised to increase significantly the railway's carrying capacity, in part because the Paris Rothschilds now entered the fray and advanced small refiners loans for tank wagon purchases and expansion.

Increased railway investments also raised the state's financial interest in the Transcaucasian railway, leading logically to its nationalisation in 1889. Within the interministerial decision-making process, a petroleum pipeline running parallel to the railway loomed increasingly as either an unwanted private competitor or an unnecessary state expense. Thus private and state-owned pipelines were repeatedly approved by the government as being highly desirable for the petroleum industry between 1887 and 1894. Yet neither was built because private ownership was subsequently ruled unacceptable and the state was unable actually to appropriate the funds. Rather, the state concentrated on expanding the militarily significant Transcaucasian railway, creating for itself an unassailable monopoly over the transportation of petroleum products for export that did not include any pipelines.

Almost simultaneously with its transport decisions, the government took a major fiscal initiative. Never completely abandoned after 1877, the idea of a new oil tax had reappeared on the agenda of the Ministry of Finance after 1883. Regarding some new taxation as inevitable, Ludwig Nobel and the pioneering industrialist V.I. Ragozin advocated a tax on crude oil of 15 to 20 kopecks per pud as the best means to raise prices, discourage waste, hinder crude oil exports, and increase state revenues. But because this idea was anathema to crude oil producers and small refiners, in 1886 Finance Minister Bunge proposed instead an excise tax on lighting oil, with a rebate on exports to permit competition with the Standard Oil Company in foreign markets.

Narrowly rejected by a badly split special conference of officials, businessmen and technical experts, the proposal was taken up again by Bunge's successor, Ivan Vyshnegradskii. Vyshnegradskii argued that the industry was now strong enough to support the measure, although he offered little evidence to support his assertion. The key points for Vyshnegradskii were the 'urgent necessity to increase state revenues' and kerosene's ability to provide considerable, easily collected revenues.[16] These considerations apparently dominated the interministerial discussion.

In November 1887, the State Council approved a heavy tax of 40 kopecks per pud on kerosene consumed within the empire. The new excise tax was three or four times as great as the wholesale price for kerosene in Baku. Combined with the state's emerging transport policy, the tax redirected market forces and helped restructure the petroleum industry.

MARKET FORCES IN THE 1890s

How, then, did state initiatives in transportation and taxation interact with market forces in the late 1880s and 1890s? In addressing this question certain underlying conditions should be kept in mind. First, whereas more than 70 per cent of light Pennsylvania crude oil could be refined into kerosene, only roughly a third of heavy Baku crude could be refined into a comparable lighting oil. Therefore, Baku always produced a joint-product – kerosene and the heavy residual oil left over after refining kerosene. Second, the demand for Russian kerosene at home and abroad came primarily from consumers for household lighting. Initially discarded, residual oil was in some demand as liquid fuel by the mid-1880s, although kerosene accounted for 80 to 90 per cent of revenues and profits.[17]

Table 5.1 summarises the Russian petroleum industry's development from 1883 to 1900 – from the beginning of kerosene exports through the industrialisation surge of the 1890s. It shows the well-known growth of kerosene exports in the standard Russian unit, as well as rarely presented data on the industry's two main products.

Table 5.1 suggests that Vyshnegradskii's heavy excise tax in 1888 went a long way toward choking off the growth of the domestic kerosene market. If we take two-year averages to dampen the effect of abnormally large shipments in 1887 in anticipation of the new tax and to smooth the base period, we find that domestic shipments of kerosene almost doubled in the four years from 1882–3 to 1886–7. But after the tax was introduced they increased by only a third (32.1 per cent) in the subsequent four-year period to 1890–1. Since general economic and social conditions were little changed in the two periods, higher prices due to taxation appear as the reasonable explanation for sharply reduced growth of domestic kerosene consumption.

Incomplete price data for the 1880s support this interpretation. The 40-kopeck excise tax quadrupled the Baku wholesale price of kerosene ready for shipment to the domestic market – from the teens to the 50s – in one fell swoop. It more than doubled the wholesale price at Tsaritsyn, the Volga River city long-established as the principal distribution point for the domestic market. Thus, whereas the average wholesale price at Tsaritsyn had declined from 65 kopecks in 1883 to 35 kopecks in 1885, it rose to 80–85 kopecks per pud by late 1888 with the inclusion of the tax. Limited data also suggest that the average retail price in major urban markets was twice the Tsaritsyn wholesale price. Therefore consumers probably experienced a 40

TABLE 5.1 *The Russian petroleum industry, 1883–1900*
(in millions of puds)

Year	*Crude oil production*	*Russian kerosene* – *Shipped to empire*	*Exports*	*Total shipments*	*Exports as per cent of total shipments*	*American kerosene exports*	*Russian kerosene as per cent of Russian & American exports*	*Russian fuel oil shipments*	*Russian kerosene as per cent of total volume of kerosene and fuel oil*
	(1)	(2)	(3)	(4)	(5)	(6)	(7)	(8)	(9)
1883	60	11.6	2.4	14.0	17.0			18.8	42.7
1884	90	17.5	3.9	21.4	18.2			29.2	42.3
1885	116	19.4	7.4	26.8	27.6			33.9	44.2
1886	150	20.0	14.0	34.0	41.2			36.2	48.4
1887	165	25.4	17.0	42.4	40.0			41.5	50.5
1888	192	24.0	27.9	51.9	53.8	84.3	24.9	61.8	45.6
1889	206	28.1	35.1	63.2	55.5	93.4	27.3	88.9	41.6
1890	239	28.7	41.3	70.0	59.0	97.3	29.8	96.9	41.9

1891	289	31.2	45.0	76.2	59.1	106.2	29.8	103.8	42.3
1892	298	32.1	48.9	81.0	60.4	105.1	31.8	117.3	40.9
1893	324	37.9	50.0	87.9	56.9	129.8	27.8	143.5	38.2
1894	297	30.1	43.3	73.4	59.0	133.7	24.5	193.6	27.5
1895	377	32.3	51.3	83.6	61.4	124.7	29.1	180.4	31.7
1896	386	37.6	52.5	90.1	58.3	137.9	27.6	185.0	32.8
1897	421	41.6	52.4	94.0	55.7	146.5	26.3	221.7	29.8
1898	436	42.5	56.2	98.7	56.9	140.1	28.6	242.4	28.9
1899	525	40.0	69.0	109.0	62.4	132.6	34.2	244.9	30.8
1900	601	54.6	75.3	129.9	58.0	134.1	36.0	264.4	32.9

Note All figures relate only to Baku. The northern Caucasus added 2 per cent to crude oil production by 1893 and 5 per cent by 1900.

SOURCES S.L. and L.L. Pershke, *Russkaya neftyanaya promyshlennost´: ee razvitie i sovremennoe polozhenie v statisticheskikh dannykh* (Tiflis, 1913), pp. 26, 29, 32, 37, 55–56, and 191–2, except for columns (1) and (8) for 1883–7 from Sovet s"ezda neftepromyshlennikov, *Sravnitel´nye statisticheskie dannye o Bakinskoi neftyanoi promyshlennosti, 1889, 1890, 1891, 1892* (Baku, 1893) p. 1.

to 50 per cent increase in price – certainly enough to slow significantly the growth of demand.[18] As one contemporary observer put it, 'The price of kerosene in the major consuming areas rose to the former levels of the 1870s. Since the purchasing power of the Russian consumer was in this time hardly able to increase, the demand for kerosene was abruptly arrested.'[19]

In December 1892, in the depths of a general depression which hit Baku hard, the government raised the excise on kerosene from 40 to 60 kopecks per pud. Tax now accounted for about three-quarters of the wholesale price and about three-eighths of the common retail price of 1.60 rubles per pud.[20] The increase in taxation helped slow the growth of domestic kerosene shipments to only 7.3 per cent between 1890–91 and 1894–95. Annual Russian kerosene consumption stagnated at about 10 lbs. per capita, even as it increased from 31 to 38 lbs. in Germany and 24 to 32 lbs. in Great Britain in the same four years. Modest expansion in the late 1890s (see Table 5.1) brought Russian per capita usage to only 13 lbs. in 1900, as opposed to about 42 lbs. per capita in both Great Britain and Germany.[21] The consumer paid more for kerosene in Baku than in London.

The heavy excise tax checked especially the growth of peasant usage and Russia's more prosperous urban population remained the primary market for kerosene until 1900 and even 1914. Peasants certainly used the product. Mendeleev wrote in 1886 that, 'almost every peasant cottage lights with a kerosene lamp.'[22] But peasants used the article only on special occasions. 'They burn kerosene at tea time and on holidays, when they have guests, but at other times they always use the wooden splinter', wrote one observer in 1909.[23]

Sluggish demand at home made foreign markets all the more critical. As Table 5.1 shows, Russian kerosene exports did surge almost threefold (178 per cent) from 1886–87 to 1890–91, at the same time domestic shipments were growing by only a third. In 1890–91, Russian exporters had challenged the Standard Oil Company's global monopoly to the extent of supplying about 30 per cent of world export demand for kerosene. The Russian petroleum industry had also restructured itself in the process: exports accounted for 60 per cent of all kerosene sales and drove the industry in terms of profits and expectations. More generally, rapid success in the world kerosene market reflected the relatively sophisticated, 'European' nature of the Russian economy and its foreign and domestic entrepreneurs.

The rapid expansion of Russian kerosene exports stalled in the 1890s. Indeed, Russian exporters maintained the 30 per cent market share they had won with difficulty throughout most of the decade. With the foreign market now stagnating like the domestic market even as crude oil output continued to grow, overproduction and much lower prices for crude oil and all refined products returned to Baku. The wholesale price of kerosene in tankers ready for shipment to the domestic market fell from an average of 16.0 kopecks per pud in 1888–90 to 6.5 kopecks per pud in 1892–94.[24] Profits fell dramatically for all participants in 1892–94. Yet all this adversity failed to spur exports and one must ask why.

Part of the answer is that total Russian and American kerosene exports slowed down in the economically depressed 1890s, growing by only about 50 per cent between 1890 and 1900. Yet suppose for a moment that Russian refiners had continued to use their very cheap crude oil to gain market share and achieve, say, 66 per cent of the world export total by 1899. This would have required neither special technology nor more crude oil production than was actually achieved. Yet Russian kerosene exports would have practically doubled.[25] With a dominant position as world price leader the Russian industry and its participants would have presumably profited handsomely in the end.

The Russian industry's failure to become the dominant factor in the world kerosene market in the 1890s was due to various factors. Three are well-known. First, American crude oil production, declining throughout much of the 1880s, recovered. It supplied American refiners with adequate if relatively expensive raw materials necessary to maintain their world market share. Second, the Standard Oil Company struck back hard. Beginning in 1888 in Great Britain, the powerful firm turned away from using independent price-conscious importers and integrated forward in its principal markets. That is, Standard Oil purchased tankers, built bulk storage facilities, and bought up European petroleum importers and even retailers. By building its own captive distribution system Standard Oil was not only able to cut significantly its distribution costs, but also succeeded in limiting severely the access of Russian exporters to British and continental consumers.[26]

Third, the Standard's energetic response effectively checked the ambitions of Nobel Brothers Petroleum and the Paris Rothschilds, the firms most responsible for the late 1880s surge of

Russian kerosene exports. By 1890, both firms were avidly seeking market-sharing agreements that would recognise Standard Oil's dominance and guarantee Russian firms only a modest 25 to 30 per cent of the European kerosene market in return. Both firms pursued variations of this restrictive policy throughout the 1890s, as Soviet scholars have painstakingly shown,[27] and thus the foreign market's growth potential was of necessity severely limited.

There was, however, another, generally neglected factor in the picture – continued inadequate transportation for export needs. The government monopoly on export transport, embodied in the nationalisation of the Transcaucasian railway and the prohibition on long-distance pipelines, saddled the industry with expensive and limited capacity to supply foreign markets. The normally prevailing freight rate of 19 kopecks per pud for shipping kerosene from Baku to Batum was three times what Standard Oil paid to pipe its crude oil from western Pennsylvania to its Atlantic refineries in the late 1880s; it was about six times as much as the company paid a decade later after further technical improvements. Moreover, even after the construction of the Suram tunnel the rail link was physically incapable of shipping much more than about 50 million puds of petroleum products annually throughout most of the 1890s.[28]

The chronic deficiency in export transport was most dramatically seen in the different prices at Baku for kerosene in railway tank wagons and in tankers. Except in rare circumstances, the price in tank wagons was always substantially higher than in tankers (for the Caspian Sea) because demand for tank wagons exceeded the inelastic supply. Thus Russian producers as a group could supply at most a third of world export demand for kerosene. They had no incentive to cut prices to gain a greater market share that they could not supply. Rather, the best strategy was clearly to seek an agreement with Standard Oil as cooperative co-monopolist.[29] In short, whereas the export market for kerosene had appeared as a viable alternative to a home market burdened by heavy taxation in the late 1880s, the export market ceased in its turn to continue developing in the early 1890s, in part because of the state's expensive, restrictive monopoly on transport to export markets.

The result was an unexpected second restructuring in the Russian petroleum industry, a restructuring which has gone largely unnoticed in a scholarly literature that stresses international 'oil wars' between big firms and their backers. To a large extent Baku turned from kerosene to fuel oil, which came to provide the bulk of revenues and sharply rising profits in the late 1890s. The Russian petroleum industry became an energy industry and lighting oil for consumers became a by-product.

This striking reorientation may be shown in numerous ways. Column 9 in Table 5.1 shows how kerosene comprised fully 50 per cent of the physical joint product in 1887 and less than 30 per cent in most years from 1894 onward. Even more striking was the changing mix of revenues from kerosene and residual fuel oil, which is presented in Table 5.2. Whereas fuel oil accounted for less than 20 per cent of joint-product revenues in 1889, it jumped to 60 per cent in 1894 and usually averaged more than 50 per cent thereafter.

Detailed calculations by the Baku Petroleum Association, which were accepted by several contemporary writers (Brandt, Pershke and Pershke, Startsev), showed that a Baku refiner who had to buy all his crude oil on the open market actually lost money on the kerosene portion of his output in 1894 and 1897–1900. Accordingly, profit-minded refiners pushed kerosene runs down from 32 per cent of crude oil produced in 1889 to a low in 1897 of only 19 per cent, which was close to the minimum run consistent with obtaining a good quality fuel oil.[30] The importance of kerosene sales after 1893 lay increasingly in permitting the industry to refine more crude oil and therefore produce more fuel oil.[31]

Untaxed and unregulated, the Russian fuel market has been little studied. Nevertheless, the basic outlines seem clear. As Table 5.2 suggests, the upturn of the business cycle in the later 1890s brought sharply rising prices that consolidated the shift away from kerosene. Demand for fuel oil came primarily from transportation and industry. In 1890, when roughly 102 million puds of fuel oil were shipped from the Baku region, 17.6 million puds were used by railways, 35 million puds by ships on the Caspian Sea and Volga River network, and 49 million puds by industrial establishments along that network, which included the Moscow region.[32] In 1899, when about 245 million puds of fuel oil were shipped from Baku, 73 million puds were used by railways, 84 million puds by the inland fleets, and 88 million puds by industrial and other users.[33] Large quantities of fuel oil

TABLE 5.2 *The market for Russian kerosene and fuel oil, 1889–1900*

	Kerosene			*Fuel oil*				
Year	*Average Baku price (kopecks per pud)*	*Total shipments (million puds)*	*Total revenues (million rubles)*	*Average Baku price (kopecks per pud)*	*Total shipments (million puds)*	*Total revenues (million rubles)*	*Total revenues (3) & (6)*	*Fuel oil revenues as per cent of total*
	(1)	(2)	(3)	(4)	(5)	(6)	(7)	(8)
1889	26.0	61	15.9	4.0	88.9	3.6	19.5	18.5
1890	19.0	67	12.7	6.5	96.9	6.3	19.0	33.2
1891	10.2	74	7.6	3.3	103.8	3.4	11.0	30.9
1892	7.7	79	6.1	1.5	117.3	1.8	7.9	22.3
1893	6.7	86	5.7	2.1	143.5	3.0	8.7	34.5
1894	7.1	71	5.0	3.9	193.6	7.6	12.6	60.3
1895	16.2	81	13.1	6.1	180.4	11.0	24.1	45.6
1896	20.6	86.5	17.8	7.7	185.0	14.2	32.0	44.4
1897	12.7	90.2	11.5	8.2	221.7	18.2	29.7	61.3
1898	13.5	95.0	13.0	10.7	242.4	25.9	38.9	66.6
1899	24.9	109.0	27.1	13.1	244.9	32.1	59.2	54.2
1900	27.4	129.9	35.6	16.0	264.4	42.3	77.9	54.3

SOURCES Sovet s´´ezda neftepromyshlennikov, *Obzor Bakinskoi neftyanoi promyshlennosti za 1897* (Baku, 1898), pp. 167, 169; . . . *za 1898* (Baku, 1899), p. 198; *za 1900* (Baku, 1901), p. 290, for all data, except for column (2), 1899–1900, and columns (4)–(6), 1889–90, which are taken or calculated from S.L. and L.L. Pershke, *Russkaya neftyanaya promyshlennost´*, pp. 64–5, 191.

not included in such statistics on shipments from Baku were consumed by the petroleum industry itself and the rapidly growing Baku region – about 30 million puds in 1890 and 143 million puds in 1899.

Liquid fuel was distributed cheaply by tankers and barges as part of a high volume wholesale trade. Thus the fuel market contrasted sharply with the kerosene trade, which rested ultimately on a more fragmented retail trade with much higher distribution costs. Efficiently organised and serving large portions of the empire, the domestic market for convenient, high caloric fuel oil was practically unlimited in the eyes of its enthusiasts.[34] More precisely, the demand for fuel oil was limited primarily by competition from other energy sources, especially coal. Yet Russian coal was as relatively expensive by international standards as Russian petroleum was cheap. In 1899, fully 20 per cent of the empire's total energy requirements were supplied by petroleum, while coal supplied 38 per cent, wood 39 per cent and peat 3 per cent.[35] A weak second as an exporter of kerosene, Russia was the world's undisputed pioneer in using petroleum as an industrial fuel.

GOVERNMENT REACTIONS TO MARKET FORCES

Thus market forces interacted with government policies to restructure increasingly the Russian petroleum industry as a domestic energy producer in the 1890s. Still building upon Olga Crisp's paradigm, let us consider briefly how government policy makers continued in their turn to interact with this and other aspects of the industry's development in the Witte era.

One interpretation, which has been advanced by the Dutch historian Gerretson in his study of the Royal Dutch Petroleum Company before 1914, is that the industry's reorientation conformed neatly to the desires of the state, in the person of the finance minister, Sergei Witte. According to Gerretson, the excise tax on kerosene had the desired effect of limiting domestic consumption of the 'unnecessary luxury' and deflecting production toward 'cheap and abundant fuel for railways and industry'.[36] Gerretson provided little direct evidence, but his interpretation is not inconsistent with Witte's raising the kerosene tax from 40 to 60 kopecks per pud in December 1892, shortly after he became finance minister in August 1892.

Gerretson's interpretation, which has not been shared to my knowledge by any contemporary or Soviet source, seems a variation on the *post hoc propter hoc* fallacy. Rather, as well-informed contemporaries noted, the increase of the excise in 1892 was again the result of the 'urgent necessity to increase state revenues'.[37] There was simply no alternative to more taxes at a time when generalised depression and specific calamities (the bad harvest of 1891 and the cholera epidemic of 1892) pressed hard, and serious governments had not yet rediscovered currency debasement as fiscal policy. Moreover, there is Witte's own testimony on the matter. Speaking in 1898 to a special interministerial conference considering state policy toward foreign investment in the petroleum industry, Witte repeatedly deplored the industry's 'abnormal condition'. That abnormality consisted precisely in the production of as much fuel oil and as little kerosene as possible, when kerosene was by rights the more valuable product. Understandable to Witte as the rational response to market forces ('Only the market for residual oil as fuel brings profits, while the foreign kerosene trade gives nothing but losses'), the chief minister now advocated governmental measures that might partially reverse the unwanted restructuring that had taken place.[38]

Action on export transportation also strongly suggests that revenues and financial considerations continued to dominate state petroleum policy under Witte as it had under Vyshnegradskii. Witte certainly followed the monopolist's classic strategy of restricting investment in order to maintain unsatisfied demand, high prices, and maximum return on existing railway investment. In 1893, the Ministry of Transportation accumulated overwhelming evidence regarding the inadequate carrying capacity of the nationalised Transcaucasian railway. It now proposed in its turn to build a 'very profitable' kerosene pipeline from Baku to Batum for 19 000 000 rubles. Cutting down the proposal in early 1894 with a two-page sentence of convoluted bureaucratese, Witte noted with amazement that the Ministry of Transportation was 'contradicting all its previously expressed opinions' and stressed the state's 'enormous investments' in the Transcaucasian railway.[39] He called for yet another in-depth study and effectively buried the project. More generally, the state maintained high freight rates for kerosene shipments by rail, although it would temporarily lower those rates when foreign competition was particularly intense. The high but adjustable freight rate was, in reality, a variable export levy.[40]

The enduring primacy of financial considerations was matched by a similar continuity in government policy toward foreign capital. Witte's spirited support of growing British investment in Russian oil at the end of the century echoed Vyshnegradskii's defence of the Rothschilds in the late 1880s: the foreign infusions quickened the industry's development and facilitated exports.[41] Equally continuous were successful state efforts to exclude the Standard Oil Company from the Baku petroleum industry, on the grounds that the American monopoly would injure both Russian private and public interests. The petroleum industry was an excellent example of the state's willingness to accept direct foreign investment because it could control and channel such investment, which I have argued elsewhere was generally the case.[42]

State policy on industrial competition and petroleum cartels revealed somewhat similar thinking, although only the briefest remarks are possible here. As the holder of extensive oil-bearing reserves and a major buyer of fuel oil, the state sought to preserve competition and refused to sanction a cartelisation of the domestic petroleum market in the 1890s. At the same time, the government was not unwilling to approve private efforts to unify Russian kerosene exporters in order to negotiate effectively with Standard Oil or to impose higher prices on foreign consumers, provided that the firms could first agree among themselves and that private export syndicates did not slight state interests.[43] Different policies toward cartels operating at home and abroad may be seen as reflecting the state's continued respect for market forces even after economic liberalism was officially abandoned, as well as the self-imposed limitations of government intervention in the economic development process in the 1890s.

In conclusion, the development of the Russian petroleum industry provides little support for the standard stress on the leading role of the state in late-nineteenth-century Russian industrialisation. Rather, this major industry's growth places in bold relief the great importance of purely financial considerations in government policy, an importance that Olga Crisp fully recognised in her influential reassessment of the Russian experience. Moreover, the petroleum industry's evolution to 1900 clearly shows the continuity and strength of market forces and the autonomous growth stream in the post-reform era that she also highlighted. Finally, with studies of individual firms and industries casting increasing doubt on the long-dominant paradigm of state-induced industrialisation at the micro level, it is perhaps time for Russian economic historians seriously to re-examine the state's allegedly decisive contribution to Russian industrialisation at the macro level and in quantitative terms.[44]

NOTES

1. Originally published in P. Léon, F. Crouzet and R. Gascon, *L'industrialisation en Europe au XIXe siècle* (Paris, 1972) pp. 435–66, this long study is reprinted with modifications in O. Crisp, *Studies in the Russian Economy Before 1914* (London, 1976) pp. 4–54.
2. Alexander Gerschenkron's influential papers are conveniently grouped together in *Economic Backwardness in Historical Perspective: A Book of Essays* (Cambridge, Mass., 1962). In Gerschenkron's paradigm the gradations of ever-increasing relative backwardness observed as one moved eastward from England meant that industrialisation in follower countries proceeded with a corresponding increase in institutional substitution and innovation. In quite backward Russia the state itself substituted for the 'missing prerequisites' of autonomous market demand, accumulated private capital, enterprising businessmen, and skilled labour.
3. Crisp, 'Industrialisation in Russia', *Studies*, p. 24.
4. Crisp, 'Introduction', ibid. p. 3. My emphasis.
5. John P. McKay, 'Entrepreneurship and the Emergence of the Russian Petroleum Industry, 1813–1883', *Research in Economic History*, 8 (1983) pp. 47–91.
6. A.A. Fursenko, *Neftyanye voiny (konets XIX-nachalo XX v.)* (Leningrad, 1985) p. 34.
7. McKay, 'Entrepreneurship and . . . the Russian Petroleum Industry', pp. 48–57.
8. Ibid., pp. 57–60.
9. There is a substantial but uneven literature on Ludwig Nobel and his company. Robert W. Tolf, *The Russian Rockefellers: The Saga of the Nobel Family and the Russian Oil Industry* (Stanford, 1976) and I.A. D'yakonova, *Nobelevskaya korporatsiya v Rossii* (Moscow, 1980) present important new material. Also see my 'Entrepreneurship and . . . the Russian Petroleum Industry', pp. 61–88.
10. Crisp, 'Industrialisation in Russia' *Studies*, pp. 23–4.
11. McKay, 'Entrepreneurship and . . . the Russian Petroleum Industry', pp. 76–84.

12. Charles Marvin, *The Region of the Eternal Fire: An Account of a Journey to the Petroleum Region of the Caspian in 1883* (London, 1884) pp. 141–2 and *passim*, has a good discussion of the railway's military significance.
13. L.E. Shepelev, *Tsarizm i burzhuaziya vo vtoroi polovine XIX veka: Problemy torgovo-promyshlennoi politiki* (Leningrad, 1981) pp. 122–5, 161.
14. Quoted in V.A. Nardova, *Nachalo monopolizatsii neftyanoi promyshlennosti Rossii, 1880–1890-e gody* (Leningrad, 1974) p. 42.
15. John P. McKay, 'Baku Oil and Transcaucasian Pipelines, 1883–1891: A Study in Tsarist Economic Policy', *Slavic Review*, XLIII (1984) pp. 604–23.
16. Part of Vyshnegradskii's analysis is published in Akademiya nauk SSSR, Institut istorii, Leningradskoe otdelenie, *Monopolisticheskii kapital v neftyanoi promyshlennosti Rossii, 1883–1914: Dokumenty i materialy* (Moscow-Leningrad, 1961) pp. 105–13. Also see the discussion in Nardova, *Nachalo monopolizatsii neftyanoi promyshlennosti*, pp. 94–112.
17. There were other speciality products as well, notably various lubricating oils, which were remunerative and widely sold on world markets.
18. This price information is taken from S.L. and L.L. Pershke, *Russkaya neftyanaya promyshlennost′: ee razvitie i sovremennoe polozhenie v statisticheskikh dannykh* (Tiflis, 1913) p. 41; Akademiya nauk SSSR, *Monopolisticheskii kapital v neftyanoi promyshlennosti′*, p. 70; G.E. Startsev, *Bakinskaya neftyanaya promyshlennost′: Istoriko-statisticheskii ocherk* (Baku, 1901) p. 58; and V.E. Parkhomenko, *D.I. Mendeleev i russkoe neftyanoe delo* (Moscow, 1957) p. 237.
19. Startsev, *Bakinskaya neftyanaya promyshlennost′*, p. 57.
20. B.F. Brandt, *Inostrannye kapitaly: ikh vliyanie na ekonomicheskoe razvitie strany*, 3 vols (St Petersburg, 1898–1901) vol. III, p. 365; Sovet s″ezda neftepromyshlennikov, *Obzor Bakinskoi promyshlennosti za 1897* (Baku, 1898) pp. 191–3.
21. Startsev, *Bakinskaya neftyanaya promyshlennost'*, pp. 57–9.
22. D.I. Mendeleev, *Sochineniya*, vol. X (Leningrad, 1934–54) p. 532.
23. Parkhomenko, *D.I. Mendeleev i russkoe neftyanoe delo*, p. 132.
24. Sovet s″ezda neftepromyshlennikov, *Obzor Bakinskoi neftyannoi promyshlennosti za 1900* (Baku, 1901) p. 312.
25. As may be seen in Table 1, 66 per cent of total American and Russian kerosene exports of 201.6 million puds in 1899 would have required 133 million puds of Russian kerosene for export. With domestic shipments equalling 40 million puds, total kerosene requirements would have been 173 million puds. Assuming the technical maximum of about 33 per cent of Baku crude was refined as kerosene, the crude oil requirements necessary for a dominant role in the world market would have been roughly 525 million puds in 1899 – exactly what Baku actually produced in that year.
26. Ralph W. Hidy and Muriel E. Hidy, *Pioneering in Big Business, 1882–1911: History of Standard Oil Company (New Jersey)* (New York, 1955) pp. 146–54, 245–54, and Harold F. Williamson and Arnold Daum, *The American Petroleum Industry: The Age of Illumination* (Evanston, Ill., 1959) pp. 647–57.
27. The recent work by A.A. Fursenko, *Neftyanye voiny* (Leningrad, 1985), provides the best point of departure to the voluminous study of interfirm and intergovernmental relations in the petroleum industry by Soviet scholars.
28. Williamson and Daum, *American Petroleum Industry*, 586–7; Brandt,

Inostrannye kapitaly, vol. III, pp. 288, 376–7; Pershke and Pershke, *Russkaya neftyanaya promyshlennost'*, pp. 53–9, 142.
29. F.C. Gerretson, *History of the Royal Dutch*, 4 vols. (Leiden, 1953–57) vol. II, p. 33.
30. Sovet s"ezda neftepromyshlennikov, *Obzor Bakinskoi neftyanoi promyshlennosti za 1898* (Baku, 1899) p. 174. The slight difference from Table 1 is due to Table 1's use of kerosene actually shipped as opposed to kerosene refined. Also see Brandt, *Inostrannye kapitaly*, vol. III, p. 363, for a different set of calculations making the same point.
31. Pershke and Pershke, *Russkaya neftyanaya promyshlennost'*, pp. 64–5.
32. V.I. Bovykin, *Zarozhdenie finansovogo kapitala Rossii* (Moscow, 1967), p. 151.
33. Brandt, *Inostrannye kapitaly*, vol. III, p. 355.
34. Sovet s"ezda neftepromyshlennikov, *Obzor za 1898*, pp. 178–81; Brandt, *Inostrannye kapitaly*, vol. III, pp. 343–60.
35. Ibid., vol. III, pp. 352, 370–2.
36. Gerretson, *Royal Dutch*, vol. II, pp. 148–9.
37. Pershke and Pershke, *Russkaya neftyanaya promyshlennost'*, p. 46.
38. Akademiya nauk SSSR, *Monopolisticheskii kapital v neftyanoi promyshlennosti*, p. 223.
39. *Tsentral'nyi Gosudarstrennyi Istoricheskii Arkhiv SSSR* (in Leningrad) fond 37, opis' 33, delo 42, ll. 59–60.
40. Pershke and Pershke, *Russkaya neftyanaya promyshlennost'*, p. 142. Eventually, the state also imposed high rates on its Baku-to-Batum kerosene pipeline, a section of which was reluctantly begun in 1896 in connection with relaying railway tracks washed out by floods and which was completed only in 1903.
41. Akademiya nauk SSSR, *Monopolisticheskii kapital v neftyanoi promyshlennosti*, pp. 114–16, 223–6.
42. John P. McKay, *Pioneers for Profit: Foreign Entrepreneurship and Russian Industrialization, 1885–1914* (Chicago, 1970) pp. 268–86, 385–7, and 'Foreign Businessmen, the Tsarist Government and the Briansk Company', *Journal of European Economic History*, 2 (1973) pp. 273–93.
43. Fursenko, *Neftyanye voiny*, is the best introduction to these complicated negotiations and agreements relating to the world market in the 1890s.
44. See the suggestive article by Arcadius Kahan, 'Government Policies and the Industrialization of Russia', *Journal of Economic History*, 27 (1967) pp. 460–77.

6 British Merchant Houses in Russia before 1914

Stuart Thompstone

From the beginning of direct commercial relations with Western Europe in the mid-sixteenth century until the 1917 Revolution, Russia's international commerce was conducted predominantly through the intermediary of foreign merchants. And as Arcadius Kahan observed, this foreign element remained a distinct group for an inordinately long time, as has Russian interest in it: 'Even now the problem of foreigners and nationals in the foreign trade of Russia occupies the attention of contemporary Soviet historians.'[1] Certainly it was common in nineteenth-century Russia, and indeed elsewhere, to discuss participation in international commerce in terms of national groups, though the trading houses involved were frequently not so much 'national' as international in the sense that they operated simultaneously in two or more countries and were owned by people tending towards a supranational outlook.

Notwithstanding these caveats, an examination of the fortunes of British mercantile houses in nineteenth-century Russia can be instructive. By the end of the eighteenth century Russia's foreign trade was, after all, predominantly in their hands. However, in the nineteenth century 'German' (by nationality rather than citizenship) merchants rapidly assumed the dominant position not only in the handling of Russia's commerce with their homeland but also with neutral foreign markets too.[2] In the second half of the nineteenth century they were posing a powerful challenge to British merchants in the handling of Russo-British trade as well. To contemporary observers this reflected badly on the entrepreneurial spirit of the expatriate British community in Russia. And there was likewise concern at the lacklustre performance of British manufacturers seeking to market their products in the lands of the Tsar.

A high mortality rate among trading houses in the nineteenth century was the norm. Trading houses usually took the form of partnerships which lapsed with the expiry of time or indeed of the partners themselves. And the commercial crises which punctuated nineteenth century international commerce took their toll of British houses in Russia as elsewhere. Accentuating this trend, British houses increasingly withdrew from handling Russian foreign trade, leaving the field to others. Nevertheless, there were notable exceptions. Such prominent families in the Russian Empire's British community as the Hubbards, the Cazalets and the Whishaws, which were all involved in Russian foreign trade from the late eighteenth century, did not join the British exodus from Russian trade and remained until the 1917 Revolution.

BRITISH MERCANTILE HOUSES IN RUSSIA IN THE EIGHTEENTH CENTURY

For British governments in the eighteenth century, Russo-British trade assumed vital importance. Russia became one of the chief sources of products of strategic as well as of economic significance. In particular the needs of British dockyards for Russian naval stores gave rise in the Westminster parliament to a strong interest in Russo-British trade. The upshot of this was that, like the East India Company, the Russia Company was able to exert a considerable influence over parliament on questions of trade and international relations, at a time when other chartered companies in Britain had degenerated into formal bodies or administrations of charitable trusts. Russia Company influence is to be seen in the Anglo-Russian Commercial Treaty of 1734; the 1766 Treaty of Commerce; and its renewal under the 1793 Russo-British Convention. And finally its efforts to persuade the British government to negotiate a long term trade treaty were rewarded with the signing of the 1797 Russo-British Commercial Treaty.[3]

This close relationship between the British government and the Russia Company also manifested itself in the involvement in British politics of Russia Company merchants. It was given great force in the late eighteenth century by the vigour of the Russia Company's then governor, Edward Forster (1730–1812). During the 1780s he won acclaim in the House of Commons for his speeches on Russian trade.[4] Forster's combination of interests in the Russia trade and banking, on the one hand, and politics, on the other, was to some extent replicated in others among the elite of Russia traders. Three prominent Hull-based families involved in Anglo-Russian commerce, the Thorntons, the Wilberforces and the Porters had a total of seven members of their respective firms in the House of Commons in the 1780s.[5]

BRITISH HOUSES IN RUSSIA IN THE FIRST HALF OF THE NINETEENTH CENTURY

As the importance to Britain of Russia's staple exports declined as a consequence of both technological change and the improved accessibility of alternative sources of supply from within the British Empire, there was a corresponding decline in interest on the part of British governments to negotiate privileges for Russia's British merchant community. Moreover, with its more familiar legal system and its more buoyant reciprocal export trade, the British Empire began to be an increasingly attractive alternative to foreign-based houses seeking to supply the British market. Soon into the nineteenth century British merchant houses in Russia were handling a smaller proportion of the country's international trade than were traders of German origin. However, the speed of this relative change in the commercial fortunes of these two national groups was more apparent than real.

The late eighteenth-century predominance of the British over other foreign merchants in the handling of Russia's foreign trade was exaggerated by the widespread practice of non-British foreign merchants taking out Russian citizenship in order to qualify for the commercial privileges available to Russian nationals. These could be very compelling. By the 1780s Russian citizenship could bring a reduction in import duties of between 10 and 14 per cent and 'German' merchants made much use of the privilege.[6]

For British merchants this did not apply with anything like the same force. Quite apart from the privileges they enjoyed under commercial treaties, British merchants were predominantly involved in the export trade and were relatively less affected by tariff impositions than were the mass of international traders in Russia. Furthermore, the umbrella organisation of St Petersburg's British merchant community, the British Factory, strove hard to maintain British solidarity, deterring its members from taking out Russian citizenship.[7]

But the declining importance to Britain of Russian export commodities in the first half of the nineteenth century had its effect on the number of British mercantile houses operating in Russia. Moreover, they never became a major force in the grain trade, the largest component of Russia's exports in the second half of the century. Palmerston's 1848 survey of British mercantile houses abroad lists only 22 British houses trading in St Petersburg with a further 13 operating in Riga and Archangel. Furthermore four of these houses had ceased trading by 1850, possibly victims of the 1848 financial crisis.[8]

And in contrast to the position at the turn of the nineteenth century the national cohesion of the British merchant community was being eroded. Palmerston's survey indicated that only 15 of the 32 partners in the 22 British mercantile houses in St Petersburg were still British subjects. Most of the rest had become Russian citizens. Also discernible is what might be termed a 'germanicisation' of British houses. Two of the ostensibly British firms in the Palmerston survey, Nichols & Plincke and Thielke & Busk could better be described as Anglo-German houses.

Mirroring trends in merchant houses in Britain itself, it became common for foreign clerks, who were usually German, to take over the businesses of their erstwhile British employers. C. Smith & Co., which had traded under that name in Russia since 1800 and from 1780 under the style of E.J. Smith & Co., was taken over in 1816 by the Cramer brothers. Similar changes affected houses established by other nationalities, for example, that of the American trader John D. Lewis, which specialised in the import into Russia of Cuban sugar, dyestuffs and coffee. On his retirement in 1842 his St Petersburg house was taken over by one of his employees, the Dutchman, Abraham van Sassen, who had come to St Petersburg in 1812 and had spent the next thirty years working for Lewis, the last 12 of them as head of the house. He successfully continued the business under the title of van Sassen & Co.. In terms of the volume of trade handled it was in 1848 the tenth largest house in Russia's international trade.[9]

For British controlled houses perhaps the most important takeover of this nature occurred in 1840, when the cotton trading firm, James Holford & Co. (the largest British importer into Russia) experienced liquidity problems, much of its £300 000 capital becoming locked up in credits in Russia. Its St Petersburg house was taken over by its longest serving employee, Wilhelm Berthau, who subsequently ran the Russian branch's business under the style of Wilhelm Berthau & Co. It retained for a time a prominent position in the Russian import trade. Holford's business also had branches in Britain, the United States and Hamburg. The surviving West European ends of the business, which would more accurately be described as an Anglo-German house, were also germanicised. Holford, Sauer & Co., Manchester, was taken over by two of its German clerks, who ran it under their own names as Wolff, Hasche & Co.; while Holford, Sauer & Co., Hamburg (which was also dissolved) was continued by its German partner, Johann Jacob Sauer, under his own name.[10]

Another contributory factor to the withdrawal of British firms from the handling of Russia's foreign trade was their perception of an acceptable level of profit. Profit levels in Russian foreign trade were probably declining in the first half of the nineteenth century, making other commercial activities appear more attractive to British merchants. For German clerks taking over the businesses of their former employers such considerations were arguably less of an inhibiting factor, since they often had no direct experience of the likely higher profits of previous times. In any event there were more than four times as many German houses as British operating in St Petersburg in the 1840s.[11] However, the average British house at this time handled more than its German counterpart and the British community had the consolation of maintaining its privileged social position in Russia. According to the German observer, Kohl, the British:

> have their own chapel and despising all other nations, but most of all their protectors, the Russians, they live shut up by themselves, drive English horses and carriages, go bear hunting on the Neva, as they do tiger hunting on the Ganges, disdain to lift their hats to the Emperor himself and proud of their indispensableness and the invincibility of their fleets, defy everybody, find fault with everything they see, but are highly thought of by the government and by all, because they think highly of themselves, and reside chiefly in the

> magnificent quay named after them. . . . . The English, as a merchant once said to me, do the prettiest roundest, most solid and most pleasant business.[12]

At the very least British merchants were still cutting a dash, but by the mid-nineteenth century they came to St Petersburg increasingly with the intention of gaining overseas commercial experience before returning to London, hopefully to become a partner in the parent house there. Their attitude was not apparently shared by the majority of Germans coming to Russia to work in commerce. With the possible exception of migrants from the Hanseatic towns, Germans usually stayed longer and frequently they themselves, and more especially their children and grandchildren, became Russian citizens, often with only their names to remind them of their German ancestry. As one successful German businessman, explaining his decision to remain in Russia, put it:

> I do not want to return home and spend more time among philistines. Why should I sit in a tavern under a cloud of tobacco smoke with a mug of beer and play skat. . . . . . . with dirty cards, leaving my wife and children at home, or invite guests, such as a rich dyer, or the chief postmaster with his wife and a dozen daughters, who think they are doing me a great honour?[13]

For that German at least, mid-nineteenth century provincial life in the German principalities held few attractions.

The aura of being a commercial élite which for a long time surrounded the British community in Russia evidently had its attractions for outsiders and there are instances of other foreigners seeking to join what was described as this 'exclusive caste'. A case in point is the Blessig family. They were partners in the important trading firm, Blessig, Braun & Co., Liverpool, and Blessig & Co., St Petersburg. The firm was established in St Petersburg in 1793 under the style of Kümmel & Blessig by F.W. Kümmel (1752–1810) from Hesse and P.J. Blessig (1762–1832) from Strasbourg. It was run in the middle period of the nineteenth century by Wilhelm Blessig (1797–1862). He was also the Oldenburg Consul and a director of the Lübeck–St Petersburg Steamship Company. He married the daughter of John

Higginbotham, an English merchant in St Petersburg, while other Blessigs married into such prominent British trading families in Russia as the Cattleys and the Whishaws. The Blessigs were members of the Anglican church in St Petersburg from at least the 1830s; towards the end of the nineteenth century the family provided the treasurer of the British Factory in Russia, John Blessig, who subsequently moved to London, where in 1907 he was elected to the Court of the Russia Company.[14]

The Baltic German family the Baroths were also closely linked to the British community and to British commerce. They not only married into the Hoth family, owners of the Russian Empire's largest ropeworks, but also into the Yates family, which owned one of Russia's largest paper mills. In the 1820s Charles Baroth helped set up de Jersey & Co., Manchester, which subsequently became the conduit through which Ludwig Knoop supplied textile machinery and raw cotton to the Russian textile industry.[15]

BRITISH TRADING HOUSES AFTER THE CRIMEAN WAR

The Crimean War dealt a serious blow to the position of British traders in Russia. The benevolent neutrality exercised by Prussia boosted commercial intercourse over Russia's land frontier, which by this time could begin to take advantage of rail links. The war obliged British consumers of Russian commodities to seek alternative sources of supply. South American tallow began replacing the Russian product. Jute was used as a partial substitute for Russian hemp and alternative supplies of hemp were also imported from the East Indies, Hungary and the Philippines.[16] Britain's position as Russia's chief trading partner steadily eroded. Not only had German firms become the chief handlers of Russian foreign trade, but after the 1871 reunification of Germany their homeland soon became Russia's most important trading partner.

British trading houses in the Baltic and the White Sea ports in a sense lived off their human capital, with little replenishment from the home country. The last full breakdown of Russian foreign trade by individual merchant house was compiled by the Russian Department of Customs Collection for 1863. It shows that in that year there were only 20 trading houses of British origin operating in the Russian Empire, a marked reduction on the 34 houses revealed in the 1848 Palmerston Survey.[17] Furthermore the volume of trade they handled on average had declined. In 1864 Baring Bros agent in Russia, Charles Jutting noted that:

> The English houses here and their London connections are on the whole respectable and of fair standing but with the exception of G. Loder & Co. and perhaps Hubbard & Co. are not strictly first rate. G. Loder & Co., whose manager Mr Busk is a shrewd man of business, seldom ship merchandise on their own account and chiefly confine themselves to exchange operations which are believed to pay very well.[18]

However, Loder & Co. ceased trading altogether in the 1870s. Giles Loder, the senior partner, died in 1871 and the London and St Petersburg branches of the firm did not long survive him. His brother Sir Robert Loder M.P. (1823–88), who had married one of Busk's daughters, pursued his career in Britain and the last tenuous link the family appears to have had with Russian commerce seems to have been the marriage of his eldest son, Sir Giles Loder to the daughter of the prominent Russia trader, W.E. Hubbard in 1876. The five sons of Sir Robert Loder concerned themselves with public life in Britain.[19] In several respects the Loder family's involvement with Russia typifies the lifestyle of the élite of the British community in Russia. The sons were usually educated in England at the most prestigious public schools and at the ancient universities and the links with England were kept very much alive. The family histories of the Hubbards, the Cazalets and the Whishaws, who remained involved in Russian commerce until the 1917 Revolution, follow a broadly similar pattern. Yet in defence of a family such as the Loders, who elected to withdraw from commerce in Russia, what D.C.M. Platt observed about merchants in the Latin American market has *mutatis mutandis* some relevance for nineteenth-century Russia too:

> There are dangers in classifying a nineteenth century merchant simply as an economic man. The element of chance and the possibility, almost probability of disaster were enough to

> persuade successful merchants to sell up rather than battle indefinitely in the market place. Sharp fluctuations in trade in a period of uncertain communications could make fortunes one day and lose them the next. All successful merchants passed through such crises, even to the point of bankruptcy, and there was every incentive to move out at the crest of some wave either to try another more promising market, or to withdraw into the comfortable status of a rentier.[20]

Certainly financial crises seem to have punctuated the histories of many of the international merchant houses involved in the nineteenth-century Russian market. In 1847 the Manchester house which specialised in exporting to Russia, de Jersey & Co., temporarily ceased trading with liabilities of £600 000, a scale of debt which indicates how important in Anglo-Russian commerce it then was. An important house in the Whishaw trading network went into bankruptcy in 1882 and in the late nineteenth and early twentieth century the directors of John Hubbard & Co., London, and Egerton Hubbard & Co., St Petersburg, twice had to call on the assistance of a wealthy relative, in the first instance to the tune of £60 000, in order to save their business from financial collapse.[21]

Family links may have played their part in slowing a British exodus from Russia. Social intercourse and business relationships amongst expatriate West European merchant families in Russia frequently overlapped. The resultant intermarriage may have conceivably kept the élite of the British merchant community in Russia, when commercial considerations might have suggested a move elsewhere. Marriage ties undoubtedly strengthened the commercial bonds between trading families and it is illuminating to trace how extensive these could be. In the case of the Whishaws, for example, William Whishaw (1746–1838), who went to Russia in about 1770, married in 1777 the daughter of Bernard Fock, inspector of the Imperial Gardens in St Petersburg. Other of Fock's daughters married into the Clarke and Cazalet families. William Whishaw's eldest son, Bernard, married Elizabeth Yeames, whose family rose to prominence in the Black Sea trade exporting Russian wool to Britain in the second quarter of the nineteenth century, through a profitable tie up with L. Stieglitz & Co., St Petersburg, and Baring Bros, London. Other Whishaws married into such prominent trading families as the Hills, the Cattleys, the Blessigs and the Todds.[22]

Early in the nineteenth century Bernard Whishaw founded with his future brother-in-law, Henry Hill, the firm of Hills & Whishaw, St Petersburg. But like so many British trading partnerships it was vulnerable to capital being taken out of the firm by the death or retirement of a partner. When James Whishaw, William Whishaw's son, went to live in St Petersburg in 1877, he believed that Hills & Whishaw was the oldest firm trading there. It was certainly one of the city's leading grain exporters. In the four years from 1878 it was respectively the tenth, fourth, second and eighth largest grain exporter in St Petersburg.[23] But size in the market place proved to be no guarantee of future survival. The delay in proving the will of a deceased senior partner, William Whishaw, who died in 1879, undermined confidence in the firm. In September of the following year the Bank of England informed Hope & Co., Amsterdam, that 'the will of the senior partner has not been proved and the delay is looked upon as suspicious and as warranting belief that there is little or no capital left in the firm. Their bills should be avoided. The London firm are partners in St. Petersburg but the latter are not partners in London.'[24]

The financial consequences of the will being eventually proved were that the capital in James Hill & Sons, London was reduced from £105 000 to £75 000. In contrast to the partnership system then prevailing in most West European commercial centres, which permitted limited liability to sleeping partners, the unlimited liability of partners under British law made such a capital withdrawal inevitable. However, the effects on the commercial standing of the St Petersburg firm were fatal. Unable to secure easy credits in London, Hills & Whishaw failed in 1882. The other Russian based branches, which were deemed by the London market to have better management, survived into the twentieth century.

For James Whishaw, jnr. probably on account of being a member of the British élite in St Petersburg, the bankruptcy of the family firm did not leave him without an income. Shortly before the firm's demise he had abandoned his medical studies in London to work in his family's St Petersburg house. Despite his lack of commercial experience the British community engineered his appointment as a sworn shipsbroker in St Petersburg, putting so much business his way in his first year for his income to exceed £3000. In fact James Whishaw turned out to be a shrewd man of business. He subsequently worked hard to establish and maintain good relations with customers in England. In 1908 he became Baring Bros representative in Russia and soon afterwards he was appointed a director of the Azov-Don Bank. He acted as a trustee for a number of British firms which sought to invest in mineral extraction in Russia in the early part of this century and he owned at that time a small fleet of tugboats which operated on the Caspian Sea.[25]

The firm established by his uncle, Arthur Whishaw in 1860, A.H. Whishaw & Co., St Petersburg continued into the twentieth century. Along with Egerton Hubbard & Co. and Clarke & Co., it was in the 1880s among the top ten grain exporting houses in St Petersburg. But its dominant grain exporters by this time, however, were firms of German origin, such as E.H. Brandt & Co. and G. Süsskind. By the beginning of this century A.H. Whishaw was chiefly concerned with exporting flax to Scotland and France with a relative in London, John Todd, providing the credit, later being replaced in that function by Baring Bros (when Todd went into liquidation). In 1911 A.H. Whishaw & Co. switched from St Petersburg to Dorpat, the flax trade having 'left St Petersburg'.[26]

By this time British mercantile houses had, as it were, largely left the St Petersburg grain trade, North America in particular proving to be a more convenient source of supply for Britain. St Petersburg's leading grain exporting firms with West European origins were: (i) the famous French firm, Louis Dreyfus & Co.; (ii) Leon & Co., who were linked with Hampton & Hoskier, Paris, Bleichröder in Berlin and J. Johnson, London, with much of its trading finance being provided by the London bankers, Hambro & Son; (iii) I. Hirschfeld; (iv) Behrend & Blumberg; (v) Blessig & Co. The last mentioned three firms all operated on the basis of foreign credits. And finally, (vi) the well-known conglomerate, Wogau & Co., which conducted its grain trading operations partly on internal sources of credit and partly on international ones. Its access to London credits would have been facilitated by the existence there of its branch house, Wogau & Co. (it continues to the present as Wogau-Brameast, a commodity trading subsidiary of merchant bankers, Guinness Peat).[27]

By the early twentieth century, changing patterns of world trade and international competition resulted in there being only one port in the Russian Empire where a British trading house remained the leading grain exporter. This was Reval. Here the firm of Thomas Clayhills & Son, which was established in 1633 and which from 1770 was run continuously by the same family, managed to remain in the forefront, largely on account of its superior grain-handling facilities. These included floating elevators and canals between its warehouses and the harbour, which enabled it to cut its handling costs below those of other traders in the port.[29]

Other branches of Russia's Baltic and White Sea trading sector had likewise only a limited visible British presence by the early twentieth century. Even in an export sector where British firms might have been expected to feature fairly prominently, and the timber trade is a case in point, German houses appeared to predominate. By this time no major British houses operated in the timber trade out of Archangel, while in St Petersburg, there were only two among the top ten timber exporters: A. Moore and E. Reynolds, who were in eighth and ninth places respectively.[30]

Viewing the nineteenth century as a whole, the decline in the number and importance of British trading houses in Russia is marked. This was to be expected. With the improvement of communications in the nineteenth century, and particularly with the development of the telegraph system, economic conditions became more favourable for commission houses, acting for principals both within Russia and more especially abroad, to challenge the old style merchant houses, which bought goods on their own account for onward sale in export markets. In the second half of the nineteenth century, commission houses became the chief conduit for Russia's international commodity trade. It became relatively easy with the improved communications for those with limited capital but with some knowledge of foreign trade to set up on their own account. It became possible for the more thrusting and ambitious from the army of German clerks, in Russia as in Britain, to run their own commission houses. On the basis of the circulars received by William Brandt's Sons & Co., London, the peak period for the establishment of commission houses in Russia was 1860 to 1880. This roughly coincides with a relatively prosperous period in the country's international grain trade. But more significantly the same circulars record only eight British commission houses being set up in Russia over the longer period between 1855 and 1914.[31]

How far this is a faithful reflection of either British interest in Russia or even British entrepreneurial performance is questionable. The rise of the commission house meant that less decision-taking needed to occur physically in the overseas market. In the case of Russo-British trade more of the entrepreneurial activity could take place in London, Manchester or Liverpool. In the timber trade, for example, a partner in the important East Anglian timber company, Jewsons, claimed that 'for a long time before the 1914–18 War a large proportion of the Russian timber exporting industry was controlled by British interests and British capital.'[32] And though lists of the most prominent timber exporters in Russian ports might appear to refute this claim, it does appear to have substance, when the financial backers of such firms can be discovered. The St Petersburg timber exporter, Oscar Steveni, was effectively set up in business by the prominent London timber trading house, Foy, Morgan & Co., and according to James Whishaw, the same London company practically started in business the St Petersburg timber exporters, Edward Reynolds.[33]

Even the famous 'Russian' timber trading company, Belayev & Co., St Petersburg, had a close British connection. One of its partners was the brother of D.B. Gellibrand, a partner in Foy, Morgan & Co. and a nephew of its senior partner, Mr Foy. In 1908, with their sawmills and forests, Belayev & Co. had a capital of £100 000 but at the same time they owed Foy, Morgan & Co. £50 000.[34] Foy, Morgan & Co. also acted as agents for such Russian-based timber exporters as S.J. Rivlin, Vologda; Bache & Wager, Onega; Firschenbrüder Bros., Onega; J.E. Makarov, Archangel; and N. Rabinovitch, Narva; and it is conceivable that without a visible presence in the Russian market, Foy, Morgan & Co. handled or controlled a larger proportion of Russia's early twentieth-century timber export trade than any other trading concern.[35]

With the continued modernisation of the late nineteenth century Russian economy came further changes in the organisations handling international commerce. On the export side the export commission house and the export agent were joined by the export departments of banks and transport concerns and by the export offices of associations of manufacturers and of individual manufacturing concerns. In the import trade independent import merchants, jobbers and import commission agents were joined by branches of foreign manufacturing concerns with their own sales departments within the country.

These circumstances made the Russian market a less attractive one for British houses. On the export side these trends tended to favour domestic organisations, while in the import field any foreign manufacturer seeking to export to Russia would either wish to do so through creating its own export sales organisation in the country or more usually would tap the market using the agency system. Depending on the product being marketed it would probably require there to be a regional network of agents or sales offices, capable of giving some technical support.

The traditional merchant house, and more especially those run by expatriate Britons, whose *forte* had been commodity trading, were not the ideal channel for this new type of marketing, although a handful such as Yeames & Co., Taganrog, and even Egerton Hubbard & Co., St Petersburg, sought to adapt to the new circumstances.[36]

British houses were at a particular disadvantage in providing sales facilities outside the main population centres of European Russia. One British newcomer to Russia, R. Martens & Co., sought to provide a countrywide network of sales offices for British and American exporters in particular, but its financial resources did not match its ambitions and it went into liquidation early in 1914.[37]

For German firms seeking to find agents throughout Russia who were more likely to be in tune with their requirements, the task was relatively easier. The German population in Russia was quite widely distributed, with every Russian town (it was claimed in the mid-nineteenth century) having a German colony of 400 to 600 people.[38]

The British effort to sell manufactured goods was also hampered by the structure of British industry. British firms trading to Russia were frequently too small to be able to afford a vigorous selling effort by a salaried force of commercial travellers, and most had to rely on commission agents who were frequently German. Added to that, the system of long term credit that German banks advanced to Russian concerns purchasing German capital goods from the bank's home based industrial clients, (which was virtually unique to Russia) was a powerful disincentive to British exporters. For them more profitable markets in the British Empire in particular, where short term credit was the norm, was a more attractive proposition.

The logic of the economic circumstances affecting British houses in Russia increasingly suggested that their energies should be devoted elsewhere. Indeed the nature of Foy, Morgan and Co.'s relationship with the Russian market is not out of line with the path followed by a number of the leading international houses involved in nineteenth century Russian trade. The higher profits to be earned from the financing of foreign trade rather than trading on their own account, drew many of the leading international houses in Russia increasingly out of direct trading activity into banking. For some of them this change of function required a move of the centre of their operations to London. Quite early in the nineteenth century, firms which had accumulated capital in trade with Russia, such as the Thorntons, the Brandts, the Loders and Thomson, Bonar & Co. began to concern themselves with banking activities in London.

Thomson, Bonar & Co., which had been involved in the Russia trade since the eighteenth century, was by the early to mid-nineteenth century one of the leading export houses in St Petersburg. By the mid-nineteenth century, however, it was graduating into pure finance and was being explicitly referred to as a bank. Through its London branch it became heavily involved in exchange dealings and other financial operations on a worldwide scale. It participated in French railway flotations in 1843 and in U.S. railway issues from the end of the Civil War. It participated in the founding of the Hong Kong and Shanghai Banking Corporation, which received its charter in 1865; and it was banker for Peru until 1870. In Russia it was involved in railway flotations (Vitebsk–Orel Railway Bonds) as well as in government loans. It also participated in the establishment of the Russian Bank for Foreign Trade, on whose London Board sat one of Thomson, Bonar's partners, A.J. Eden. As with other houses in Russia, which had moved out of direct trade into finance, government loans and railway flotations could be a lucrative business, but their bread and butter work was in the financing of foreign trade.[39]

Precise data on the growing contribution of British capital to the financing of Russian foreign trade during the nineteenth century are unavailable. Nevertheless at the end of the eighteenth century it was probably well in excess of £1 million of credit per annum.[40] In 1855, a year of disrupted trade, the City of London was said to have provided some £10 million of acceptance credits for the financing of Russian international commerce; in the early 1860s Russian acceptances in London were put at between £12 and £15.5 million a year and by the early twentieth century estimates of up to £20 million have been made.[41]

As might be expected, prominent in the business of providing credit to finance Russia's international commerce were those merchant banks in the City of London that had had trading connections with Russia. J.H. Schroeder & Co. and Wm. Brandt's Sons & Co., which once had trading houses in Russia are cases in point. The latter house concentrated heavily on financing Russian commerce until 1875, when it began to concentrate on trade with Argentina. Subsequently London merchant banks seemed to have spread their risks in the field of trading finance. On the outbreak of the First World War, Brandt's Russian acceptances amounted to £860 000, just under 10 per cent of its total acceptance business. The obverse side of such risk spreading was that merchant banks with no historic trading links with Russia became involved in the financing of its trade. A case in point is S. Kleinwort & Sons, who built up a string of clients involved in Russian international trade. In the years before the First World War its Russian acceptances reached £650 000.[42]

With British merchant banks being able to earn good returns from indirect involvement in Russia's international commerce through the provision of trading credit and of shipping and insurance services too, the concerns that were increasingly voiced from the 1880s about the performance of British enterprise in Russia in the face of German competition, merits some qualification. The Russian market after all was of primary importance to Germany but to Britain it had become of secondary significance. With most of the natural advantages seeming to lie with Germany, it might be more appropriate to consider why some of the major British trading houses elected to remain in Russia rather than why the significance of British commerce there declined. A brief examination of the business activities of the Hubbards and the Cazalets, who were amongst the élite of British traders in Russia, suggests some tentative conclusions.

THE HUBBARD ENTERPRISES

The Hubbard family's links with Russia date from the second half of the eighteenth century, when William Hubbard went first to Archangel before settling in St Petersburg, where he died in 1783. His international trading business was continued by his two sons, John and William. In 1801 John married the daughter of John Morgan, subsequently a partner in the prominent London timber trading house Morgan, Gellibrand & Co.. The lifestyle of the Hubbards and the positions to which they were appointed suggest good returns from their commercial activities in Russia. John Hubbard's son, John Gellibrand Hubbard (1805–89) entered the firm in 1821 and later ran the London end of the family business. He was appointed a Director of the Bank of England in 1838 and a Public Works Loan Commissioner in 1853. He was also active in politics. He was Conservative M.P. for Buckinghamshire, 1859–68, and for the City of London, 1874–87. In 1887 he was raised to the peerage as Baron Addington. He was regarded by his commercial peers as one of the most important figures in Anglo-Russian trade and he was appointed to the honorary position of governor to the Russia Company in recognition of this. His brother William Egerton Hubbard (1812–83) ran the Russian branch of the firm, staying in St Petersburg from 1829 until 1842.[43]

In the period 1830–63 Egerton Hubbard & Co. was consistently among the top five British trading houses in Russia and often among the top ten trading houses there. In 1863, for example, in terms of the international trade it handled, it was the fourth largest trading house in Russia.[44] John Hubbard & Co., London, in essence acted as banker and London agent for the family's Russian interests.

By the mid-nineteenth century the two family partnerships, Egerton Hubbard & Co., St Petersburg and John Hubbard & Co., London, were not only involved in trading and banking, they had acquired manufacturing interests too. They began cotton spinning in their Petrovskii Mill in 1842 and weaving in 1853. They also bought the nearby Spasskii Mill and in 1867 they began textile printing in their recently purchased Schlüsselburg Printworks, which had been founded near St Petersburg in the late eighteenth century. When these three enterprises were combined into the Anglo-Russian Cotton Company in 1897, the capitalisation was £340 000. The Hubbards also had important timber concessions at Onega in Northern Russia and Utra in North East Finland. The Utra timber estates alone were valued by the Hubbards in 1899 at £250 000, which even with encumbrances on them of £60 000 still left a sizeable remainder of £190 000.

There were, however, serious weaknesses in the business by this time and these were exacerbated by the lack of business acumen shown by the successors of William Egerton Hubbard and John Gellibrand Hubbard. Both men had large families and both seem to have overestimated the capacity of their Russian enterprises to generate the consistently high profits needed to support their offspring to the extent provided for in their respective wills. The resultant financial commitments bedevilled the next generation of Hubbards in charge of the family business and on several occasions bankruptcy was only averted through the financial assistance given by the Liberal politician and industrialist Lord Stuart Rendel, who had married into the family. William Egerton Hubbard jnr., who remained in harness until his death in 1918, presided over the family's business interests in Russia, while his cousin the Hon. Evelyn Hubbard (1852–1934) ran the London end. His outside interests were evidently a mixed blessing. Evelyn was a Director of the Bank of England, 1890–1909; he was Chairman of the Guardian Assurance Company, from 1900 to 1930; and he sat as Conservative M.P. for Brixton from 1896 until 1900, when he reluctantly took the Chiltern Hundreds in order to devote himself more actively to the troubled family business. No marked improvements resulted from this sacrifice. Management continued to be appointed more to provide 'outdoor relief' for the wider family than on merit, and greater emphasis was put on commissions for the partnerships than on improving the efficiency of the cotton enterprises which were regarded as the 'milch cow of the firms'.[44] However, after financial restructuring it was reported in 1910 that 'the mills are doing fairly well considering the high price of cotton'.[45] After the 1917 Revolution Hubbards submitted to the Board of Trade in London a claim of £2.5 million for the sequestrated assets of the Anglo-Russian Cotton Co.[46]

THE CAZALET ENTERPRISES

The Cazalet family's involvement in Russian trade began when Noah Cazalet (1757?–1800) went to Russia in his early twenties. He was probably engaged in importing silk into Russia, with his eldest brother, Peter (1756–1811) being his London representative. Peter Cazalet is believed to have joined his father-in-law's banking house, Langston Poolhill, Tourgood and Amory (established in 1777) which traded subsequently as Langston, Tourgood, Cazalet & Co.[47]

With such a connection in London Noah Cazalet's Russian business prospered. He established a rope factory in St Petersburg in the 1790s. His murder at Narva in 1800 put the responsibility for running the business on to the shoulders of his son, Peter Cazalet (1785–1859). In turn Peter Cazalet was joined in the family business by his younger son from his first marriage, Edward (1827–83). Under Edward's subsequent control the family business expanded substantially. He set up a thriving candle works, which acquired the right to provide candles to the imperial palaces. In 1851 the factory became a joint stock enterprise as the Neva Stearine Co. with an issued capital of 450 000 rubles. At the end of the 1870s the Nielsen Company's Moscow stearine works was taken over, giving the company an aggregate output from its two plants of 6.7 million rubles a year. It became the Russian Empire's largest tallow processor with markets abroad as well as within Russia. Edward also acquired for the family enterprise St Petersburg's Kalinken Brewery. By 1913 the value of its output had reached six million rubles. The firm also acquired the Russian Steam Oil Mill Company.

This branch of the Cazalet family became prominent in Russia's foreign trade after Edward's marriage in 1860 to Elizabeth Marshall from Leith. She was related to the Miller family, who operated a shipping fleet dealing in the herring trade and who through their St Petersburg house, William Miller & Co. had been involved in Russian foreign trade since 1832. Until 1854 the Russian end of this business was headed by William Miller (1809–87). He later entered Parliament as a Liberal 'independent of party', representing Leith and Berwickshire. He was created a baronet in 1874.[48]

Marriage ties between Edward Cazalet and this family were followed by a business link up. Edward acquired a one-third share in William Miller & Co. and the Millers and Marshalls obtained reciprocal shares in the Cazalet concerns. In 1864 Edward Cazalet as head of William Miller & Co. became a founder and director of the St Petersburg Commercial Joint Stock Bank. It is also noteworthy that William Miller & Co. by this time were gravitating into banking, acting in this capacity for the Dunaburg-Vitebsk Railway Company.

In 1868 Edward made his home in England, leaving his extensive Russian business interests in the hands of managers. He purchased a country estate in Kent and sought unsuccessfully to enter Parliament. After his death from typhoid in 1883 his only son, William Marshall Cazalet, continued to live in England, leaving the business in the hands of managers. In 1917 the value of Wm. Miller & Co.'s Russian assets was put at 44 million rubles.[49]

Another branch of the Cazalet family also enjoyed commercial success in Russia. Peter Cazalet's half brother, Alexander (1793–1879), who is believed to have worked for a time with his brother in the family firm, later set up his own trading house, Alexander Cazalet & Sons. It would appear that he took over the Cazalet rope factory. He ran these three businesses until his retirement in 1875, when he handed over to his three sons, Clement, Louis and Edward. They continued until 1890, when it was wound up. Edward returned to live in England, where in 1893 he founded the Anglo-Russian Literary Society.

The interests in Russian commerce of this branch of the family were continued by Louis Cazalet. After the death of his first wife he emulated his cousin Peter by making a significant marriage into a Scottish family, the Mirrielees from Aberdeen. The two sons from this marriage, William Lewis Cazalet (1861–1953) and Frederick Archibald Cazalet (1871–1945) played an important part in the management of the business owned by Archibald Mirrielees, their maternal grandfather. Archibald Mirrielees had begun trading in his own name in St Petersburg in 1843 and shortly afterwards in Moscow too. In 1889 the foreign trading house and the wholesale side of the business in both St Petersburg and Moscow, trading under the style of Muir & Mirrielees, was converted into a limited liability company with the title 'Oborot'. This company continued until the Revolution.

Much more famous, however, was the retailing side of the business which continued to trade under the name of Muir &

Mirrielees. William Cazalet became its Managing Director and Frederick its chief cashier. The company's profits for the 1908–9 financial year were 263 414 rubles, rising to almost 660 000 rubles in 1909–10 and to almost 700 000 rubles and over 900 000 rubles respectively in the next two financial years. In addition to the celebrated Moscow retail store, Muir & Mirrielees also owned a substantial furniture factory in the city's Presnya District. The value of their company's assets in 1918 was calculated at £1 740 000 with the Cazalet family being major shareholders.[49]

CONCLUSION

By the early twentieth century the ranks of Russia's British merchant community had been considerably thinned. In his memoirs James Whishaw painted a picture of rapid change in its St Petersburg component:

> The English colony (especially those in society) was a large one and one could dine out practically every evening without meeting the same family twice. It was to decline all too rapidly in this respect, for the senior residents either retired or died off, and by the time of the Great War very few of the old families remained.[50]

In 1914 a few second-rate British houses in Russia were still involved in commodity trading (exporting timber, hemp, flax and grain and importing coal) but what is significant about the two leading British houses still operating in Russia – William Miller & Co. and Egerton Hubbard & Co. – is that they had long diversified out of their purely trading role into finance and industry. Their industrial concerns arguably kept them in Russian international trade, when international trading considerations alone might have suggested a move elsewhere.

Once the necessity for Britain to import particular products specifically from Russia had declined, as was increasingly happening from the early nineteenth century onwards, it was only to be expected that British trading houses would focus their attention elsewhere and particularly in the British Empire. Nevertheless, through the provision of banking, shipping and insurance services, Britain retained an important role in Russia's international commerce. And it did so in those trading functions that were considered the most profitable. The growing concern in late nineteenth-century Britain at the poor performance of its international traders in Russia may have some foundation but there are mitigating circumstances.

NOTES

1. A. Kahan, *The Plow, the Hammer and the Knout* (Chicago and London, 1985), pp. 262–3.
2. Assessing the German contribution to Russia's international commerce is problematic for the period before the 1871 unification of Germany, the more so because of the Baltic German component in the Russian Empire's population. 'German' in this chapter refers to nationality rather than citizenship. For an assessment of the 'German' contribution to Russia's international trade in the late 18th and early 19th centuries, see C.F. Menke, 'Die Wirtschaftlichen und Politischen Beziehungen der Hansastädte zu Russland im 18 und Frühen Jahrhunderte' (Unpublished PhD, University of Göttingen, 1959) pp. 126–40.
3. D.K. Reading, *The Anglo-Russian Commercial Treaty of 1734* (New Haven, 1938); J. Ehrmann, *The British Government and Commercial Negotiations, 1783–1793* (London, 1962) p. 125; and The Public Record Office (PRO) FO 65/14, 17/11/1787; FO 65/15/164, 24/4/1787; FO 65/36, 21/3/1797.
4. D.S. Macmillan, 'The Russia Company of London in the 18th Century: The effective survival of a Regulated Chartered Company', *The Guildhall Miscellany*, IV, 4 (1973) pp. 222–36.
5. G. Jackson, *Hull in the Eighteenth Century* (London, 1972) pp. 253–4. The close connection between the élite of Russia traders and British politics continued into the 19th century, though to a lesser extent, when the strategic importance to Britain of Russia's staple commodities had evaporated.
6. D. Gerhard, *England und der Aufstieg Russlands* (Berlin, 1933) p. 4.
7. PRO FO 65/15/164, Shairp to Carmarthen, 24/4/1787 and FO 65/15/214, Frazer to Carmarthen, 3/7/1787.
8. British Parliamentary Papers (BPP) XXXIX (1847–48) pp. 309–24 and PRO FO 83/110, Circulars to Ministers and Consuls abroad, 14/9/1848.
9. Baring Bros. Records, Guildhall Library (BBGH) HC10.1.29 Stieglitz to Baring Bros. 15/2/1833; HC 10.11/1, 2, 6, 9, and 10, Gibson to Barings and Van Sassen to Barings, 1841–51; and Brandt Circulars, Nottingham University Library (BCNU) 1829, p. 302.
10. BCNU 1825, pp. 242–45 and p. 301; and S.D. Chapman, *The Rise of Merchant Banking* (London, 1984) p. 73.

11. J.G. Kohl, 'Sketches of Russian Commerce', *Hunts Merchants Magazine*, X, 3 (1844) p. 216.
12. Ibid., pp. 209–10.
13. E. Kolbe, *Unterhaltungen über Russland* (1853) p. 30.
14. Guildhall Library, Church of England Registers, ms 11, 194/1, part II, 27/5/1837, 2/1/1839 and part III, 12/4/1846; Russia Company Records, Guildhall Library (RCGH), Minutes, vol. XV, pp. 81–5; BCNU, 1862–1866, p. 3 and 1911–12, p. 28; and Menke, *Wirtschaftlichen und Politischen Beziehungen*, p. 343.
15. RCGH, ms. 11, 753.
16. L.S. Semenov, *Rossiya i Angliya: Ekonomicheskie otnosheniya v sredine XIX veka* (Leningrad, 1975) p. 156.
17. *Vidy gosudarstvennoi vneshnei torgovli za 1863* (St Petersburg, 1864) Table XLII.
18. BBGH HC 10.28.2, Jutting to Baring Bros., 7/3/1864.
19. *Who's Who* (London, 1911) cols. 1231–2; and BCNU, 1872–4, pp. 165 and 485.
20. D.C.M. Platt, *Latin America and British Trade, 1806–1914* (London, 1972) p. 52; D. Morier Evans, *The Commercial Crisis, 1847–1848* (London, 1849) p. lvi; and S. Thompstone, 'Ludwig Knoop: The Russian Arkwright', *Textile History*, xv (1984) p. 48.
21. Anglo-Russian Cotton Co. Records, Guildhall Library (ARCCO) ms. 10/314, file no. 1, W.E. Hubbard to Lord Stuart Rendel, 20/7/1899 and ms. 10/364, file no. 2, Report by J.E. Hubbard, June, 1910.
22. M.S. Leigh (ed.), *James Whishaw: A History of the Whishaw Family* (London, 1935); and BCNU, 1849–55, p. 319.
23. Uncatalogued Brandt Papers, Nottingham University, box 1, Grain Circulars of Charles Prevost, St Petersburg Grain Broker, for years p. 1878 to 1881.
24. Baring Bros. Records, Bishopsgate (BBBG), Character Reference Book no. 2, entry for 15/12/1881.
25. Leigh (ed.) *James Whishaw*, pp. 85–8; and D.S. Guseinova, *Rabochie-moryaki Kaspiya* (Baku, 1981) pp. 33 and 37.
26. *Spravochnaya kniga S. Petersburgskoi kupecheskoi upravy*, (St Petersburg 1902), p. 666; and BBBG, London Credit Registers, vol. iii, p. 12.
27. T.M. Kitanina, *Khlebnaya torgovlya Rossii v 1875–1914 gg.* (*Ocherki pravitel'stvennoi politiki*) (Leningrad, 1978) p. 156; and BBBG, London Credit Registers, vol. II, p. 209.
28. RCGH, box 2, letter 631, de Soucanton to C. Taylor, 26/11/1880.
29. M.P. Fedorov, *Khlebnaya torgovlya v glavneishikh russkikh portakh i Kenigsberge* (Moscow, 1888) pp. 248–50.
30. J.N. Lodyzhensky, *Russia: Its Industries and Trade* (Glasgow International Exhibition, 1901) p. 322.
31. BCNU, calculated from the data in volumes for the period 1855–1914.
32. C.B. Jewson, *The Timber Trade with Russia* (Privately published, Norwich, 1948) p. 1.
33. BBBG, London Credit Registers, vol. II, pp. 59, 103 and 159.
34. Ibid. p. 52.

35. L. Bamberger, *Memories of Sixty Years in the Timber Trade* (London, 1929) pp. 11, 45, 56 and 69; and sundry uncatalogued letters held by Foy, Morgan and Co.'s successors, Price, Pierce & Co., London.
36. ARCCO, ms. 10/364, file no. 2.
37. R. Martens & Co., *The Russian Market and British Enterprise* (London, n.d.) p. 4; and PRO Records of Defunct Companies, BT31/21001/125031.
38. J.G. Kohl, *Petersburg in Bildern und Skizzern*, 2 parts (Dresden and Leipzig, 1841) part 2, pp. 221–3.
39. L.H. Jenks, *The Migration of British Capital to 1875* (New York, 1927) pp. 143, 176 and 271; and BBGH HC10.28.2., 7/3/1864/ HC10.15, 4/2/ 1877 and HC10.28, 29/12/1874.
40. PRO FO65/47/228, Shairp to Hammond.
41. S. Diaper, 'The History of Kleinwort & Sons Co. in Merchant Banking', (PhD, University of Nottingham, 1983) p. 152; and Chapman, *Rise of Merchant Banking*, p. 107.
42. Diaper, 'History of Kleinwort and Sons', pp. 152 and 169–72.
43. Compiled from ARCCO records.
44. ARCCO, ms 10, 364, file no. 2 Lord Rendel to W.E. Hubbard, 11/12/1911.
45. Bank of England Records, B. of E. Discount Department, Entry for John Hubbard & Co. (provided by S.D. Chapman).
46. PRO FO371/14836.
47. Compiled from Cazalet papers and unpublished family history in family possession.
48. The Times, 11/10/1887; and M. Stenton (ed.) *Who's Who of British Members of Parliament*, vol. I, 1832–85, p. 270.
49. PRO FO371/14836.
50. Leigh (ed.) *James Whishaw*, p. 88.

7 Defence Industries in Tsarist Russia, 1908–13: Production, Employment and Military Procurement

Peter Gatrell

Many aspects of defence in later imperial Russia have come under detailed scrutiny by western scholars in recent years. Walter Pintner, in a study of defence spending during the eighteenth and nineteenth centuries, concludes that the burden of defence, defined as the military share of the budget, tended to decline over time.[1] The struggle between the Ministry of War and the Ministry of Finances over the size of the defence budget in the aftermath of the Russo-Japanese War has been analysed by William Fuller, in a book which has wider implications for our understanding of the tsarist state.[2] Other authors have researched the social composition of the imperial army, including the officer corps, and have demonstrated its social heterogeneity.[3] The decision-making process in defence policy looms large in a wide-ranging book by Dietrich Geyer and in specialised studies.[4] Finally, Dietrich Beyrau and John Bushnell have drawn attention to the character of military procurement during the second half of the nineteenth century. Their studies highlight the importance of the 'regimental economy', namely a system of military supply in which rank and file soldiers were obliged to manufacture their own uniforms and other items from materials they had purchased or with which they had been supplied. The inefficiency of this system, and the problems associated with military supply during the Russo-Japanese War, led to the formal abandonment of the regimental economy, although elements of it probably survived, even into the early Soviet period.[5] These and other issues have also been treated in the work of Soviet historians.[6]

The focus of the present study is on the industrial implications of pre-war rearmament and on the problems encountered in administering budgets, materials and industrial manpower in the defence industry. The first section presents estimates of defence production and the workforce engaged in defence industry. The second section deals with the organisation of the defence industry. The final section considers some general issues in military procurement between 1908 and 1914.[7]

I

The most readily available indicator of the dynamics of tsarist defence preparations is the published defence budget. The combined defence budget grew from just over 600 million rubles in 1908 to 960 million rubles in 1913. Defence absorbed 28 per cent of total government spending in 1913, compared to 23 per cent in 1908. During these six years, 4240 million rubles were assigned to defence.[8] The bulk of this expenditure went, as before, on pay, food, uniforms and fodder.[9] But a rising share of total spending was devoted to armaments, and in particular to the acquisition of new military vessels. In line with the programme for reconstruction and expansion of the Baltic and Black Sea fleets, the allocations for shipbuilding (including repairs) increased from 31 million rubles in 1908 to 108 million rubles in 1913. Shipbuilding thus claimed over 11 per cent of total defence spending in 1913, compared to five per cent in 1908. In all, the tsarist government purchased ships to the value of 302 million rubles between 1908 and the outbreak of war. Total allocations for land-based armaments, including fortress artillery, amounted to around 521 million rubles (1908–13). Of this total, some 200 million rubles were actually spent in this period. The Chief Artillery Administration (GAU) spent just over 30 million rubles in 1908 on the acquisition of armaments (this figure excludes repairs and maintenance); by 1913, actual outlays had risen to 50 million rubles.[10]

If we add the two major components, namely weaponry and military vessels, we find that government purchases increased from around 60 million rubles in 1908 to 160 million rubles in 1913, an increase of 167 per cent. Some of these orders were placed abroad. Unfortunately, there is no reliable information on the extent of foreign orders for armaments, except for 1908–10 (in the case of the Ministry of War) and 1908–9 (Navy Ministry), when 9.6 per cent and 23 per cent respectively of all orders were placed with foreign suppliers.[11] If these proportions applied throughout the period 1908–13, then imports of military vessels and other armaments would amount to 70 and 19 million rubles respectively. Correspondingly, the government purchased ships from domestic suppliers to the value of 232 million rubles and other armaments to the value of 181 million rubles. But these figures must be regarded as tentative.

A reasonable approximation can be made of the value of total defence production and armaments production in particular. The starting-point of any such calculations is the industrial census that was conducted in 1918. The census identified 2287 enterprises that had operated without interruption between 1913 and 1918. Respondents were asked to categorise their output according to end-product for each successive year. In 1913, 5.3 per cent of total industrial production at this sample of enterprises was classified as 'defence' production.[12] The same source also yields an estimate of the proportion of machine-building production that was destined for military use. In 1913, 26.2 per cent of the output of 120 engineering enterprises represented military production. The application of these percentages to the available data on total industrial production and machine-building production in 1913 yields the results shown in Tables 7.1 and 7.2, which together indicate that armaments production accounted for around 44 per cent of total military industrial production in 1913 (48 per cent on USSR territory).

How does this compare with the situation in 1908? In principle, it should be possible to reconstruct the value of military

TABLE 7.1 *Defence production in 1913 (million rubles)*

Empire		*USSR*	
Total industrial production	*Defence production*	*Total industrial production*	*Defence production*
7358	390	6098	323

SOURCE Cols. 1 & 3 from *Dinamika rossiiskoi i sovetskoi promyshlennosti* (Moscow-Leningrad, 1929–30) vol. III, pp. 176–7. Cols. 2 & 4 represent 5.3% of these totals, based upon the proportions reported in *Trudy TsSU*, vol. XXVI (Moscow, 1926) p. 41.

TABLE 7.2 *Armaments production in 1913 (million rubles)*

Empire			*USSR*		
military share of:			*military share of:*		
machine-building	*metal-working*	*chemicals*	*machine-building*	*metal-working*	*chemicals*
134	17	20	104	13	17

SOURCE Col. 1, 26.2% of total reported machine-building, from *Dinamika*, vol. III, pp. 176–7. Col. 2, 5.3% of total reported metal-working, in ibid. Col. 3, 5.3% of total chemicals production, in ibid. Col. 4, 26.2% of total reported machine-building, taken from *Trudy TsSU*, vol. XXVI, pp. 41, 70. Col. 5, 5.3% of total reported metal-working, ibid. Col. 6, 5.3% of total reported chemicals production, ibid., pp. 84–5.

TABLE 7.3 *Defence production in 1908–13 (million rubles)*

	Index of defence spending	*Value of defence production (empire)*	*Value of defence production (USSR)*
1908	69	269	223
1909	71	277	229
1910	73	285	236
1911	73	285	236
1912	87	339	281
1913	100	390	323

SOURCE Col. 1 total defence expenditure from P.W. Gatrell, 'Industrial Expansion in Tsarist Russia, 1908–1914', *Econ. Hist. Rev.* XXXV, (1982) 104, deflated in accordance with the index given in P.R. Gregory, *Russian National Income, 1885–1913* (Cambridge, 1982) pp. 254–5, table F3. Cols 2 & 3 from Table 1, backcast to 1908.

output, by drawing upon the scattered information contained in the 1908 industrial census. But the aggregation of these data would involve considerable effort. A less laborious procedure is to backcast from 1913, by applying an index of defence spending. The appropriate index, along with an estimate of military production for the period 1908–13, is given in Table 7.3.

Adopting a similar procedure, we can derive an estimate of armaments production between 1908 and 1913 (see Table 7.4).

TABLE 7.4 *Armaments production in 1908–13 (million rubles)*

	Index of armaments expenditure	*Empire*	*USSR*
1908	43	74	58
1909	41	70	55
1910	44	75	59
1911	57	97	76
1912	73	125	98
1913	100	171	134

SOURCE Col. 1 armaments expenditure from *Econ. Hist. Rev.*, XXXV (1982) 105 (cols 4 & 5 only), deflated as in table 3 above. Cols. 2 & 3 derived from Table 2 above, backcast to 1908.

Table 7.4 implies that armaments output accounted for 28 per cent of total military production in 1908, compared to 44 per cent in 1913.

Throughout the period 1908–13 the most significant component in the total output of armaments was shipbuilding. There are no direct figures for the total value of naval construction in 1913. However, it is possible to derive the value of output at the four main state shipyards from official figures and to offer an approximate value for output at the private yards, based upon data on labour productivity in the state sector. Similar procedures can also be adopted for 1908. The results of these investigations are presented in Table 7.5.

The data on the size of the labour force in armaments production are somewhat patchy, especially where the private sector is concerned. Table 7.6 presents the results of an attempt to calculate the total numbers employed, for both state and private enterprise, in 1908 and 1913.

The state sector employed a considerable number of workers on armaments production. Total numbers employed in state defence works increased by 23 per cent (and by 45 per cent, if we exclude the state-owned metallurgical enterprises). This compares with a likely increase of 29 per cent in Russian industry as a whole.[13] However, it is apparent that by 1913 the balance of employment had begun to shift towards the private sector, thanks to the very substantial growth of employment in the private shipyards after 1908.

TABLE 7.5 *Military shipbuilding, 1908 and 1913 (million rubles)*

	Empire	*USSR*	*Empire*	*USSR*
state yards	30	28	49	47
private yards	23	22	66	63
Total	53	50	115	110

SOURCES Col. 1 state yards' output is taken directly from *Vsepoddaneishii otchet morskogo ministerstva za 1909* (St Petersburg, 1911); private sector output is calculated by applying a coefficient of output per person in state sector (from ibid.) to the labour force in private yards in 1908. The labour force for 1910 is given in L.G. Beskrovnyi, *Armiya i flot Rossii v nachale XX veka* (Moscow, 1986) pp. 198–9, and is estimated for 1908 by applying an index of expenditure on shipbuilding, derived from *Econ. Hist. Rev.*, XXXV (1982) p. 105. Col. 2, figures in col. 1 multiplied by 0.95, representing the coefficient for shipbuilding on USSR territory, as reported in *Dinamika rossiiskoi i sovetskoi promyshlennosti*, vol. II, pp. 128–41. Col. 3, state yards output from *Vsepoddaneishii otchet morskogo ministra za 1914* (Petrograd, 1915); private sector calculated on same basis as col. 1 above, i.e. 1913 output per person in state yards multiplied by private sector workforce in 1913. Col. 4 is based on same procedure as col. 2 above.

TABLE 7.6 *The labour force in the armaments industry, 1908 and 1913*

(Empire)	*1908*	*1913*
A. State sector		
1. Gau factories	33 000	47 400
2. Department of Mines	30 733	27 552
3. Shipyards	11 173	16 970
B. Private sector		
1. Shipyards	8 720	23 100
2. Other armaments	2 000	5 000
Total	85 626	120 022

SOURCES A.1 from G.K. Miftiev, 'Artilleriiskaya promyshlennost′ Rossii v period pervoi mirovoi voiny' (kand. diss., Leningrad, 1953) p. 100 (1909 figure adjusted in line with armaments index); A.2 from *Otchet gornogo departamenta*, various issues, less 22%, representing the average proportion of work completed for private customers; A.3 from Beskrovnyi, *Armiya i flot*, 1986, pp. 198–9 and K. F. Shatsillo, *Russkii imperializm i razvitie flota nakanune pervoi mirovoi voiny* (Moscow, 1968) p. 223; B.1 in ibid., 1910 figures adjusted in line with shipbuilding index; B.2 derived indirectly from L.E. Mints, *Trudovye resursy SSSR* (Moscow, 1975) p. 87. For further details see P.W. Gatrell, *The Last Argument of Tsarism: Government, Industry and Rearmament in Russia, 1900–1914*, forthcoming.

Preliminary calculations suggest that there was a significant overall improvement in labour productivity in the armaments industry between 1908 and 1913. Some of the measures taken to improve productivity in state enterprise are mentioned below. At the same time, it is worth pointing out that the labour force, particularly in the GAU enterprises, was very large in relation to estimated output. This raises interesting but so far unresolved questions about the respective strategies pursued by the Artillery Administration and the Department of Mines.

It would appear from the above estimates that armaments constituted a much larger proportion of metal-working and machine-building in Russia than in France, the only other country whose armaments industry has been subject to this kind of investigation. According to François Crouzet armaments accounted for less than six per cent of the total output of this sector (1905–13), whereas the proportion in Russia was probably closer to 18 per cent, at least in 1911–13. It may be that the proportion in France is biased downwards by the inclusion in total output of small-scale enterprise, whose armaments manufacture must have been non-existent.[14]

Total arms spending in Russia amounted to 1120 million rubles in 1908–13, or 6.5 per cent of total budget expenditure. In France, the corresponding figure (1905–13) was around 4.5 per cent. As a proportion of total defence spending, armaments accounted for around one-quarter in Russia, compared to 14 per cent in France.[15] Expressed in terms of national income, however, Russia probably spent just over four per cent on defence in 1913, compared to a figure of around five per cent in France. In Germany the figure was around 4.5 per cent. In a European context, therefore, the burden of defence in Russia was comparatively light.[16]

II

The manufacture of armaments in tsarist Russia had long been the responsibility first and foremost of state enterprise. But it should not be imagined that the state sector constituted an integrated whole. The administration of production was in the hands of three separate agencies: the Chief Artillery Administration (GAU), under the aegis of the War Ministry; the Department of

Mines (*Gornyi departament*), part of the Ministry of Trade and Industry; and the Department of Shipyards, within the Navy Ministry. The GAU was responsible for 18 separate enterprises in 1913, including the six state arsenals. The Department of Mines had overall charge of 13 metallurgical and metalworking enterprises, all of which (with the exception of the Aleksandrovsk Works, in Olonets province) were located in the Urals. Of these, the largest and single most important was the Perm Cannon Works. Many of the others manufactured shell cases. Finally, there were four state-owned shipyards, the Admiralty, Baltic, Izhorsk and Obukhov yards, as well as wharves and workshops in Kronstadt, Sevastopol and Nikolaev.

There was little coordination of production between factories, even when they were administered by the same ministry and manufactured the same products. The Tula, Izhevsk and Sestroretsk works specialised in the production of rifles, and two other factories, at St. Petersburg and Lugansk, concentrated on cartridges. All of these enterprises were administered by the GAU, but there seems to have been no technical or other collaboration between them. A somewhat different situation applied in shipbuilding. In 1907, the Navy Ministry established a council 'to unify and coordinate the productive activity' of shipyards. However, the council was a purely deliberative body and in this branch of defence as well there was plenty of scope for collaboration that went unrealised before 1914.[17]

Where enterprises were administered by different authorities, the potential for collaboration was even less. The obvious example here was the production of artillery pieces, which were manufactured by three state works: the St. Petersburg Gun Works (under GAU control), the Perm Cannon Works (Department of Mines) and the Obukhov Shipyards. Similarly, the Department of Mines administered one factory (Zlatoust) which produced rifles on a small scale, but which did not cooperate with the GAU enterprises.

Individual enterprises were administered in the following way. The GAU factories, termed 'technical artillery establishments', were run by a director (*nachal'nik*), appointed by the GAU. The director in turn appointed an 'economic committee' for the day to day management of the factory (curiously, its members could not serve for more than three years). This committee was responsible for the supervision of work in progress (except where 'technical' questions such as the design and specification of weapons were concerned), for checking equipment and for planning construction programmes. Its other main function was to arrange for the purchase of raw materials. In order to indicate how seriously it took this question, the GAU placed its own nominee on the committee, to ensure that its members adhered strictly to the War Ministry's guidelines on the prices at which raw materials could be procured. The GAU regulations spelt out in laborious detail the limited extent to which the economic committee could take the initiative in raw materials procurement (see below). In addition to the economic committee, other boards were charged with responsibility for technical questions and for the supervision of the labour force. The director of the factory had the right to hire and fire workers, to determine wage and piece rates and to fix the hours of work.[18] His autonomy in this sphere contrasted sharply with the constraints to which he was subject in respect of procurement prices.

The system described above persisted until at least 1914. In other branches of state armaments production, however, the administrative arrangements changed during the period under consideration. In December 1907, for example, the Tsar approved a 'Regulation for the Administration of Factories under the Naval Department', which replaced a statute that had been in force since 1864. The new rules required state yards to rely less heavily on credits from the government. In future, they were to meet their operating expenses out of recurrent income and, where necessary, from accumulated reserves. The aim of this reform was to encourage such enterprises to have a more accurate idea of costs of production and of the current value of their inventories. Within the individual enterprise, each workshop was to 'purchase' its inputs from other workshops and thus monitor its operating costs.[19]

These reforms led in the first instance to compulsory redundancy for scores of workers in the state yards. According to the Soviet historian K.F. Shatsillo, management also exploited the remaining workforce still more rigorously, in order to keep down production costs.[20] But the scale of rearmament after 1910 required that the labour force be expanded to cope with the influx of orders for vessels. In addition, the need for additional funds to finance new capital investment undermined attempts to place shipyards on a self-financing basis. Although profits could be quite high, as in the case of the Obukhov shipyard in 1911–12, state enterprises continued to call upon government for the injection of funds. To this extent, administrative reforms had a limited impact in shipbuilding.[21]

Parliamentary pressure, which had played an important part in forcing through reform of state shipyards, also produced changes in the administration of state-owned enterprise in the Urals. Some idea of existing management procedures can be gleaned from a summary of the changes that were recommended by the Duma in 1909. These included: proper commercial accounting procedures; recruitment of more highly-qualified technical personnel on a 'voluntary' basis; greater specialisation of production; inter-enterprise cooperation in the allocation of orders, especially for shell; reduction of excess stocks of raw materials; reduction in the number of unfinished orders; and the elimination of enterprises' debts.[22]

These changes were eventually enacted in December 1910. To what extent did they have the desired effect? Government inspectors made fewer complaints in 1910 about the lack of attention given to the storage of raw materials and the inadequate care of instruments and other equipment. But other projected reforms were not carried out before 1914: for example, the production of shell was not concentrated at two or three enterprises, as the Duma proposals had envisaged. Other reforms proved difficult to implement in Russian conditions. The management of the Perm Cannon Works sought to ensure that supplies of raw materials did not exceed actual requirements for current production, but this was only feasible where factories were not isolated; at many factories it was essential to maintain adequate stocks against the possibility of non-delivery.

Raw materials were acquired either by purchase from other state enterprises or at special auctions (*torgi*). Some state works were of pivotal importance in the supply of raw materials and semi-finished goods. For example, the Izhevsk steel works supplied quality steel billets and other goods to a range of state enterprises, including the rifle factories at Sestroretsk and Tula. Neither Perm nor Votkinsk had their own iron- and steel-making facilities and bought metal from Zlatoust, Kushvinsk and other enterprises in the Urals.[23] As we have already seen, the government placed great importance on keeping down costs of procurement in order to avoid being thought of as a milch-cow for

Russian merchants. For this reason, the conduct of auctions was subject to detailed scrutiny.[24] However, the price of raw materials on the open market rose sharply between 1908 and 1913, and in the long run the government was obliged to pick up the bill. In passing, it may be noted that the private armaments industry responded to the inflation in input prices by integrating backwards into the production of coal, iron and steel, and copper.[25]

III

Procurement of weapons, army uniforms and footwear, and military vessels was handled respectively by the GAU, the Chief Commissary Administration (GIU) and the Chief Shipbuilding Administration (GUK). The GIU also had responsibility for the procurement of food and fodder. Military vehicles were purchased by the Chief Military-Technical Administration (GVTU) and rolling-stock and communications equipment by the Chief Engineering Administration (GInzhU). From the point of view of the economic historian, however, the important distinction is not to be drawn between the different procurement agencies, but rather between the products that were being procured. A brief glance at procurement arrangements may make this clear.

In principle, the purchasing departments could transfer semi-finished materials from one state enterprise or shop to another, and could therefore supervise the entire production process. Alternatively, the department might purchase materials (either at auction or by commission) and then allocate them to its chosen contractor. A third variation involved simply the acquisition of the finished product from a supplier (state or private), which otherwise had no contact with the procurement agency.

These different arrangements coexisted in each branch of procurements. Even the Chief Commissary Administration administered a small number of state-owned workshops which produced army uniforms and boots.[26] The question then arises as to the reason for adopting one method of procurement as against another. Although it would be wrong to attribute too much consistency to tsarist policy in this sphere or in any other, it may be suggested that the procurement agencies exercised closer supervision in respect of items where quality control was at a premium. This applied, for example, to the production of rifles and machine-guns, involving high-precision engineering, which was a virtual monopoly of state works and under the complete control of the GAU. By contrast, the manufacture of uniforms and boots was normally handled by contractors to whom cloth and leather were 'put out'.[27] With products where there was a direct overlap between civilian and military requirements (as in the case of rolling stock), the procurement authorities normally bought the finished product direct from the producer, implicitly counting upon the market to ensure that quality was maintained.[28]

According to defence regulations, tendering for contracts was the normal means of procurement.[29] In 'exceptional' circumstances, such as were dictated by the nature of the product or by the failure of the auction to yield a satisfactory outcome, the procurement agency was entitled to award contracts directly. In advance of the auction, the procurement agency had to submit to the Ministry a schedule of prices: the price paid on previous occasions, the current 'recorded' (*spravochnaya*) price, the prevailing market price (if applicable) and the price at which it expected to procure the product on this occasion. The latter price was officially subject to the most stringent secrecy, but in practice the secrecy was breached by officials whose modest salaries made them liable to corruption by defence producers in the private sector.[30]

Many of the procedures laid down in these regulations were doubtless standard European practice, but there were also instances of peculiarly Russian convention. *Dvoryane* who supplied food and fodder from their own estate, or who supplied manufactured goods from a factory they owned, were alone exempted from the requirement to leave a deposit (as evidence of good faith), at the time of submitting a bid. The main features of the 'auctions' that took place are clear from the annual reports of the State Comptroller and from the senatorial investigations that were carried out between 1908 and 1911. Private firms concluded preliminary agreements among themselves about the prices at which they were willing to sell. Senator Garin concluded that 'the artillery industry is not united into one permanent syndicate, but it effectively forms a syndicate for every large order'.[31] At the auction, prices would gradually be forced down by spurious competition, towards the basic price which the members of the ring were prepared to accept. The unsuccessful bidders would then be compensated from a fund to which all members had contributed. Procurement officials turned a blind eye to this behaviour.[32]

Documentary evidence for the survival of this practice is not available for the period after 1911. The Tsar abruptly stopped the senatorial inspections in October 1911, in circumstances that are still unclear. Since it began (in 1906–8) at a time of severe depression in the metal-working and machine-building industry, it may be that the practice declined in the years immediately preceding the war, when abundant orders were being issued. But one cannot be certain.

What is more certain is that Soviet historians such as Livshin and Bovykin have exaggerated the economic significance of such rings. Garin's original report estimated that the GIU paid an average of two million rubles annually in 1908–10. But this represented no more than four per cent of the GIU equipment budget.[33] The government had a clear idea of what was taking place. What leverage did it have to exercise in the face of such collusion? The authorities could – and did – refuse to accept the prices reached at auction; they could award contracts to state factories; or they could go abroad. But on occasions the government decided not to exercise its choice; at times, the choice did not exist.

On the eve of the War the tsarist government abandoned the auction as a major method of military procurement. Experience had shown, according to the State Comptroller, that 'not all those who came forward have been in a position to fulfill the obligations they took upon themselves'.[34] Such criticisms were not new: in 1905, an official in the GAU complained that the entire system of tendering led to the award of contracts to a firm that offered the lowest price, irrespective of its reputation, its existing commitments and its capacity.[35]

In place of auctions, the government drew up a list of approved manufacturers with whom contracts might be placed. The main aim of the reform was to improve the speed with which products were delivered as well as the quality of the finished goods. Particular concern had been expressed by the Chief Commissary Administration about the delivery of cloth and leather. Implicit here was a criticism of the prior reliance by the GIU on small-scale producers (including *trudovye arteli*), since these had frequently failed to meet agreed deadlines (lack of sufficient working capital was cited as one reason). The greater reliability of larger-scale enterprise, together with the scope given for closer supervision of production, led the government to abandon its previous willingness to deal with small-scale producers.[36]

The success of the tsarist procurements system may be judged by reference to three key areas in any system of military procurement: quality control, price and delivery date.

As we have already seen, the government did respond to complaints from the military about the quality of finished goods. The authorities advised the Urals metallurgical enterprises that an unacceptably high proportion of output of shell and guns was defective.[37] But these critical comments became less commonplace by 1912 and 1913, suggesting that the reform of factory administration had left its mark on defence production. In 1913, one official compared the quality of cannon produced at Perm very favourably with that produced abroad.[38] So far as the private sector is concerned, Garin had poor things to say in 1910 about such major armaments firms as Putilov and Sormovo. Perhaps the quality of output improved as such firms gained greater experience in the manufacture of weapons.

The government sought to keep down procurement prices, directly, through the system of tenders and, indirectly, through the system of procurements of raw materials. In addition, the government expressed the hope that the competition between state and private sectors would act as a restraint on price inflation. The evidence on this last point is inconclusive. The State Comptroller believed that competition was desirable and successful, and there is some evidence from shipbuilding to suggest that this was indeed the case.[39] On the other hand, Garin argued that the state works often charged higher prices than the private sector, thereby undermining the principle that they should 'regulate' procurement prices.[40] Besides, whatever moderating influence may have been exerted on prices by such rivalry, the fact remains that the general tendency was for costs and prices to rise, as a result of the inflation in raw materials prices before 1914. This inflation was reflected in the Treasury assessment of spending, where the excess of actual armaments spending over projected spending was substantial.[41] In shipbuilding, there were specific forces at work, such as the transition to more advanced and costlier technologies in propulsion and armament, that resulted in higher procurement prices.[42]

No less important was the question of delivery dates. Delays were common in state and private enterprise alike, as Garin discovered. The annual reports of the State Comptroller testify to delays in the Urals complex, especially between 1907 and 1909. In 1907, for example, arrears (*nedoimki*) in production at the Perm works amounted to 173 per cent of its total output in that year.[43] Sometimes, there were quite specific explanations for delays, such as problems with the supply of foreign parts for military vessels.[44] But there were other, more systemic problems. One of these was the excessive observation of formalities at the level of individual enterprises in the state sector. We have already noted some of the constraints to which management of state industry was subjected. The regulations on procurement included 250 pages of forms that the management had to return, sometimes daily, to the GAU.[45] Another problem had to do with the constant changes in product specification which were imposed on contractors, a problem that also had implications for costs. Some of Vickers' strongest criticism of tsarist procurements practice was reserved for the tendency of the authorities to set new specifications after the contract had been agreed.[46]

The government tried to alleviate these problems in various ways, including the imposition of fines on private enterprise for delays in completion of work. This, it has recently been suggested, could have repercussions in other spheres. For example, engineering firms in the capital preferred to make concessions to workers' demands, rather than risk the interruption of production schedules by stoppages of one kind or another.[47] It is difficult to know how common this particular strategy may have been.

Two more aspects of procurement should be raised. The first concerns the choice of domestic or foreign suppliers. The desire to place orders with domestic rather than foreign suppliers was a deep-seated and longstanding one. An imperial edict in 1860 had instructed government departments to order manufactured goods from Russian factories wherever possible. The Ministry of Trade and Industry sought to give a practical meaning to previously pious expressions of support for domestic producers, by insisting (in 1902) that all departments of government should inform it of orders that were given to foreign suppliers, in order to encourage stricter adherence to the principle of domestic supply. In 1907, any order worth more than 10 000 rubles had first to be cleared with the Ministry.[48] In the same year, the Navy Ministry resolved that vessels should in future be built or re-equipped so far as possible at Russian yards.[49] However, there was a limit to what could be done to implement these aims. The contracts that were made on the eve of the First World War between Russian firms and major European arms firms (Vickers, John Brown, Schneider-Creusot) provided for the possibility of significant import substitution, but there remained many items which Russian firms could not supply, such as turbines and pumping equipment for modern vessels.[50] And even orders for relatively straightforward armaments could sometimes slip through the net, as the result of GAU impatience with domestic suppliers. In 1913, for example, the GAU issued orders for high explosive shrapnel, worth a total of 10 million rubles, but one-third of the orders went to German firms.[51]

The second issue relates to the choice of private as against state enterprise. We have already seen that in some spheres, notably small arms, the state monopolised production and that in others, such as artillery and explosives, production was shared by both sectors. In shipbuilding, private industry claimed an increasing share of output (see Table 7.5), mainly because the large new private firms could trade on the close technical collaboration they enjoyed with advanced foreign enterprise.

The relations between state and private enterprise were always strained. In the depths of the industrial depression in 1908, a meeting of private entrepreneurs in the Baltic engineering industry urged the government to forbid the expansion of production at state factories.[52] Six years later, on the eve of the War, the Eighth Congress of the Association of Trade and Industry complained that state works 'do not confine themselves to the fulfilment of orders for state defence, but are attempting to compete with private industry on the domestic market'.[53] However, by this time the enterprises in question had all but abandoned such 'private' work in the face of substantial defence orders.[54]

The main bone of contention for the private sector concerned the 'artificially' low prices charged by state enterprise. Private industry complained that state works took no account of overhead costs and made no allowance for amortisation of capital, and that this explained the disparities in contract prices – where they existed.[55] However, as we have seen, reforms before 1914 led to a greater emphasis on commercial management, which required state factories to make more realistic calculations of costs. This drew the teeth of critics in the arms trade. In any case, private enterprise took comfort from the realisation that the government bestowed significant fresh orders on private firms, especially for ships.

IV

The evidence suggests that we can speak of the partial modernisation of armaments production and procurement on the eve of the First World War. The naval authorities switched to more commercial principles of shipyard administration after 1908, although they were hampered by the scale of naval rearmament. The Department of Mines similarly adopted more commercial management in the state-owned metallurgical industry from 1910 onwards. The practice of awarding contracts at public auctions was abandoned after 1913. The initiative for such changes did not invariably emanate from the procurements agencies themselves; sometimes, change was the result of parliamentary pressure and senatorial investigation.

Before concluding, one should note two other aspects of arms production and procurement. First, experience elsewhere suggests that inefficiency and corruption were not exclusive to tsarist Russia.[56] One might, for instance, contrast the limited impact of the Boer War on British procurements policy and administration with the more far-reaching effects of the Russo-Japanese War on Russian practice. Second, the rearmament drive that took place before 1914 did not simply affect procurement practices and factory administration. It also impinged upon the Russian working class, in ways that have yet to be fully explored. Nevertheless, there seems to have been no clear correlation between the growth of employment in the defence industry and the well-documented resurgence of labour protest between 1910 and 1914. Heather Hogan has suggested that there was such a link, in so far as management of engineering enterprises enforced changes in the labour process which were intended to improve labour productivity, but which tended to 'deskill' and thus alienate skilled craftsmen. But other historians have observed that managers in defence industry sought to avoid confrontation with the labour force, in order to maintain production.[57] The evidence also suggests that workers in the defence industry, especially the state sector, enjoyed significant advantages over those in other occupations, both in the length of the working day and in welfare provision.[58] Here is one area in which the social historian and the economic historian of pre-war Russia might usefully collaborate.

NOTES

1. W.M. Pintner, 'The Burden of Defence in Imperial Russia, 1725–1914', *Russian Review*, XLIII (1984) pp. 231–59. In the short run, of course, as in 1905–14, the burden could, and did increase.
2. W.C. Fuller, *Civil-Military Conflict in Imperial Russia, 1881–1914* (Princeton, 1985). Fuller demonstrates among other things the increasing reluctance of professional officers to tolerate the use of the army as an internal policing mechanism.
3. P. Kenez, 'A Profile of the Pre-Revolutionary Officer Corps', *California Slavic Studies*, 7 (1973) pp. 121–58. A.K. Wildman, *The End of the Russian Imperial Army* (Princeton, 1980).
4. D. Geyer, *Russian Imperialism* (Leamington Spa, 1986). M. Perrins, 'The Council for State Defence, 1905–1909: A Study in Russian Bureaucratic Politics', *Slavonic & East European Review*, LVIII (1980) pp. 370–98.
5. D. Beyrau, *Militär und Gesellschaft im vorrevolutionären Russland* (Cologne and Vienna, 1984). J. Bushnell, 'Peasants in Uniform: The Tsarist Army as a Peasant Society', *Journal of Social History* XIII, (1980) pp. 565–76. See also J. Bushnell *Mutiny amid Repression: Russian Soldiers in the Revolution of 1905–1906* (Bloomington, Indiana, 1985).
6. References to the work of Soviet scholars, such as Sidorov, Shatsillo and Beskrovnyi, will be found in the following footnotes.
7. Further discussion of production and procurement, with particular reference to shipbuilding, will be found in P.W. Gatrell, 'After Tsushima: Economic and Administrative Aspects of Russian Naval Rearmament, 1905–1913', *Economic History Review* XLIII (1990) pp. 255–90. The present study forms part of a larger work, entitled *The Last Argument of Tsarism: Government, Industry and Rearmament in Russia, 1900–1914*, forthcoming.
8. Calculated from P.A. Khromov, *Ekonomicheskoe razvitie Rossii v XIX–XX vekakh, 1800–1917* (Moscow, 1960) pp. 526–9.
9. Pintner, 'The Burden of Defence', pp. 241–5.
10. *Smeta voennogo ministerstva po GAU na 1909* (St Petersburg, 1908); ibid., *na 1914* (St Petersburg, 1913). Other information is derived from A.L. Sido-

rov, *Finansovoe polozhenie Rossii v gody pervoi mirovoi voiny* (Moscow, 1960), pp. 68, 81.
11. *Otchet otdela promyshlennosti za 1911* (St Petersburg, 1911) pp. 146–7.
12. *Vserossiiskaya promyshlennaya i professional'naya perepis' 1918 goda: fabrichno-zavodskaya promyshlennost' v period 1913–1918 gg.*, *Trudy TsSU*, vol. XXVI, vyp. 1–2, (Moscow, 1926) vyp. 1, p. 41. The original figure has been adjusted to take into account raw materials, which were listed separately in the source.
13. Calculated from L.E. Mints, *Trudovye resursy SSSR*, (Moscow, 1975) p. 40.
14. F. Crouzet, 'Recherches sur la production d'armements en France, 1815–1913', *Conjoncture économique, structures sociales: hommage à E. Labrousse* (Paris, 1974) p. 304.
15. Ibid., p. 303.
16. The estimate for Russia is derived from P.R. Gregory, *Russian National Income, 1885–1913* (Cambridge, 1982) p. 57. The estimate for France is taken from *Industrielle Mobilmachungen: Statistische Untersuchungen* (Hamburg, 1936), and for Germany, from P. Witt, 'Reichsfinanzen und Rüstungspolitik, 1898–1914', *Marine und Marinepolitik im kaiserlichen Deutschland, 1871–1914* (Düsseldorf, 1972), p. 177. The proportion in the U.K. was probably around three per cent.
17. *Svod morskikh postanovlenii*, vol. V (St Petersburg 1910) para. 35. See *Tsentral'nyi gosudarstvennyi arkhiv voenno-morskogo flota* (*TsGAVMF*), f. 410, op. 3, d. 822, 11.318–22, for initiatives taken after 1908; and *Vsepoddaneishii doklad po morskomu ministerstvu za 1915* (Petrograd, 1917), p. 109.
18. *Svod voennykh postanovlenii*, vol. XIII (St Petersburg, 1910) paras. 8, 16, 65, 66.
19. *Vsepoddaneishii otchet morskogo ministra za 1906–1909* (St Petersburg, 1910) pp. 198, 202–3. K.F. Shatsillo, *Russkii imperializm i razvitie flota nakanune pervoi mirovoi voiny* Moscow, 1968) p. 221. For some of the difficulties faced by state yards as a result of these changes, see *TsGAVMF*, f. 401, op. 5, d. 178, 11.2–17; ibid., f. 401, op. 6, d. 1, 11.142, 175ob.
20. Shatsillo, *Russkii imperializm*, p. 221.
21. See Gatrell, 'After Tsushima', and *Vsepoddaneishii otchet morskogo ministra za 1913* (Petrograd, 1914) pp. 318–9; *Vsepoddaneishii doklad po morskomu ministerstvu za 1912* (St Petersburg, 1913) p. 122; ibid., *za 1914* (Petrograd, 1915) p. 111.
22. *Smeta dokhodov i raskhodov gornogo departamenta na 1911* (St Petersburg) 1912, pp. 73–8; I.Kh. Ozerov, *Gornye zavody Urala*, Moscow, 1910. For recent discussion, emphasising the obstacles to reform, see V.V. Polikarpov, 'O "kommercheskom" upravlenii gosudarstvennoi promyshlennost'yu v Rossii nachala XX v.', *Vestnik MGU*, istoriya, 4 (1988) 48–61.
23. E.K. Germonius, 'Izhevskii oruzheinyi zavod i rol' kazennykh zavodov v dele oborony' *Russian Economist* (1922) pp. 2901–15; *Vsepoddaneishii otchet gosudarstvennogo kontrolera za 1908*, (St Petersburg, 1909) p. 145.
24. *Svod voennykh postanovlenii*, vol. XVIII (St Petersburg, 1907).
25. Details in V.I. Bovykin, 'Banki i voennaya promyshlennost' Rossii nakanune pervoi mirovoi voiny', *Istoricheskie zapiski*, LXIV (1959) pp. 82–135.
26. *Vsepoddaneishii otchet gosudarstvennogo kontrolera za 1909* (St Petersburg, 1910) pp. 31–2.

27. The production of boots at state workshops led to complaints about the quality of the finished product, so it did not follow that supervision led to higher quality. See the comments in *Tsentral'nyi gosudarstvennyi istoricheskii arkhiv SSSR (TsGIA)*, f. 1393, op. 2, d. 455, 11.85ob–88.
28. P.G. Ivanov, *Ocherk istorii i statistiki zavodskogo parovozostroeniya* (Petrograd, 1920) p. 4, for the production of locomotives, largely concentrated in private hands.
29. *Svod voennykh postanovlenii*, vol. XVIII, (St Petersburg, 1907) para. 11.
30. *TsGIA*, f. 1393, op. 2, d. 455, 11.17–101.
31. Ibid., d. 456, 1.367.
32. Ibid., d. 455, 11.21, 97–100ob. See also Ya.I. Livshin, 'K voprosu o voenno-promyshlennykh monopoliyakh v Rossii v nachale XX veka', *Voprosy istorii*, 7 (1957) pp. 62–3.
33. *TsGIA*, f. 1393, op. 2, d. 455, 1.84. *Proekt gosudarstvennoi rospisi dokhodov i raskhodov na 1911* (St Petersburg, 1911). V.I. Bovykin, 'Monopolisticheskie soglasheniya v russkoi voennoi promyshlennosti', *Istoriya SSSR*, 1 (1958) pp. 125–9; Livshin, 'K voprosu', p. 63.
34. *Vsepoddaneishii otchet gosudarstvennogo kontrolera za 1914* (Petrograd, 1915) p. 29.
35. Yu.F. Subbotin, 'Voennaya promyshlennost' Rossii vo vtoroi polovine XIX-nachale XX veka' (kand. diss., Leningrad, 1975) p. 125.
36. *Vsepoddaneishii otchet gosudarstvennogo kontrolera za 1910* (St Petersburg, 1911) p. 48ff.; ibid., *za 1912* (St Petersburg, 1913) p. 33.
37. Ibid., *za 1908* (St Petersburg, 1909) pp. 142–3.
38. M.P. Vyatkin, *Gornozavodskii Ural v 1900–1917* (Moscow-Leningrad, 1965) p. 265.
39. *Vsepoddaneishii otchet gosudarstvennogo kontrolera za 1913* (Petrograd, 1914) p. 98. See evidence presented in Gatrell, 'After Tsushima'.
40. *TsGIA*, f. 1393, op. 2, d. 456, 1.367ob.
41. See *Proekt gosudarstvennoi rospisi dokhodov i raskhodov*, various issues.
42. *TsGAVMF*, f. 410, op. 3, d. 822, 11.75ob–76, and discussion in Gatrell, 'After Tsushima'.
43. *Vsepoddaneishii otchet gosudarstvennogo kontrolera za 1908* (St Petersburg, 1909) p. 141.
44. Ibid., *za 1912* (St Petersburg, 1913) p. vi.
45. A.A. Manikovskii, *Boevoe snabzhenie russkoi armii v mirovuyu voinu 1914–1918 gg.*, 3 vols (Moscow, 1930) vol. II, pp. 28–9.
46. G. Jones and C. Trebilcock, 'Russian Industry and British Business, 1910–1930: Oil and Armaments', *Journal of European Economic History*, 11 (1982) pp. 61–103.
47. R.B. McKean, *St Petersburg Between the Revolutions: Workers and Revolutionaries, June 1907–February 1917*. New Haven, Conn., 1990, pp. 273–5.
48. *Otchet otdela promyshlennosti za 1910* (St Petersburg, 1911) pp. 134–9.
49. R. Girault, 'Finances internationales et relations internationales (à propos des usines Poutiloff)', *Revue d'histoire moderne et contemporaine*, 13 (1966) p. 220.
50. K.F. Shatsillo, 'Inostrannyi kapital i voenno-morskie programmy Rossii nakanune pervoi mirovoi voiny', *Istoricheskie zapiski*, LXIX (1961) pp. 75–6, 86; Jones and Trebilcock, 'Russian Industry'; E.R. Goldstein,

'Vickers Ltd. and the Tsarist Regime', *Slavonic & East European Review*, LVIII (1980) pp. 561–71.

51. A. Bart, 'Na fronte artilleriiskogo snabzheniya', *Byloe* 6 (1925) pp. 147–91.
52. Manikovskii, *Boevoe snabzhenie*, vol. II, p. 63. For further evidence of entrepreneurial disquiet see *Stenogramma soveshchaniya o polozhenii metallurgicheskoi i mashinostroitel'noi promyshlennosti, mai 1908* (St Petersburg, 1908).
53. Quoted in M.Ya. Gefter, 'Tsarizm i zakonodatel'noe "regulirovanie" deyatel'nosti sindikatov i trestov v Rossii nakanune pervoi mirovoi voiny', *Istoricheskie zapiski*, LIV (1955) p. 189.
54. *Smeta dokhodov i raskhodov gornogo departamenta na 1913* (St Petersburg, 1912) p. 37; ibid., *na 1914* (St Petersburg, 1913) pp. 21–2.
55. Ibid., *na 1914*, p. 37; Subbotin, 'Voennaya promyshlennost'', p. 127.
56. W. Ashworth, 'Economic Aspects of Late Victorian Naval Administration', *Economic History Review*, XXII (1969) pp. 491–505. R.C. Trebilcock, 'War and the Failure of Industrial Mobilization', in J. Winter (ed.) *War and Economic Development* (Cambridge, 1973) pp. 139–64. For recent corruption scandals in the U.S. Defense Department, see *The Washington Post*, 15 June 1988.
57. H. Hogan, 'The Reorganization of Work Processes in the St. Petersburg Metalworking Industry, 1901–1914', *Russian Review*, XLII (1983) pp. 163–90. McKean, *St. Petersburg Between the Revolutions*, pp. 273–5.
58. This comment is based upon material contained in *Workmen's Insurance and Compensation Systems in Europe*, 2 vols. (Washington, 1911) vol. II, pp. 2259–97; *Polozhenie o vol'nonaemnykh i pravila o naime masterovykh i rabochikh v tekhnicheskikh artilleriiskikh zavedeniyakh* (Petrograd, 1915); S.V. Murzintseva, 'Iz istorii ekonomicheskogo polozheniya rabochikh na predpriyatiyakh voennogo i morskogo vedomstv v 1907–1914gg. v Peterburge', *Uchenye zapiski LGU*, CCLXX (1959) pp. 217–41; and I.I. Shelymagin, *Zakonodatel'stvo o fabrichno-zavodskom trude v Rossii v 1900–1917gg.* (Moscow, 1952).

8 1917 in the Rear Garrisons

Howard White

THE REAR ARMY IN THE RUSSIAN REVOLUTION

The role of the armed forces in the Russian Revolution has attracted quite a lot of attention from Western historians, with the primary focus on the great naval bases and the army units of the Front. The importance of the garrisons of the Rear is universally acknowledged, but not much studied. There is one major monograph by the émigré historian Mikhail Frenkin, available only in Russian. Soviet literature is somewhat richer, but has yet to free itself from the well-known constraints upon interpretation highlighted by Frenkin (through his own liberation from them). This essay is intended as a brief preliminary survey of the process of revolution in the Rear garrisons, with some comment on its significance in the revolution as a whole. It draws conceptually on the existing Western literature on the armed forces, itself a component of what has been identified as the new 'dominant paradigm' in historiography; it draws empirically upon Western and Soviet literature and some primary sources.[1]

Armies are obviously important in political crises – to use S.E. Finer's classic analysis – because of their organisation and coherence, symbolic status, and monopoly of arms.[2] In revolutions armies may shift allegiance or disintegrate: either can be crucial in depriving ruling élites of direct coercive power and of authority – on the symbolic level, by demonstrating that the nation-in-arms rejects the regime – on the practical level, by causing economic and administrative chaos.[3] In the specific circumstances of the Russian Empire in 1917, however, there are a number of nuances and additional complications that should be noted.

First of these is the omnipresence of the Army. The number of servicemen deployed in the Rear was officially estimated at 2 265 000 in January 1917, compared to over 7 000 000 at the Front. The scale was partly dictated by the Army's enormous appetite for cannon fodder in the conditions of world war – constant early mobilisation of new cohorts of conscripts, to be hurriedly trained and rushed to the Front. Other factors included the extensive use of military personnel instead of civilians for logistical support of troops in the field, and none-too-veiled concern for policing the interior in the event of crisis. In its deployment the Rear Army combined huge bases at the centre of Military Districts with a network of smaller garrisons. This reflected practical problems, connected with the induction of men and supply of food and material in conditions of poor transport infrastructure, as well as considerations of policing. The result was that almost every urban centre had a garrison, sometimes of a size equalling the civilian population. The Moscow Military District had 155 garrisons, the Kazan Military District 98. While there are difficulties in establishing precise figures, some idea of the number of men deployed in the 12 Military Districts (technically, five of these were attached to Fronts; they do not include the Cossack Hosts) can be given.[4]

Kazan:	853 000	Caucasus:	153 000
Moscow:	750 000	Dvinsk:	153 000
Kiev:	568 000	Minsk:	138 000
Petrograd:	540 000	Irkutsk:	100 000?
Omsk:	191 000	Turkestan:	32 000?
Odessa:	168 000	Priamursk:	?

A second feature of the Rear Army was its blurring of social and ethnic location. Most obviously it brought peasants from the village into the towns, but it also brought rural ethnic minorities into Russian urban centres and Russians into minority regions. The tsarist military authorities had always been careful to distribute ethnic minorities evenly (the Moscow Military District included parts of the Ukraine, and Ukrainian conscripts were dispersed amongst Russian-dominated units). Also, according to Frenkin, they stationed peasants from the most 'backward' northern provinces in Petrograd; however, these endeavours may have been hampered by transport difficulties as the war progressed.[5]

The presence of the Rear garrisons injected into interior politics a separate set of issues arising from the conditions of service and aspirations of the soldiers which might otherwise have been geographically confined: some of these will be identified below.

As well as affecting the host communities, these last two factors together surely contributed to a blurring of social identities amongst the soldiers themselves: men put into uniforms and made to think of themselves as soldiers, peasants uprooted from rural isolation and exposed to the excitement of urban revolution, members of ethnic minorities suddenly made aware of ethnic differences and disadvantage.[6]

It should also be noted that the Rear garrisons had some impact beyond their host communities – through men sent on delegations, deserters, and (most numerous) men sent on leave to their farms.

In terms of organisation and coherence it should be noted that the revolution in the garrisons did not generally lead to physical dispersal: men remained organised into units, sub-units, barracks etc; some sense of military virtues like team-spirit and (revolutionary) hierarchy may even have persisted; and the communications systems also seem to have remained intact. On the level of symbolic status there was no difficulty in seeing the armed forces as the *narod* in uniform, although they could also be identified as the peasantry in uniform by those for whom the distinction mattered. As concerns monopoly of armed force, it should be noted that the tsarist police had effectively been abolished in the February Revolution, replaced by a civilian militia which swiftly became legendary for its cowardice and incompetence. While armed workers' militia units also appeared, they only became extensive in the autumn of 1917, and even then could not match the immense resources of the military.[7]

The role of the Rear garrisons in 1917 may thus be assumed to have been complex. Their presence was clearly an exacerbating factor in disorder, not merely passively through repudiation of authority and refusal to act as the coercive arm of the government, but also actively through the fomentation of local disturbances and the exacerbation of local supply problems. Their presence was also a unifying factor in the development of the revolution, bringing the same issues and internal processes to widely differing regions. These issues and processes are consequently worth further investigation.

THE PROCESS OF REVOLUTION IN THE GARRISONS

The survey offered in this section is necessarily limited and impressionistic: it reflects the limitations of the readily-available literature and primary sources. It is not possible to offer a comprehensive profile either of every Military District (the Caucasus, Central Asia, Siberia and the Cossack Hosts are largely excluded) or of every garrison within the major Military Districts. This does leave open the risk of underestimating local variation, which must simply be acknowledged. It is also not possible to arrive at any precise analysis of the extent of radicalism measured by support for the Bolsheviks (or even Left SRs) or the impact of Bolshevik agitation and manipulation. The extensive Soviet literature on this topic, and even Frenkin's heavily-documented account, suffers from a marked paucity of reliable indicators.

It is, however, possible to explore the way in which garrison soldiers became radicalised. Evan Mawdsley has pointed out that the existing literature offers distinct models of the process of revolution in the armed forces.[8] The first is that of John Bushnell, who argues that the Russian Army is essentially peasant with a self-reinforcing feudal lifestyle; the key to its behaviour is the peasant mentality. A second model is that of Allan K. Wildman, who stresses the importance of a 'radical intermediate stratum', at first the natural representative of the dark masses, but gradually losing their confidence: this places emphasis both on specific experience and underlying mentality. Mawdsley offers a more detailed analysis of the specific experience, which has parallels with work on other social groups, distinguishing an initial process of democratisation superseded by radicalisation – an approach which will be followed here.[9]

A number of points can be made about the character of the garrisons. They are overwhelmingly peasant by social origin, but do contain several structurally distinct groups. First there are new recruits of the November 1916 and February 1917 call-ups, aged 18–20 (some 345 000 were in the garrisons in October). Then there are evacuated soldiers, mostly sick or injured: a net influx of 400 000 of these during 1917 adding to those already present. Finally there are Home Guard units permanently based in the garrisons on logistical support duties. Further recruits were added during 1917: a major call-up of reservists in September according to Frenkin (he concludes that the central figure in the garrisons in October was the reservist aged 30–40), and those who lost exemptions: the Petrograd Committee on the Review of Deferments found 900 'workers' at the Post Office and 50 at the Artillery Works who were owners of businesses. There was considerable turnover in the garrisons: large numbers of men were released for agricultural work (200 000 in the Moscow Military District) and there was considerable transfer of units to the Front (probably 1 500 000 men, mostly in June and July. Finally, the relatively low number of professional NCOs should be noted.[10]

The February Revolution would seem, on the whole, to have had more immediate impact on servicemen in the Rear (the naval bases being an exception). As in Petrograd, garrison troops were frequently participants, and in almost all major centres there was some sort of psychological turning point at which the relations between officers and men were changed forever. In Tver, for example, the troops were aroused to great tension on 1 March by rumours and a workers' demonstration in the town centre. After a sleepless night of debate in the barracks, the men burst onto the streets – shooting wildly in the air and rushing from barracks to barracks to force everyone to join in. They attacked the governor's house and Jewish shops, destroyed the town prison, and eventually lynched the governor, Fon-Bunting. Such extreme outbursts were not common, although some sort of break-out by troops frequently occurred. In Kazan, troops were deployed on 2 March to defend strategic points against student demonstrators, but were withdrawn the next morning when news arrived by telegraph from Stavka of the abdication. The commander, General Sandetskii, issued an order recognising the new government – as he thought – of Grand Duke Michael. This created extreme alarm in the barracks, and next morning the four largest units mutinied. Even in towns where the officers were wary enough to accommodate swiftly to the new regime, some symbolic form of revolt often occurred. In Tsaritsyn on 2 March, the 141st Regt. was led through the streets in marching order, with the band playing, as a gesture of solidarity with the revolution; but that evening the soldiers took to the streets to join a mob engaged in burning down the town prison. All over Russia, unpopular commanders were arrested, and occasionally beaten up or even killed. Frenkin cites the figure of 100 arrests in the Volga garrisons. The few major exceptions were garrisons near the Front, where discipline seems to have been better (except on the Northern Front), and garrisons where there was a popular commander or senior officer. Thus in Moscow, Colonel Gruzinov could be brought in by hasty agreement between the Committee of Public Organisations and the military authorities; in Odessa, the Chief of the District Staff was a well-liked (and aptly named) Popular Socialist, General Marks.[11]

The revolt of the garrison usually culminated in the formation of a committee or soviet to represent the soldiers. This first act of democratisation was an immediate reaction – sometimes modelled on the workers' soviet, occasionally fostered by agitators from the civil population, but usually a more-or-less automatic reflex from within the garrison. The committee or soviet created was very often quite separate from the workers' soviet, although moves would generally be made to merge the two quite swiftly – initiative in this respect varying from place to place. It is clear that the 'committeefication' of the army began much earlier in the Rear than at the Front – denying the government and military authorities even the modicum of initiative in this respect that they were able to exploit outside the Northern Front. It does not appear that Order No. 1 had an enormous impact – the details often arrived only after the revolutionary upheaval had occurred.

The second act of democratisation, again arising spontaneously in the course of the February unheaval, was the attempt to introduce election of officers – or at least some form of control or veto over them. Soldiers usually pressed for election but settled for the removal of the most unpopular or suspect officers, whether or not it was implied that such action was acceptable only as a one-off response and implied no permanent rights.

Soldiers then began to assert further 'rights' through their committees, as well as through petitions and telegrams addressed to the new revolutionary authorities of the locality and the centre. The first set of rights concerned army life: freedom to determine their own lives 'off-duty', including full freedom to go into town, attend meetings, join organisations etc; concomitant with this was rejection of the authority of officers off-duty, particularly in the symbolic issue of saluting; also universal was the demand to be treated with dignity on and off duty – not to be sworn at or addressed as *ty*. The second set of rights concerned the local community: soldiers demanded concessions like free use of public transport, and more generally to be recognised as legitimate participants in local politics, with the right to take part in municipal elections, be represented in municipal institutions, and have a say on all local issues.[12]

The initial wave of democratisation was very rapid, and generally successful on all counts except the election of officers. It seems to have been a uniform process – most importantly because it reflected the basic concerns and aspirations of soldiers, but also because it was endorsed by the local revolutionary authorities and by the Provisional Government; hence it was exported to outlying areas when necessary.

The initial demands gave way during March and April to demands on a series of issues growing out of the soldiers' conditions of service and sense of rights: these too seem to have been almost universal, and certainly were the major preoccupations of garrison troops (and often of the host communities) in the spring. First to emerge, very often, were demands about the system of deferments. There was considerable feeling that the burden of military service was not being spread equitably, and demands were made that all the *belobiletniki* (holders of exemptions) be conscripted. Soldiers not infrequently organised 'raids' into town to seek out deserters and persons evading conscription: a late example occurred in Odessa in May. There were some instances of hostility to factory workers exempted from service, but mostly anger was directed at social groups perceived as evading service en masse and/or having profited from the war – note that the round-up in Petrograd mentioned above netted a large number of traders and clerical workers. A second concern was that of benefits for dependants, the value of which had been considerably eroded by inflation; moreover common-law wives had been ruled ineligible under the tsarist system, causing much hardship. In Kazan there was a demonstration of soldiers' wives in early May, which focused attention on the issue. Other demands which surfaced at this time included payment for militia duties (troops were often used for routine policing because of the difficulty of recruiting and training the new civil militia), reflecting a strong sense that this was not part of a soldier's 'normal' obligations – an extension of the early rejection of absolute military authority over servicemen, with overtones almost of contract.

Some of the issues that began to surface in March and April had more open political implications, and mark the transition between democratisation and politicisation. There were increasing calls for the demobilisation of older conscripts (43 year olds) and for the temporary release of younger men for agricultural labour. This provided a vehicle for discussions of the land question. Similarly, soldiers began to protest at routine plans to move to camps for spring training, insisting that they remain in barracks in the towns; since this carried with it the threat of subsequent rotation to the Front, it concentrated minds on the war. Finally, the first demands for the formation of ethnically segregated units began to be heard at the end of March – again linked to conceptions of rights and justice, but raising the larger issue of national relations in the new Russia.[13]

Gradually these assertions of rights arising from immediate conditions of service fed into a broader politicisation, in which the immediate concerns became linked to the major political issues of the day, were taken up by political parties, and acquired an increasingly anti-government flavour. These issues became the centres of debate, agitation and protest – often as part of deliberate campaigns to involve the soldiers in what the revolutionary parties thought of as mainstream politics. All the parties made conscious efforts to reach the garrison soldiery, by propaganda and by incorporating them into the soviets and other 'democratic' institutions; the Bolsheviks were by no means neglectful of this, making a point of setting up military organisations wherever possible. This politicisation was a uniform process in terms of its issues and chronology, if not in terms of degree and extent – which could be affected by local variables. Amongst these would be the degree of initial mutiny, the presence or absence of 'democratic' officers enjoying the confidence of the men, proximity to the major bases of revolution, ethnic composition of the garrison, local supply conditions, and the strength of political consensus in the host communities.

Frenkin, in common with Soviet historians, highlights the land question as a key issue for garrison soldiers; given the plethora of contemporary reports of soldier-inspired disorders, as well as the records of soldiers' demands and the concentration of the SR press on the issue, the coincidence of soldier and peasant values seems beyond dispute. The question of whether soldiers did actually take the lead in agrarian revolution must remain open; there is much circumstantial evidence that they did, but as individual deserters or men on leave or small-scale deputations, rather than in any organised form. A number of Soviets of Peasants' Deputies were formed in garrisons, but this does not seem to have been universal: a sense of separate identity was maintained, along with primary loyalty to the existing soldiers' committees. The land question was intricately bound up with the broader issue of power – loss of confidence in the Provisional Government, expectations of the Constituent Assembly – and was central to the radicalisation of opinion in the garrisons, even if it did not directly engender much conflict.[14]

The second key issue, in the spring and early summer, was that of peace and war. Initially there was little anti-war feeling, but the Petrograd Soviet's defence policy with its emphasis on a 'democratic peace' struck an immediate chord. As Wildman has documented for the Front, this anticipated the April crisis – although the impact of this affair on the credibility of the Provisional Government should not be underestimated. The government's 'Liberty Loan' was an important early touchstone, with units in Kazan Military District and elsewhere refusing to participate in fund-raising. The war issue became serious in May–June, when normal rotation of units to the Front was linked with preparations for the June Offensive; leave for agricultural work began to be cancelled for the same reason. In the aftermath of the offensive (and the July Days) pressure to despatch reserve units increased. As in Petrograd, many units refused to leave. T.F. Kuz'mina charts the departure of 29 reserve infantry regiments from the Moscow Military District in July and August: for eight of these there is no clear indication of the response, but amongst the remaining 21 there were disturbances or refusals to take up positions in 16 (two succeeded in entirely frustrating the order). Two major mutinies occurred on the issue, in Tsaritsyn in May and Nizhnii Novgorod at the end of June; in both cases pacification expeditions were sent (from Saratov and Moscow), the latter more successfully.[15]

Frenkin highlights the campaign for national units as the third issue of the spring and summer; one which Soviet historians are generally less prone to stress. It would certainly appear that the

Rear garrisons were at the centre of the growth of national consciousness and self-assertion in 1917. The tsarist army had some ethnically separate units, notably the eight Latvian rifle regiments and the famous Savage Division, and a Polish Army was also being formed, but the army command and the Provisional Government were hostile to the extension of this principle. As suggested above, demands surfaced early. In the Kiev Military District it appeared almost at once; by April a Ukrainian Military Committee was established and units were unilaterally formed, emerging as two Ukrainian Regiments from the deal between the Provisional Government and the Central Rada; in July one of these units attempted to seize power in the city causing a major crisis. The Second Ukrainian Military Congress in early June united 2500 delegates representing 1 700 000 servicemen all over the empire. In Odessa there was a similar swift assertion of separatism, with Ukrainian soldiers and junior officers establishing their own committee. By the autumn, according to Frenkin, 130 regiments with 120 000 men had been Ukrainianised on Ukrainian territory. In Petrograd there was a Ukrainian demonstration in March, and formation of a Ukrainian fraction in the Soviet, which was bound up with the demand for separate Ukrainian units; Ukrainians in the Tsarskoe Selo garrison made similar demands. In Moscow a Ukrainian Regiment was formed after the Government-Rada agreement. Nor was the movement confined to Ukrainians: in Tallinn and Petrograd Estonian troops set up committees to organise separate units, and the government conceded the formation of an Estonian Regiment (to be stationed away from Tallinn). In Kazan garrison a Moslem committee was set up in March, Chuvash and Ukrainian committees in April; the Moslem Congress in July set up an All-Russian Moslem Military Organisation. Frenkin also records the formation of a Union of Jewish Soldiers in the Kiev garrison at the end of July, leading to a nationwide conference in October.

The formation of national units obviously involved soldiers in conflict with the government – which could not be confined to this particular issue alone. Frenkin cites more general demands for federalism from Ukrainian soldiers' organisations. Moreover, it involved some conflict inside the 'democratic' camp: Russian soldiers were often hostile, and members of the socialist parties were uneasy at the spread of nationalism; many garrison committees passed resolutions against the practice. There was considerable conflict on the issue in Kiev and Odessa.[16]

The collapse of the June Offensive and the July Days prodded the Provisional Government into an effort to improve discipline in the armed forces, first and foremost by eliminating the Bolsheviks. Resistance to the discipline campaign became an important issue in the Rear garrisons in July and August. At the Front there were armed clashes and arrests; in the Rear protest was generally less violent. The restoration of the death penalty became a key symbolic focus. Soviet historians stress the emergence of counter-revolutionary organisations in these months: it is not clear how much of an issue this was to soldiers at the time, but the psychological basis for the response to the Kornilov affair was being laid.

Counter-revolution inevitably became the major issue as news of the Kornilov affair broke; its impact was enormous and immediate. Garrison committees and soviets immediately responded, assuming that there was a nationwide conspiracy and a serious threat to the revolution. A plethora of extraordinary 'Committees for the Salvation of the Revolution' were set up, some already assuming the title of 'Military-Revolutionary Committee': these assumed all power in the localities. Kuz´mina traces at least 51 such committees in the Moscow Military District founded between 28 August and 1 September. Soldiers also responded spontaneously by arresting officers and releasing weapons to workers' guard units. There were demands for the widespread arrest and trial of counter-revolutionaries, and the dissolution of the Union of Officers.[17]

In the autumn of 1917 two further issues fuelled discontent in the garrisons. The first concerned belated efforts by the government to deploy troops in support of the civil authorities, occasioning many refusals to participate. The second concerned living conditions. In many towns the situation was becoming quite bad in terms of supply of food and clothing (especially footwear), and as winter approached concern grew over reserves of fuel and food. In Saratov and a number of other towns, soldiers began to demand to be moved into civilian billets instead of their barracks. It does not seem that any real attempt was made to incite soldiers against workers or peasants on the supply issue – social solidarity reinforced by the socialist parties would have made this difficult.[18]

Finally, in sketching the process of revolution in the Rear garrison some mention must be made of the role and experience of officers; their behaviour is of relevance to the disintegration of authority and the failure to establish counter-measures. Like other middle social strata in tsarist Russia, the officer corps had undergone a process of imperfect professionalisation in the pre-revolutionary decades; the new wartime officers reflected this general social trend. It undermined their social solidarity and sense of identity, which helps explain the failure to set up a strong officers' association in 1917. At least three sub-groups might be distinguished. Fully-professionalised officers, particularly of the General Staff, would be disinclined to be involved in politics and prone to helplessness. 'Democratic' officers, like Marks or Gruzinov mentioned above, were far more numerous; indeed, Ronald G. Suny estimates that in the Caucasus Army they were almost half of the officer corps. They would be reluctant to shoulder a middle-class or *tsenzovyi* identity, looking rather to intelligentsia traditions which presumably carried many into the Red Army. Then there were traditional aristocratic officers (and non-aristocrats who emulated them), tending to be older, and prone either to apathy or a sort of apocalyptic 'the worse the better' gloom; even though these should have been the standard-bearers of counter-revolution. Wildman concludes that there was little real muscle and will behind Kornilov, even at the Front. Wartime conditions would have magnified these divisions: the middle ground was physically destroyed in battle, leaving the professionals and the older cohort to face a new officer corps very much younger and different in outlook. Moreover the Rear garrisons were the natural home for the most liberal officers, sent into a sort of exile because of their suspect views, as well as the oldest and least competent or least healthy. (A favourite example of the tragedy of the garrison officers is that of Colonel Timchenko of the 149th Infantry in Ekaterinburg. Transferred to the Rear after dismal performance at the Front, he was persuaded to stand for election to his command – received no votes at all, and shot himself.)[19]

PROVISIONAL GOVERNMENT POLICY

The Provisional Government's overall policy towards the Rear Army in the first part of the year was in essence the same as toward the Front, as documented by Wildman and V.I. Miller. This amounted to a recognition of the democratisation of the armed forces and an attempt to co-opt and control the committee structure, with some limits – notably on election of officers and formation of national units. As at the Front, this was initially effective: most problems were successfully defused. In this period the government did not attach great importance to the internal policing role of the armed forces. In this it was under pressure from the High Command, which was both reluctant to get sucked into local politics and extremely worried about manpower for prosecuting the war. Priority was firmly placed on the war effort. This meant no permanent transfer of soldiers to militia service, and no exemption from military service for militia personnel, despite considerable pressure from local authorities. Inevitably, at local level there was use of troops for routine urban policing, and I.I. Mints has identified a number of cases of use in more serious incidents – 17 in May and 39 in July–August; but on the whole this was a local matter, with little central involvement or coordination, and relatively infrequent. In Kazan the soviet and army committees debated forming armed teams to enforce the grain monopoly, but nothing seems to have come of this. The priority given to the war effort also meant that the military authorities refused to budge on the issue of the demobilisation of older men, and were grudging about the temporary release of men for agricultural work despite strong evidence of rural shortage of labour. Finally, the authorities used every occasion to send their most reliable units to the Front – denuding the Rear garrisons by creation of shock-battalions, units of Cavaliers of St George; even insisting on sending national units to the Front instead of exploiting the potential for divide-and-rule. Cossacks were also chiefly deployed at the Front, as were units of former tsarist policemen (although some reports indicate that their reliability was questionable). It is hard to escape the conclusion that the Provisional Government's basic strategy for managing the revolution remained to pre-empt the Constituent Assembly and win the war.

Only in the autumn did the government seriously begin to

consider a radically different policy. This amounted to recognition of an internal policing role, in Verkhovskii's order of 11th October:

> One of the tasks placed upon the army in the transition period is that of guaranteeing within the country the physical safety and genuine civil liberties of the people. The existing militia is incapable of satisfying this prime concern of the state. The Army is obliged to assist by all its means and with all its expertise the commissars of the government and urban and rural self-government organs.

The order divided Russia into regions, to which military units were assigned for deployment at the request of local civil authorities. The new approach was also linked to a major restructuring of the armed forces as a whole: memoranda by Kerenskii and Dukhonin refer to a drastic reduction in the size of the Army, concentrating on new volunteer units organised on a territorial basis. No concrete steps, however, could be taken before October.[20]

The moderate socialists, who had considerable influence within the government and dominated most local institutions, did not develop any distinct policy towards the Rear army. A certain ambivalence towards the soldiery is clearly evident, even amongst left-wing Mensheviks like Sukhanov: images of 'dark people' in 'grey coats' reflect fear of the potential association of the armed forces with the peasantry, and hence anarchy and/or counter-revolution. There were initial hesitations amongst Mensheviks about allowing the soldiers entry to the soviets. Later in the year, as Rex Wade notes in his study of the Red Guard, there was no little distrust of the garrison troops even amongst Bolsheviks (Lenin also hinted that 'a wave of real anarchy may become stronger than we are' in urging a timely seizure of power). Yet the moderate socialists had no strategy other than attempting to control the garrisons from their initial base in the committees; the Mensheviks' fears were possibly allayed by the SRs' apparent dominance.[21]

OCTOBER

The role of garrison troops after the Kornilov affair becomes harder to assess. On the one hand they certainly supported the Committees for the Salvation of the Revolution, many of which refused to disband once the emergency was passed, forming instead an institutional wedge between the Provisional Government and the High Command and local civil and military authorities (many of the latter, of necessity, cooperated with the Committees). This was half-way to Soviet power: the spirit manifested at the Democratic Conference. Soviet historians are also able to point to an impressive record of Bolshevisation of army committees in the Rear. Yet it is also clear that there were strong tendencies towards anarchy: revolts in Tambov, Orel and Tashkent in September were not so much concerted attempts to establish Soviet power as riots. It is equally clear that the garrison role in the Bolshevik revolution was limited: there was a great deal of 'neutrality', and a considerable role played by the Left SRs (around half the deputies of the Kazan garrison, for example) which has yet to be investigated. The new national units were not generally well-disposed towards the Bolsheviks. There are shades of opinion in the specialist literature on the armed forces, but it may be fair comment to suggest that it is readier than the literature on the workers to accord a manipulative role to the Bolsheviks, stressing their command of soldiers' institutions and ability to exclude other voices. Nonetheless the ability of the Bolsheviks to mobilise their own Army is prima facie a warning against dismissing its predecessor as the epitome of peasant anarchy.[22]

If there is still much work to be done on the role of the Rear garrisons in 1917, it should at least be apparent that it will be worth the effort. A survey of the impact of these soldiers on the revolution suggests that it was crucial, both in intensifying disorder and rendering Russia ungovernable, and in homogenising the experience of revolution across different regions. A survey of the process of revolution in the garrisons suggests that the dominant paradigm of Western historiography is indeed powerful in explanation – but two qualifications might be made, of some significance: first, that it overstates the unity of the middle and upper strata of society; second, that it understates manipulation, fragmentation, diversity and neutrality in the camp of 'revolutionary democracy'.

NOTES

1. The principal western works are Allan K. Wildman, *The End of the Russian Imperial Army*, 2 vols (Princeton, 1980 and 1987); Evan Mawdsley, *The Russian Revolution and the Baltic Fleet: War and Politics, February 1917–April 1918* (London, 1978); Mikhail Frenkin, *Zakhvat vlasti bol'shevikami v Rossii i rol' tylovykh garnizonov armii: Podgotovka i provedenie oktyabr'skogo myatezha* (Jerusalem, 1982). Recent Soviet works include A.M. Andreev, *Soldatskie massy garnizonov russkoi armii v oktyabr'skoi revolyutsii* (Moscow, 1975); T.F. Kuz'mina, *Revolyutsionnoe dvizhenie soldatskikh mass tsentra Rossii nakanune Oktyabrya* (Moscow, 1978); I.M. Ionenko, *Soldatskie massy v oktyabr'skoi revolyutsii: Po materialam Povolzh'ya i Urala* (Kazan, 1982). The 'dominant paradigm' was first identified by Ronald Grigor Suny, in 'Towards a Social History of the October Revolution', *American Historical Review*, LXXXVIII, 1 (1983).
2. S.E. Finer, *The Man on Horseback: The Role of the Military in Politics* (London, 1963) pp. 6–12.
3. Recent theoretical literature on revolution stresses the importance of 'states as administrative and coercive organizations'. See Theda Skocpol, *States and Social Revolutions* (Cambridge, 1979) p. 14.
4. These figures are for general guidance only. They are taken from Frenkin, *Zakhvat vlasti*, ch. 1; Kuz'mina, *Revolyutsionnoe dvizhenie*, ch. 1; Andreev, *Soldatskie massy*, ch. 1. Frenkin discusses the difficulties in some detail, and often seems ambivalent himself. See also L.M. Gavrilov and V.V. Kutuzov, 'Perepis' russkoi armii 25 oktyabrya 1917g.', *Istoriya SSSR*, 2 (1964); L.M. Gavrilov, 'Sostoyanie rezervov fronta nakanune Oktyabrya', *Istoriya SSSR* 4 (1967).
5. Frenkin, *Zakhvat vlasti*, pp. 16–18.
6. See L. Haimson, 'The Problem of Social Identities in Early Twentieth-Century Russia', *Slavic Review*, XLVII, 1 (1988).
7. On the militia see H.J. White, 'Civil Rights and the Provisional Government', in Olga Crisp and Linda Edmondson (eds) *Civil Rights in Imperial Russia* (Oxford, 1989), pp. 287–312; A.P. Zvyagintseva, 'Organizatsiya i deyatel'nost' militsii Vremennogo pravitel'stva Rossii v 1917 g.' (kand. diss., Moscow State University, 1972).
8. To a seminar at the School of Slavonic and East European Studies, London, 5 March 1987.
9. Wildman, *End of the Russian Imperial Army*, vol. I p. xix; Mawdsley, *Russian Revolution*, chs 2–3. See S.A. Smith's image of the workers' struggle for a 'constitutional' factory as a microcosm of class struggle in which class consciousness developed and class aspirations were defined. *Red Petrograd: Revolution in the Factories, 1917–18* (Cambridge, 1983) p. 256.
10. Data on garrison composition are from Frenkin, *Zakhvat vlasti*, ch. 1; Andreev, *Soldatskie massy*, ch. 1; Kuz'mina, *Revolyutsionnoe dvizhenie*, ch. 1. The campaign against evaders of conscription is noted by N.A. Vostrikov, *Bor'ba za massy: Gorodskie srednie sloi nakanune Oktyabrya* (Moscow, 1970) p. 21, and Smith, *Red Petrograd*, p. 22.
11. Tsuyoshi Hasegawa, *The February Revolution: Petrograd 1917* (Seattle, 1981); V. Zakharov, *Soldaty. (Vospominaniya)* (Tver, 1917) pp. 23–31; N. Ezhov, *Voennaya Kazan' v 1917 godu* (Kazan, 1927) pp. 24ff; V.V. Vas'kin and G.A. Gerasimenko, *Fevral'skaya revolyutsiya v Nizhnem Povol'zhe* (Saratov, 1976)

pp. 30–1; G.T. Gavrilov, *1917 god v Stalingradskoi gubernii* (Stalingrad, 1927) p. 4; Frenkin, *Zakhvat vlasti*, p. 53; V. Konovalov, *Krasnyi flag nad Odessoi* (Odessa, 1977) passim.

12. See works cited in n. 11. Also Andreev, *Soldatskie massy*; Kuz´mina, *Revolyutsionnoe dvizhenie*; scattered references in the national press; much useful information in Donald J. Raleigh, *Revolution on the Volga: 1917 in Saratov* (Cornell, 1986); M. Ferro, *The Russian Revolution of February 1917* (London, 1972) pp. 130–6.
13. Ibid.
14. Frenkin, *Zakhvat vlasti*, ch. 3.
15. Ezhov, *Voennaya Kazan´*, p. 84; Kuz´mina, *Revolyutsionnoe dvizhenie*, pp. 62ff., 290–1; Donald J. Raleigh, 'Revolutionary Politics in Provincial Russia: the Tsaritsyn "Republic" in 1917', *Slavic Review*, XL, 2 (1981); Andreev, *Soldatskie massy*, pp. 129ff.
16. Frenkin, *Zakhvat vlasti*, ch. 4; *Odesskie novosti*, for 1917; *1917 god na Kievshchine* (Kiev, 1928); Ezhov, *Voennaya Kazan´*, pp. 53ff.
17. For Soviet views of counter-revolution, see N.Ya. Ivanov, *Kontrrevolyutsiya v Rossii v 1917 godu i ee razgrom* (Moscow, 1977); Andreev, *Soldatskie massy*. On 'Salvation Committees' see reports of provincial commissars in *Tsentral´nyi Gosudarstvennyi Arkhiv Oktyabr´skoi Revolyutsii*, f. 1788, op. 2, d. 69; also Kuz´mina, *Revolyutsionnoe dvizhenie*, pp. 292–302.
18. Rex A. Wade, *Red Guards and Workers' Militias in the Russian Revolution* (Stanford, 1983) ch. 10; other sources as in n. 11.
19. Many of these points were made by Evan Mawdsley in his 1987 seminar paper (n. 8). On officers, see M. Mayzel, *Generals and Revolutionaries: The Russian General Staff During the Revolution* (Osnabruck, 1979); Peter Kenez, 'A Profile of the Pre-Revolutionary Officer Corps', *California Slavic Studies*, 7 (1973); Ronald Grigor Suny, *The Baku Commune, 1917–1918: Class and Nationality in the Russian Revolution* (Princeton, 1972). On professionalisation generally, see Howard White, 'The Middle Classes' in Robert Service (ed.) *Society and Politics in the Russian Revolution* (forthcoming). For Timchenko, see *Stanford, Hoover Institution Archive*, mss. memoirs of V.P. Anichkov.
20. For Provisional Government policy, see esp. D.V. Oznobishin, 'O popytkakh Vremennogo pravitel´stva Rossii reorganizovat´ Armiyu', *Istoricheskii arkhiv*, 4 (1961), which reproduces a number of documents.
21. N.N. Sukhanov, *The Russian Revolution 1917* (Oxford, 1955) passim; Wade, *Red Guards*, chs. 10–11; V.I. Lenin, 'Letter to the Central Committee, the Moscow and Petrograd Committees and the Bolshevik Members of the Moscow and Petrograd Soviets', 1 Oct. 1917, *Selected Works* (Moscow, 1975) vol. II, p. 390.
22. National Press reports, e.g. *Vestnik Vremennogo Pravitel´stva*, 17 Sept. 1917; *Otkrytoe pis´mo ispolnitel´nogo komiteta Tambovskogo soveta soldatskikh deputatov i bol´shinstva aktyvnykh ego sotrudnikov po povodu besporyadkov 12–13 sentyabrya k rabochim, soldatam i vsem grazhdanam Tambova* (Tambov, 1917); Kuz´mina, *Revolyutsionnoe dvizhenie*, pp. 234–8.

9 Lenin and Agrarian Economics in 1917

Robert Service

Lenin was among his party's experts on many subjects in 1917 and especially on the countryside. His words had always been taken seriously by Bolsheviks on agrarian economics, on the sociology of the peasantry and on rural political tactics. His articles in the 1890s had been distinguished by their attention to agriculture, and his *Development of Capitalism in Russia* (1899) had emphasised the technical and organisational advances already made by Russian farming. It was Lenin who had initiated the Bolshevik discussion of 'the agrarian question' before the First World War. At party congress after congress he had delivered speeches on the peasantry. Upon his return from Switzerland in April 1917, Lenin led the debate on agrarian affairs at the seventh party conference in Petrograd.

His general project for a transfer of power from the liberal-led Provisional Government to a socialist administration is well known. Lenin aimed at a European socialist revolution. In Russia he wanted 'a dictatorship of the proletariat and the poorest peasantry'.[1] His administration was meant to combine centralism with latitude for local freedom and initiative. The middle and upper classes were to be disenfranchised, but the vast majority of the population would engage in mass participatory politics. Workers, soldiers and peasants would rule. Lenin also devised policies for the economy. He envisaged a government take-over of banking institutions and the establishment of a single central bank. He urged, too, the nationalisation of the largest industrial enterprises along with schemes for the compulsory amalgamation of smaller enterprises into larger ones, so that further nationalisation might eventually be undertaken. He stressed that this would not amount to the introduction of socialism by decree. There would still be capitalism in the industrial sector, but the socialist administration would aim at its ultimate replacement. Lenin in April also called for land nationalisation, and throughout 1917 urged that the land be put at the disposal of local elective peasant bodies.[2]

Thus the seventh party conference was asked to make a drastic revision of the party's objectives. Before 1917 the Bolsheviks had expected the next revolution to be a 'bourgeois' one. The Mensheviks agreed with this, and Bolsheviks and Mensheviks had concurred that Russia's level of economic and cultural development as yet precluded the inauguration of a socialist order. But the Bolsheviks had also maintained that the bourgeoisie was incapable of carrying through a bourgeois revolution in Russia, and that only a provisional 'revolutionary democratic dictatorship of the proletariat and the peasantry' would be adequate for such a task. In 1917 Lenin and like-minded Bolsheviks abandoned the notion that the beginning of the transition to socialism could not be attempted until years after that bourgeois revolution.

All this raised fundamental questions, among which were several relating to economics. What kind of economic order could be constructed in Russia, in town and countryside? What had changed in the country's economic and cultural level to justify such a revision of party policy? How would production be organised in industrial and agricultural enterprises? What kind of society would exist after the establishment of a soviet administration? Lenin's reply in its broadest terms was that Europe stood on the verge of socialist revolution and that Russia could and would benefit from fraternal revolutions elsewhere. He also affirmed that the war had led to a massive growth in industrial output and to a concentration of capital in ever vaster companies, and that Russia had partaken of this growth.[3] Unlike all politicians outside the Bolshevik party and many Bolshevik leaders too, Lenin in spring and summer 1917 made light of the contention that his country faced economic problems that were not easily soluble.[4] He added that Russian workers had acquired a deepened political consciousness through and after the February Revolution. They were capable of exerting 'workers' control' in their respective enterprises. Lenin, who had once derided notions of 'primitive democracy', now stated that a mass participatory system of politics in the soviets was possible and necessary.[5]

But what about the countryside? Most works on Lenin's rural perspective in 1917 have focused on social and political themes.[6]

And yet the economic theme was obviously also of immense importance. The greatest proportion of the sum of human endeavour in the Russian economy was located on the land. Lenin wished to elaborate a future policy for agriculture so that his general project to begin the 'transition to socialism' might attract support inside and outside his party.

His *April Theses* proposed the slogan of 'land nationalisation'. This was no new slogan for him; he had been advocating it since 1905. But herein lay a possible source of objections; for in 1905 he had proposed land nationalisation as a bourgeois and not as a socialist measure. In Lenin's view, the temporary 'revolutionary democratic dictatorship of the proletariat and the peasantry' would take ownership of the land in order to promote the most efficient method of agrarian capitalist development in Russia. Nationalisation, he had argued, would enable the authorities to do away with peasant practices deemed to be inimical to modern farming. Sub-letting of land by inefficient cultivators would be banned. Only efficient farmers would survive. Lenin also sought to remove the impediments to technical innovation thought by him to result from the existence of the Russian peasant land commune. He believed that this was 'the American path' to modernisation; and that the faster that Russia undertook the journey, the sooner it could move towards its eventual socialist revolution.[7]

For some weeks after the February Revolution, Lenin simply advocated the slogan without mentioning the kind of economy it involved. At the seventh party conference in April he gave lengthy speeches on the agrarian question. On land nationalisation, he repeated that he regarded it as 'a bourgeois measure' (*mera burzhuaznaya*).[8] This appeared to imply that he still felt that a further epoch of capitalist development was necessary in Russian agriculture. Thus Lenin changed his stance less on agriculture than on industry after the February Revolution: the policy that in 1905 had been designed by him as a means of modernising the technical and organisational framework of his country's farming remained unchanged.

Lenin had always recognised that Russian industry had made greater progress than Russian agriculture; and even in 1917 he was not suggesting that all Russian industrial enterprises should be nationalised. It would have been quite illogical for him to have proposed instant socialism in agriculture while refraining from proposing it in industry. His arguments in favour of land nationalisation were roughly what they had been before the First World War. He reiterated his interpretation of the aspirations of peasant deputies in the First and Second State Dumas; according to Lenin, they had supported schemes for the land to become governmental property.[9] This was a dubious interpretation – as he discovered in August 1917 when surveys of opinion of peasants' representatives were published. Nor had Lenin succeeded, before the February Revolution, in securing his party's acceptance of it. His advocacy of land nationalisation had been opposed by many fellow Bolsheviks as being impractical and likely to alienate the peasant support necessary for a worker-peasant class alliance. A dispute broke out in 1906 at the fourth party congress between S.A. Suvorov and Lenin. Suvorov led a group of Bolsheviks, which included Stalin, believing that the peasants ought to be encouraged to take over the non-peasant land without government hindrance. The seized land ought to become 'the full property of the peasantry' and should not be nationalised in the bourgeois revolution.[10]

This intra-Bolshevik disagreement was complicated by the fact that it occurred at a party congress attended by the Mensheviks. The Mensheviks gained most votes at the congress and it was their policy of 'land municipalisation' that won the day. Nevertheless more Bolsheviks supported Suvorov than Lenin.[11] So Lenin, in coming forward with his nationalisation proposal in April 1917, was seeking to have it accepted for the first time as official party policy. Expert and authoritative as he was on agrarian matters, he had not yet had his viewpoint ratified as official Bolshevik policy.

Yet in April 1917, at the seventh party conference, he succeeded at last. There are probably several reasons for his success. In the first place, the party was already accepting a more radical version of its general strategy than before and some enlargement of its agrarian objectives was to be expected. Secondly, the Bolsheviks in spring 1917 focused on urban development and perhaps most delegates simply failed to see the urgency of taking the arguments against Lenin seriously. In any case he was not proposing instant socialism, and he continued to assert that the peasants, while not owning the land, would enjoy full rights to its use. As it happens, some Bolsheviks in April continued to put the case for letting the peasants get on with land seizures as they saw fit. Stalin was among them.[12] Yet the matter did not become openly controversial in the party. Stalin did not make a major issue of his disagreements even though he had the opportunity.[13] Lastly, Lenin stressed that he did not want the peasantry to be oppressed by the implementation of his policy. He conceded that 'a gigantic bureaucratic apparatus' (*giganticheskii chinovnicheskii apparat*) would be needed to realise land nationalisation; but he claimed that it would not act despotically since it would remain under the control of the soviets.[14]

Such arguments may have stilled the worries of those Bolsheviks urging caution: but events after October 1917 were to show that a large number of leading Bolsheviks, many of whom became associated with the Left Communists, were unhappy with so limited an agrarian reform.[15] The Bolshevik party was far from being politically homogeneous. After seizing power, it was buffeted by disputes over the treatment of the other socialist parties, over industrial management and over international relations as well as over agriculture.

This poses the problem of how Lenin managed to avoid a conflict with the left wing of his party between the February and the October Revolutions. No doubt it helped that they all agreed on certain key short-term goals, especially the seizure of power. The left-wing Bolsheviks, furthermore, were just as preoccupied by urban politics as other Bolsheviks. Lenin, furthermore, was clearly the party's pre-eminent leader. His position, which had been fragile in many ways during the war, was decisively strengthened at the seventh party conference. His sway over his audience was noted by everyone. Yet a further factor must not be overlooked: namely that Lenin's speeches were not unambiguous about the kind of economy to be fostered after the seizure of power. True, he expected that capitalism in some form would exist. But he did not herald it as a positive goal. Historians have pointed out that the limited industrial nationalisations favoured by Lenin for many months after October, which he described as belonging to a system of state capitalism, accorded with his industrial project as set out in summer 1917.[16] But the tactical point, which is usually overlooked, is that he did not expressly recommend 'state capitalism' in advance of seizing power.[17] No doubt he had not yet thought through all his ideas; and he himself was affected by the utopian ambitions of the epoch. No doubt, too, his intuitive understanding of Bolshevik sensibilities told him that he would rally little support for commencing 'the transition to socialism' if he indulged in enthusiastic advocacy of further capitalist development.

Be that as it may, there were sides to Lenin's agrarian proposals that contrasted with his portrayal of land nationalisation as a 'bourgeois measure'. At the seventh conference he did not specify capitalist agricultural development as a positive objective. In a curious formulation he stated only that land nationalisation 'does not exclude capitalism'.[18]

Lenin added that his policy, while not involving instant socialism, would act as a bridgehead for 'a transition to broader measures'.[19] It is hard not to see this as an intention to move on to socialism. Lenin also urged that the larger gentry estates should not be divided up among peasant households but should be turned into 'model farms' (*obraztsovye khozyaistva*), which would be worked by agricultural labourers along with trained agronomists. As Lenin since the 1890s had been prominent in demonstrating, regions of the Russian Empire had undergone a remarkable agricultural modernisation. The latifundia of the Ukraine and elsewhere were famous for their size, their advanced equipment and their capitalist organisation; and crop diversification and technical renovation was occurring in the Baltic area and elsewhere.[20] If large industrial concerns were to be nationalised, why not large agricultural concerns? But Lenin's scheme included far more estates than the latifundia. He urged that all estates of 100–300 desyatins and upwards be turned into model farms.[21] Translated into English measurement, this would have involved gentry landholdings of roughly 270–810 acres. It has been reckoned that, in 1905, 96. 6 per cent of estates held by the landed gentry in forty-four provinces of European Russia were 100 desyatins or greater in size.[22] If Lenin's plan would have included virtually all gentry estates, it is hardly surprising that the far-left members of his party, with their leanings towards collectivisation, did not demur.

In any case, Lenin was not compelled by his colleagues to explain why the peasantry would accept his proposals. He was, after all, merely re-stating an idea he had propounded repeatedly in the pre-war years. Even the scheme for model farms had been broached in 1905;[23] but, whereas once it had been a minor and loosely-formulated feature, it had now become the principal one.

From April through to July he commented intermittently on the potential attractiveness of the proposals to the peasantry. Firstly, he urged the immediate seizure of gentry land by the peasantry. This was meant to bring Bolsheviks and peasants together politically. The long-held peasant wish to elect the gentry would be supported only by Lenin's party. No greater electoral appeal could be devised.[24] Secondly, his revolutionary strategy was based upon the imminence of European socialist revolution. Peace, Lenin thought, would be quickly brought about; and this would facilitate the reorientation of Russian industry towards production for the civilian market.[25] The result would be a massive increase in the goods demanded by the peasantry. Agricultural equipment rather than armaments would supply the thrust of the industrial drive (just as, according to Lenin in *The Development of Capitalism in Russia*, it had traditionally been).[26] Lenin also promised to keep peasant taxes low.[27] Gratitude to a Bolshevik-led government would be all the greater if the fiscal load on the peasantry were lightened and if the socialist administration drew its revenues primarily from the rich layers of the population in town and countryside.[28]

Lenin, naturally, did not think in narrowly economic terms; he emphasised that he was looking to specific sections of the population for political support. Just as in the towns he aimed to appeal mainly to the workers, in the countryside he wanted to attract chiefly the poorer peasants and the agricultural wage-labourers. The work-forces of the new model farms would be drawn from them.[29] Lenin also declared that such peasants would be encouraged to organise themselves separately, in both unions and soviets, from the rest of the peasantry.[30] Throughout the year he drew a picture of a future administration based upon support from 'the proletariat and the semi-proletariat'.[31] Recognising that this formula might not be self-explanatory to everyone, he frequently referred to 'the proletariat and the poorest peasants'.[32]

The appeal to the poorer peasants, according to Lenin, was crucial to the Bolshevik advance in the towns. He argued that the seizure of land by the peasantry as a whole would still lack the necessary finance and equipment and would not be an economic panacea for the village poor. At the First All-Russian Congress of Peasants' Deputies in May 1917 he pointed out that, however much land was acquired by a poor household, the advantage would be small if its members lacked sufficient livestock, implements and finance (and economic historians have sided with his argument here).[33] This would be a problem not only for agricultural wage-labourers but also for poor peasants.[34] The Socialist Revolutionaries proposed that, when the land was transferred to the peasantry (which they, unlike the Bolsheviks, envisaged as being tied to the decisions of the Constituent Assembly), the criterion of distribution should be either the number of mouths to be fed in a household or the amount of work which a household could undertake. This would be 'land socialisation'; it would be accompanied by periodic redivisions of the land and by prohibitions on the hiring of labour and on the renting of land.[35] Lenin dismissed such projects as unrealistic. Without model farms, the poorer peasants would not be in a significantly better position to survive economically than before 1917.[36]

He added that, whatever laws were enacted under such a system, the peasants would circumvent them. They would be constrained by the inherent logic of the economy. Lenin saw his own alternative as the sole solution to the difficulty. Model farms would save poor peasants from penury and from subjection to rich peasants and would enhance opportunities for national agricultural advance.[37]

Politically speaking, this called for a campaign to accelerate the division of the peasantry into two camps. In his 'farewell letter to Swiss socialists', delivered before mounting the train that took him across Germany, Lenin spoke of 'the inevitability of embittered class clashes between agricultural wage-labourers, along with the poorest peasants associating themselves with them, and the rich peasants'.[38] In a speech to Petrograd soldiers on 10 April, he spoke aggressively about 'the rich peasants (who are capitalists just the same)' and urged his audience to ensure that poor peasants were not tricked by the rich.[39] He claimed, at the city party conference on 14 April, that the rich peasants would prove to be 'more right-wing than Guchkov'.[40] This statement shows that, despite the modifications he made in his agrarian perspective after the experience of the 1905–6 Revolution, he still adhered to several basic tenets in his thinking from the 1890s.[41] In May 1917 he continued in this vein. His open letter to the First All-Russian Congress of Peasants' Deputies warned poor peasants not to trust the rich peasants (*bogatye muzhiki*) since the rich peasants were merely capitalists.[42]

These, then, were the outlines of Lenin's project in agrarian economics in the first months of the February Revolution. They were made in April; some details of justification were added in May, and little was modified until the end of August. Previous accounts have suggested that Lenin was happy with his policy until August, when he took account of the 242 so-called 'peasant instructions' (*nakazy*). Such an interpretation is based on his public programmatic statements; and certainly Lenin did not display his abandonment of his scheme for land nationalisation until 29 August.[43] But Lenin, while being a theorist and a formulator of projects, was also a politician. If we apply to him the kind of investigative techniques considered normal for other politicians, we need to look not only at what he said but also at what he failed to say. Let us take the slogan of land nationalisation. He rallied his party with it at the seventh party conference in April. Yet did not expressly recommend it again in the months before the October Revolution. He approached the subject only indirectly. For example, he stated in his letter to the congress of peasants' deputies on 7 May that the party disapproved of 'the seizure of land as property'.[44] This formulation could comprehend land nationalisation, but it was not exhausted by nationalisation; it could equally include land socialisation: indeed Lenin in the same letter stated: 'The whole land must belong to the people. All gentry lands must pass without compensation to the peasants.'[45]

His subsequent speech to the congress itself on 22 May failed to eliminate the vagueness. If anything, he increased it by declaring that the land should be the 'property of the entire people' and that landed property should be an 'all-people's' thing.[46] How do we explain this failure to enunciate the Bolshevik official slogan in front of the most important peasant audience addressed by Lenin in 1917? One possibility would be that he was trying to disguise his legislative intentions by means of a verbal flurry. But this itself would signify that Lenin already knew that the policy commanded little peasant support. A second possibility is therefore more likely: namely that Lenin himself either had already changed his mind or was in the process of changing it.

Lenin did not refer to land nationalisation in June, July and August. This cannot have been accidental. His reticence cannot be explained by his flight to Finland; for Lenin did not leave Petrograd until the second week in July. In addition, even when he was in hiding he was producing works on a wide range of subjects. Nor did his Finnish sojourn put him further out of contact with Russian rural developments than before. In fact he had not visited a single village in Russia since returning from Switzerland.[47] His information on the countryside came almost entirely from what he read in newspapers and what he could glean from those few Bolsheviks visiting Petrograd who had recently been in the villages. His contact with peasants at the First All-Russian Congress of Peasants' Deputies in May had been the only exception to this. The newspapers of Petrograd, which he read before his flight and which he continued to receive in Finland, were full of accounts of the increased resort of peasants to land seizure. All these reports must surely have convinced him that the peasantry as a whole was on the move; and, although he discussed the 242 peasant *nakazy* publicly only from 29 August, the basic nature of their contents had been evident at the Congress of Peasants' Deputies.[48] Such a dénouement was what the Bolshevik critics of Lenin's agrarian writings had been saying for a dozen years. His own unwonted silence on land nationalisation surely indicated that he was having to give way to them.

On 29 August he finally made his change of stance public. Characteristically he avoided putting it expressly in such terms: he did not explicitly disown nationalisation as a short-term measure. But the implied change was plain enough in his article in *Rabochii* (which was a name assumed by *Pravda* to avoid the government's harassment after the July Days). There for the first time he declared that the 242 peasant instructions compiled by the Socialist Revolutionaries should be embodied in official Bolshevik party policy.[49] The central committee took the same line on 31 August 1917, calling not for land nationalisation but for 'the immediate abolition of private property in the land of the gentry without compensation and its transfer to the disposal of peasant committees'.[50]

Nevertheless it is not self-evident that Lenin's change of mind was the major factor in the change in the party's official stance on the agrarian question in the months before the October Revolution. On 7 May 1917 the central committee published a list of suggested policy statements to be made by Bolshevik activists campaigning for election to their local soviets. It included the advice to declare that all the land should 'pass without compensation into the hands of the peasants'.[51] No mention of land nationalisation. A further piece in the jigsaw of evidence is provided by the proceedings of the sixth party congress, held in Petrograd from 26 July to 3 August (while Lenin was still in hiding). The agrarian question was not a separate item on the agenda: yet another indication of the heavy urban bias in the Bolshevik mentality. But the question was in fact discussed by Stalin as part of his report on the political situation. Not once did he mention land nationalisation. Furthermore, he announced that 'the central committee had put forward three basic slogans' in the period after the seventh party conference in April: 'all power to the soviets, control over production and confiscation of gentry land'.[52] No delegate to the congress proposed that land nationalisation should be restored to prominence; indeed no one referred to it at all. At the very least this indicates a self-distancing by the central committee from the policy on land nationalisation accepted at the seventh party conference in April.

The precise implications are obscure. We do not even know for certain that a central committee vote was taken to abandon the slogan; but it is a probable, if not a verifiable, hypothesis. In addition, the presence in the central committee of leaders such as Stalin who had always opposed land nationalisation makes it likely also that Lenin's reticence on nationalisation after April was a response to their arguments.[53] Whether he was convinced by the arguments for dropping the slogan or was told to keep quiet by the central committee is not ascertainable from the available documents. It could even have been decided to dispense with land nationalisation as a slogan without giving it up as a policy. If such a fudge was undertaken, it was no longer possible to maintain it after the publication of the 242 peasant instructions in *Izvestiya* on 19 August 1917. The central committee was obliged to state unambiguously what its policy on the agrarian question really was.

Both Lenin's article of 29 August 1917 and the central committee's decision on 31 August 1917 accept the 242 peasant instructions as the basis of party policy. This signified implicitly that the peasants should have the right to equalise landholdings among local households, to conduct periodic redistributions of landholdings and to place restrictions on the hiring of labour.[54] It involved an acceptance that the huge number of model farms originally projected by Lenin would not quickly be set up. The peasants would be allowed to take over the land unimpeded. He continued to hope that the very largest modern farms would be retained by the state; but he refrained from putting even this on the record until after he had seized power.[55] He maintained that the Bolsheviks would not be bowing altogether to peasant wishes in the longer term. His argument was that 'the dominance of the proletariat at the centre', in the new socialist state, would ensure that policies could eventually be steered towards the party's ultimate objectives.[56] Lenin's shift of policy was consequently temporary and tactical. He did not expect, any more than he ever had, that the peasantry as a whole would achieve economically what the peasants expected. He still felt that the egalitarian restrictions on landholding would be circumvented in practice. But he also believed that enough economic and political good would result from the modification of official Bolshevik policy as to justify undertaking the modification.[57]

Luckily we can make an informed guess as to what he meant by this. Earlier, while putting the case for land nationalisation, he had offered a critique of the kind of proposals that later appeared in the 242 peasant instructions. 'Land socialisation', he had insisted, would not abolish capitalism; on the contrary, capitalism would robustly survive. Indeed this had been a principal reason why Lenin had also suggested that only land nationalisation and the establishment of a vast number of model farms would enable the agricultural wage-labourers and the poor peasants to escape penury and to slip 'from under the yoke of capitalism'.[58]

Even so, Lenin omitted to say this in so many words from late August. His self-restraint stemmed not from an intellectual conversion but probably rather from a recognition that it would not be politic to dwell on the matter. Some left-wing elements in his party still remained committed to agricultural collectivisation. More than that: not even the long-standing supporters of some kind of socialisation (such as Stalin and Kalinin) specified that the future agrarian policy would foster capitalism.[59] Neither the left nor the right wing in the Bolshevik party warmed to arguments in favour of the protection of capitalism after the hoped-for establishment of a socialist administration. A blind eye was turned to the inherent tensions in the party's general strategy of revolution, and consequently the economic aspects of the Bolshevik agrarian project were less carefully sketched even than in April and May 1917. This omission was not confined to Lenin. Not even the sixth party congress in July 1917 went further than a call for the expropriation of the gentry; the details of policy were neglected. The preoccupation with other current difficulties and future policies had become intense. Perhaps if Lenin had been able to attend, there would have been a more thorough debate. Yet even he gave the topic a scant amount of thought not only before but also after his *Rabochii* article of 29 August: only one further lengthy statement on party policy on the 242 peasant instructions came forth from him.[60]

But under what conditions was capitalism expected to operate after the socialist seizure of power? Again we search in vain for an answer that was either direct or comprehensive. Certainly Lenin openly advocated the retention of the state grain-trade monopoly; certainly he still wanted to establish model farms on the very largest of the estates already under intensive cultivation. But he did not specify to what extent, if any, such farms would be subject to market pressures.[61]

Lenin's project of agrarian economics at the moment of the October Revolution remained patchy and vague, and his vision was blurred not only about the next 'stage' in his country's future but also about its current economic condition. His comments on the reasons for the disruption of the economy in general and the agricultural sector in particular lacked his usual incisiveness. This was not a subject which could lightly be ignored. For the choice of cure would depend on the diagnosis of the malaise. Lenin might have been expected to provide a running commentary on current economic ills. He had broad access to the pages of *Pravda* until the July Days, and even afterwards could get his material published as long as it did not involve a threat to the party's existence by calling for the violent overthrow of the Provisional Government. His articles reveal little endeavour to account for the break-up of the Russian imperial economy in 1917. Liberal, Menshevik and Socialist Revolutionary newspapers were full of such attempts, pointing to the crippling strains imposed by prolonged involvement in war with an advanced industrial and military power such as Germany. They detailed the shortages of raw materials and fuel to the factories and of food-stuffs to the towns; they dealt with transport difficulties, inflation and the peasantry's reluctance to release grain to the state procurement agencies.[62]

Lenin noted the empirical data and acknowledged that economic crisis was imminent under the Provisional Government. But he repudiated the assertion that catastrophe was inevitable. He even tried to demonstrate that, however bad the situation was in Russia, it was a lot worse in Germany; and he repeatedly stated that the country had an abundance of grain, cotton, fuel and metal.[63] His occasional allusions to a coming crisis were overshadowed by his disquisitions on the ability of a socialist administration to solve all economic and political problems quickly.[64] Only in September 1917 did he change his approach, and the title of his major essay on the future economic policy of a Bolshevik-led government signalled this: 'The Imminent Catastrophe And How To Combat It'.[65]

Even so, his projected measures were not accompanied by a sustained analysis as to why the economy had got into such difficulties. This may have stemmed partly from the fact that he had always taken a rather favourable view on the economic effects of war. Whereas others had emphasised its dislocating consequences, Lenin had emphasised that modern war strongly stimulated industrial growth in Russia and elsewhere.[66] No wonder he was late in perceiving the de-industrialisation of Russia that was already beginning in 1917. In addition, many of Lenin's proposals for industrial reorganisation in 1917 were in many ways not vastly different from those of the Mensheviks. Indeed the Mensheviks had suggested several of them before him.[67] Nevertheless he wanted to go further than they did with the nationalisation of large-scale factories and with the establishment of 'workers' control'; and he never ceased to call for a 'merciless struggle' with the capitalist class in general, including resort to executions and terror.[68] He tended to lay blame on capitalists for their 'greed'' as an explanation of the economy's troubles.[69] This was paradoxical. Lenin in his earlier years as a political and economic theorist had characteristically urged that the subjective motivations of social groups were less important than objective material pressures for a Marxist analysis of economic trends; he had regarded moralism in economics as mere romanticism.[70]

This had a heavy bearing on the prospects of success for

Bolshevik economic policy after the October seizure of power. Lenin rightly maintained that peasant land seizures would not necessarily involve a disruption of agriculture. For a time he even contended that land redistribution would not affect the army's fighting capacity through desertions. Thus the cycle of ploughing, sowing, weeding and reaping was expected by Lenin to proceed as normal.[71]

And yet the incentive to maintain acreages and, even more importantly, to trade with the towns was linked to the chances of boosting production of the industrial goods demanded by peasants. Lenin banked upon a rapid end to the war, and here he was disappointed. Worse than that: Brest-Litovsk robbed the Soviet republic of a huge portion of its best agricultural soil. Even without the collapse of the party's foreign policy there would have been grave problems. The programme of industrial nationalisation and anti-capitalist social legislation was bound to cause a flight of capital and capitalists from Russian industry. Here was Russia's tragedy in 1917. The Mensheviks overestimated what could be obtained through continued cooperation with and moderate pressure on bankers and industrialists, while the Bolsheviks overestimated what would accrue from hostility towards them and intensive pressure on their financial operations. Lenin made no secret of his will to tax the rich extremely heavily and to use violence if the need seemed to arise. He also admitted, and indeed boasted, that his land redistribution policy would involve an assault on private enterprise in the towns since so many estates were mortgaged to banks which were about to be nationalised.[72]

In such circumstances the tacit assumption that state industrial capitalism would long survive was light-headed. Further disruption of the urban sector would consequently have occurred even without Brest-Litovsk. This in turn meant that the rural sector would take all the longer to re-establish its links with the towns. In such circumstances the Bolsheviks under Lenin had no better chance of succeeding with the policies announced by them before October 1917 than the Mensheviks and Socialist Revolutionaries were having with theirs while in ministerial office.

Nothing, however, shook Lenin from his course until he had first tried out his ideas. They were embodied in the 'Decree on the Land' on 26 October 1917. He was not the only author. On the night of the seizure of power, 24–25 October, he and

V.P. Milyutin hastily composed a series of short clauses to deal with the matter.[73] The 242 peasant instructions were declared as government policy. It was still asserted that large capitalist farms would be preserved for the state. But peasants were enjoined to take over the rest of the land through their own local peasant soviets.[74] No mention was made of the food-supplies crisis in the towns.[75] It was hoped that the crisis would somehow be resolved either as a result of an end to the war or because the revolutionary reforms in the towns would rapidly have a beneficent effect on the countryside. The scale of the economic crisis facing the country was not addressed. Nor was the problem of the country's long-term agricultural development. This was an anomalous development for a man who had first come to prominence as a revolutionary theorist for his writings on the agrarian economy. But it was not so surprising for a politician who wanted to seize power, who had limited time for thought and reflection and who needed to inspire his party with the notion that a socialist revolution was both necessary and not unduly difficult.

Not that this means that Lenin misread the entire economic situation. At least he recognised that the peasants were going to get the land and that governmental policy should recognise the fact. Only very belatedly, on the eve of the October seizure of power in Petrograd, did the Mensheviks come to their senses and decide to approve of an immediate expropriation of the gentry;[76] and the Socialist Revolutionaries, despite all the bluster of Chernov in the Provisional Government, never got near to implementing their policy of land socialisation. Moreover, both the Mensheviks and the Socialist Revolutionaries suggested an abolition of the government grain-trade monopoly only months after the October Revolution. They were right to identify this as a principal block to economic reconstruction; but this had not been their perception in 1917. It is anyway far from being self-evident that a programme of privatisation was feasible while Russian armed forces remained at war and millions of soldiers and armaments-producing workers needed to be fed by the state. Lenin and the Bolsheviks were even less inclined than Kadets, Mensheviks and Socialist Revolutionaries to promulgate privatisation, even on a limited scale, until fear of being swept away by a general peasant revolt terrified them into accepting the New Economic Policy in 1921.

From such a vantage point it is hardly astounding that politicians in the period discerned only parts of the problems rather than the problems in their entirety. If Lenin were not so often touted as an all-seeing genius, the verdict on him would not need to be so severe. No one in Russia had the right solution to the economic difficulties. In truth, there was no immediate panacea. Lenin's attitude to the agrarian question shifted in the period of his party's April conference and fell closer into line with the ideas of Stalin and others in the central committee; but the modifications, although they took greater cognisance of the politics of the Russian peasantry, were bound to prove to be inadequate to deal with an horrendous economic emergency.

NOTES

I am grateful to Olga Crisp for lengthy and valuable lunchtime discussions on the theme of this piece. Thanks also to John Channon for pointing me towards the importance of Stalin's articles in 1917; and to Olga Crisp, Maureen Perrie and Bob Davies for alerting me to a statistical blunder in the original conference paper.

1. See, for example, V.I. Lenin, *Polnoe sobranie sochinenii*, 5th edn (Moscow, 1959–65) vol. XXXIV, p. 134. (This edition hereafter *PSS*.)
2. Ibid., vol. XXXI, p. 115.
3. *Sed'maya (aprel'skaya) vserossiiskaya konferentsiya RSDRP (bol'shevikov). Aprel' 1917 goda. Protokoly* (Moscow, 1958) pp. 75–6. (Hereafter abbreviated as *Sed'maya konferentsiya*).
4. See, for example, 'Grozyashchaya katastrofa i kak s nei borot'sya', *PSS*, vol. XXXIV, p. 194. There was not a universal optimism among Bolsheviks about the potential economic efficacy of their measures. See the remarks of their spokesman on economic affairs, V.P. Milyutin, as early as 27 June 1917, in D. Koenker (ed.) *Tret'ya vserossiiskaya konferentsiya professional'nykh soyuzov* (New York and London, 1982) p. 294.
5. See *Gosudarstvo i revolyutsiya*, in *PSS*, vol. XXXIII, pp. 86–91.
6. See E. Kingston-Mann, *Lenin and the Problem of Marxist Peasant Revolution* (Oxford, 1985) pp. 140–4, 149–51 and 172–5; and N. Harding, *Lenin's Political Thought*, vol. II, *Theory and Practice in the Socialist Revolution* (London, 1981) pp. 208–16.
7. See R. Service, *Lenin: A Political Life*, vol. I, *The Strengths of Contradiction* (London, 1985) pp. 132–3, 151–3 and 163.
8. See *Sed'maya konferentsiya*, p. 246 for the incorporation of this phrase in the conference resolution. In his report he had referred to land nationalisation as 'the great bourgeois project', p. 188. See also ibid., p. 235.
9. Ibid., p. 187.

10. *Chertvertyi (Ob"edinitel'nyi) s"ezd RSDRP. Protokoly. Aprel' (aprel'-mai) 1906 goda* (Moscow, 1959) p. 492.
11. Ibid., p. 132.
12. For Kalinin, see *Pravda*, no. 13, 19 Mar. 1917; for Stalin, see ibid., no. 32, 14 Apr. 1917. See also Stalin's speech along the same lines at the sixth party congress: *Shestoi s"ezd RSDRP (bol'shevikov). Avgust 1917 goda. Protokoly.* (Moscow, 1958) pp. 26–7.
13. Ibid. However, Stalin did state in *Pravda* that he favoured the takeover of uncultivated gentry land by peasant communes: see no. 48, 4 May 1917. This was in line with his general wish to let the peasantry get on with the rural revolution.
14. *Sed'maya konferentsiya*, p. 189.
15. However, it must be emphasised that prominent leftists like Bukharin and Osinskii did not expressly espouse collectivisation, or even transitional measures towards it, before the October Revolution. They were satisfied by the formulations produced by Lenin at the April party conference in favour of seeing land nationalisation as a bridgehead towards socialist measures; and they did not take issue with him about the other side of his thinking which dwelt on the survival of capitalism after the socialist seizure of power. Thus the topic became an acute political dispute only in January 1918.
16. See H.R. Buchanan, 'Lenin and Bukharin on the Transition from Capitalism to Socialism: the Meshchersky Controversy, 1918', *Soviet Studies*, 1 (1976) pp. 66–82.
17. For a detailed post-October statement on state capitalism, see *PSS*, vol. XXXVI, pp. 254–5.
18. *Sed'maya konferentsiya*, p. 235.
19. Ibid., p. 190.
20. See O. Crisp, *Studies in the Russian Economy Before 1914* (London, 1976) p. 70; S.M. Dubrovskii, *Sel'skoe khozyaistvo i krest'yanstvo Rossii v period imperializma* (Moscow, 1970) pp. 225; P. Gregory, *Russian National Income, 1885–1913* (Cambridge, 1982) p. 274.
21. *PSS*, vol. XXXI, p. 109.
22. See A.P. Korelin, *Dvoryanstvo v poreformennoi Rossii, 1861–1904 gg. Sostav, chislennost', korporativnaya organizatsiya* (Moscow, 1974) p. 62. I am grateful to Roger Munting for bringing this statistic to my attention.
23. The idea as advocated by Lenin in 1905 was for a limited number of transfers of gentry-owned estates to *assotsiatsii rabochikh* ('associations of workers'). See *PSS*, vol. XI, pp. 220–2.
24. *Sed'maya konferentsiya*, p. 189.
25. *PSS*, vol. XXXII, pp. 195–7.
26. See Service, *Lenin*, vol. I, pp. 66–7.
27. *Resheniya partii i pravitel'stva po khozyaistvennym voprosam*, vol. I, 1917–1928 gody (Moscow, 1967) p. 23. (The promise comes in an announcement of 5 Nov. 1917.) See also *PSS*, vol. XXXIII, pp. 45–6.
28. See n. 26.
29. *PSS*, vol. XXXII, p. 186.
30. Ibid., vol. XXXI, pp. 56, 188, 270, 377.
31. Ibid., pp. 334, 446, 452.

32. Ibid., vol. XXXIV, pp. 206–7.
33. Ibid., vol. XXXII, p. 182.
34. Ibid.
35. Ibid., p. 183.
36. Ibid., pp. 186–8.
37. Ibid., p. 187.
38. Ibid., vol. XXXI, p. 92.
39. Ibid., p. 188.
40. *Sed'maya konferentsiya*, p. 10.
41. For the literature on the shift in Lenin's agrarian ideas after 1905–06, see Service, *Lenin*, vol. I, p. 228.
42. *PSS*, vol. XXXII, p. 44.
43. Ibid., vol. XXXIV, pp. 115–16.
44. Ibid., vol. XXXII, p. 132.
45. Ibid., p. 43.
46. Ibid., pp. 169, 172.
47. *Vladimir Il'ich Lenin. Biograficheskaya khronika*, vol. IV (Moscow, 1973) pp. 56ff.
48. *PSS*, vol. XXXIV, pp. 115–16. See also G. Gill, *Peasants and Government in the Russian Revolution* (London, 1979) ch. 3.
49. *PSS*, vol. XXXIV, pp. 115–16.
50. *Protokoly Tsentral'nogo Komiteta RSDRP (b). Avgust 1917–fevral' 1918* (Moscow, 1958) p. 38.
51. *Pravda*, no. 51, 7 May 1917.
52. *Shestoi s"ezd*, pp. 14–20.
53. See notes 12 and 13.
54. *Shestoi s"ezd*, pp. 14–20.
55. Ibid.
56. *PSS*, vol. XXXIV, p. 115.
57. Ibid., pp. 115–16.
58. Ibid., vol. XXXII, pp. 186–7.
59. See n. 12.
60. *PSS*, vol. XXXIV, p. 234.
61. Ibid., pp. 109–16.
62. See P.V. Volobuev, *Ekonomicheskaya politika Vremennogo pravitel'stva* (Moscow, 1962) *passim*, for a discussion of the governmental and soviet data.
63. *PSS*, vol. XXXIV, p. 194.
64. This is not to say that he did not talk of the 'ruin' and 'crisis' facing the country. See, for example, ibid., vol. XXXII, pp. 74–6 and 105–11.
65. Ibid., vol. XXXIV, pp. 151–99.
66. See, for example, ibid., vol. XXXI, pp. 355, 443.
67. R. Browder and A.F. Kerensky (eds) *The Russian Provisional Government 1917: Documents* (Stanford, 1961) vol. II, pp. 674–5, vol. III, pp. 1481, 1484–6; and *Tret'ya vserossiiskaya konferentsiya professional'nykh soyuzov*, pp. 305–14.
68. *PSS*, vol. XXXIV, pp. 37, 174.
69. See, for example, his stinging remarks on fraud and corruption in ibid., pp. 173–4.
70. See Lenin's economic writings against the narodniki in the 1890s, especially

The Economic Content of Narodnichestvo, in ibid., vol. I, pp. 347–534.
71. *PSS*, vol. XXXII, pp. 178–9.
72. Ibid., vol. XXXIV, pp. 110–11.
73. See the account by E.A. Lutskii, 'Zasedanie TsK RSDRP (b), noch'yu 24–25 oktyabrya 1917 g.', *Voprosy istorii KPSS*, 11 (1986) 89–90.
74. *Resheniya partii i pravitel'stva*, pp. 15–17.
75. Ibid.
76. F. Dan, 'K istorii poslednikh dnei Vremennogo pravitel'stva', *Letopis' revolyutsii*, I (1923) pp. 170–4.

10 Land Revolution and Land Reform:

The Case of the Central Black-Earth Region, 1917–24

John Channon

INTRODUCTION

For the half-century preceding the 1917 Revolution, the central black-earth region (hereafter the CBE) had been the area of European Russia most associated with agricultural backwardness. Land and labour productivity were low and the degree of commercialisation and capitalist relations minimal, while the commune, with its myriad inconvenient land arrangements, remained dominant. Loss of land and the new economic burdens resulting from the emancipation from serfdom 'pushed' the CBE peasants into a national market at a time when the region was at the forefront of Russia's grain marketing, but the region proved unable to cope with competition on both the internal and external fronts. The subsequent fall in international agricultural prices principally affected landowners' incomes but had a knock-on effect for peasants via increased rent levels.[1] Notwithstanding current debates as to whether there was a general 'agrarian crisis' in the late nineteenth century, few would deny the appropriateness of such a term to the CBE. While distribution of land per capita was one of the lowest in the country by 1917, more general agricultural decline in the region can be witnessed by the statistics on gross output per person in four of its provinces between the late 1880s and 1913.[2] (See Table 10.1). Such impoverishment was an important factor in explaining the widespread peasant unrest in the region during 1905–6, while peasant rental of non-peasant lands, indicative of the intricacies of landowner-peasant ties, was most widespread in this region (as well as the neighbouring middle Volga) and was a major peasant grievance a decade later. In 1917, five of the CBE

TABLE 10.1 *Gross output per person, four provinces, 1887–1913 (in rubles, at pre-war prices)*

Province	*1887*	*1901*	*1913*
Orel	51.9	37.4	28.5
Kursk	51.9	36.8	35.7
Voronezh	55.3	34.3	39.1
Tambov	52.1	41.8	32.1

SOURCE I.D. Balashov, ed., *Agrarnoe dvizhenie v TsChOv v 1917 godu*, vyp. I (Voronezh, 1930) p. 16.

provinces (*gubernii*) were amongst the twelve in European Russia most affected by peasant unrest. The height of unrest that year was reached in early September and centred on Kozlovsk district (*uezd*) in Tambov province.[3]

Such relative backwardness had other implications for the region's agrarian development. Firstly, the insignificant degree of differentiation within the peasantry in the CBE has been seen as a consequence of a predominantly subsistence agriculture.[4] This provided a rationale for strong communalism, manifested in the risk-averse strategies and subsistence insurance mechanisms of land redivision, three-field strip farming and so forth. It naturally followed that in the CBE the mir should constitute the chief vehicle for rural revolution. Secondly, as is well known, some of the most violent excesses of the agrarian revolutions of both 1905 and 1917 occurred here. This was a manifestation of the serf-like landlord-peasant relations that still persisted in the region, as well as a symptom of the conflict sown amongst the CBE peasantry by the Stolypin land reforms. The failure of the reform here was probably due as much as anything to the immiseration of the peasantry, while many separations appear to have been executed against the will of the community.[5]

The CBE was clearly one of the regions most in need of agricultural assistance before the 1917 Revolution, while the acute land shortage made the acquisition of additional land a central peasant demand. In this respect, the region provides a good case study for examining the impact of revolution on peasant land use and the effects of land reorganisation in mitigating or eliminating its worst aspects in the early years of Soviet power.

THE LAND REVOLUTION 1917–18

The events of the 1917–18 revolution in the CBE countryside have been discussed elsewhere.[6] Attention in this paper is focused on its outcome. Even though many writers have stressed that much non-peasant land was already used by the peasantry (through renting, for example) before 1917, they often fail to stress that peasants were unable to rearrange this land with their own, to enable greater efficiency in land use. Thus, land additions after the Revolution may have been smaller than expected, but there were other advantages which could accrue to the peasantry from gaining direct control over the land. The main problem stemmed from the fact that a locally determined land reform, which pitted village against village and community against community (and even in some instances volost against volost), only served to worsen the organisation of land now under peasant use, thus making land reform all the more necessary.

To appreciate why land use arrangements in some areas of the CBE became even more complex after 1917 requires some discussion of the reasons for the more radical redivisions of land in the region. A peculiar situation had developed by the spring of 1918 which reduced the potential area available to those CBE peasants primarily engaged in agriculture before the Revolution. Although relatively rare in European Russia generally, radical or general redivisions, where all land was pooled and redivided – in the parlance of rural Russia, black repartitions or *chernye peredely* – were most common in the CBE. In some respects this was not surprising. The region had been known previously for its radical stance on the land issue, a reputation that was confirmed by peasant deputies when they expressed their views in the Duma and to the Constituent Assembly.[7] Several reasons, relating to the region's backwardness, may be also be adduced to explain this phenomenon, although communal forms of land holding and redivisional land practices had remained alive and strong. Thus if the land issue were to be determined locally, it would be natural for the peasantry in the CBE to seek solutions within a communal framework. Other factors, however, operated in the spring to complicate matters.

Instances of general redivisions in the CBE resulted from particular circumstances that arose in the spring of 1918. Before the Revolution, a large number of peasants in the region sought

TABLE 10.2 *The number of families returning to the CBE countryside, spring 1918*

No. of villages replying	*No. of families which returned on average per village*
103	6.6

SOURCE Ya. Blyakher, 'Sovremennoe zemlepol'zovanie po dannym spetsial'noi ankety TSSU 1922 g.', *Vestnik statistiki*, vol. XIII, nos. 1–3.

TABLE 10.3 *The attitude of communities to families returning and to their setting up households (CBE), Spring 1918*

Land allocated to returning families			*Returning families who established households*		
No. of villages replying	*% of villages*		*No. of villages replying*	*% of villages which*	
	allotted land	*not allotted land*		*established households*	*did not establish households*
150	97	3	122	52	48

SOURCE Blyakher, as above, p. 143.

off-farm earnings (the so-called *otkhodniki*), while there was a considerable number of full-time workers in the cities who still maintained links with their villages. Many full-time workers and peasants returned to their villages during the winter of 1917–18 and the early spring (many *otkhodniki* never leaving for work in the first place that year) to claim a share of land. A large number of landless and poor peasants, many of whom had formerly provided the labour force for the estates, now clamoured for land or more of it. This was at the same time as many younger, better-educated peasants, imbued with radicalism from the army, were returning from the front. According to one survey, 97 per cent of those returning to the CBE provinces received land and just over half were able to establish their own households.[8] [See Tables 10.2 and 10.3].

An additional factor was to place further pressure on land resources in the region. Not only did people migrate back to their native villages. There was also an influx of individuals from other areas (sometimes accompanied by families too) referred to

TABLE 10.4 *Land allocated to newcomers in CBE, Spring 1918*

No. of villages replying	*% of villages in which newcomers*	
	received land	*did not receive land*
177	74	26

SOURCE Blyakher, as above, p. 144.

as 'newcomers' or 'aliens' (the *prishlye*). The attitude of the CBE peasants towards these newcomers appeared welcoming in the extreme, with 74 per cent of them being allocated land, the highest percentage so favoured of all the regions covered by the survey.[9] [see Table 10.4] To be sure, this situation was due to pressure exerted on the CBE by outsiders, though there was also good reason locally for accepting some such migrants. A shortage of agricultural equipment and other metal items, caused by the economic situation in the spring of 1918, meant that these newcomers were welcomed if they possessed the necessary skills (and equipment) and could assist the local peasant economy.[10] The greatest incidence of those returning to their native villages, and of newcomers being accepted, occurred in the CBE.[11] Furthermore, the elements of justice and fairness contained in the peasant notion of *chernyi peredel*, provoked calls for land to be allocated to all tillers, that is, all those who were prepared to cultivate it without hired labour, and this could include former gentry landowners (*pomeshchiki*) and clergy, further increasing the number of recipients of land.

In the light of this, the occurrence of general repartitions should not seem surprising. The mir was responding to the economic and social circumstances of 1918 in precisely the same way as it had always done under similar conditions. Whenever the population to land ratio and/or demands from outsiders changed dramatically, the redivisional community had activated its function of land repartition.[12] As before 1917, when periodic repartition of land was the only method by which individual cases of severe land shortage could be alleviated, the mir responded to the mass influx into the community in 1918 by the only means at its disposal – the redivision of all land now under the community's control. This included all peasant land, both communal and privately-owned, as well as all non-peasant privately-owned lands, even though the latter was often divided separately from former peasant lands.[13] As of old, the only way in which newcomers into the community could enforce their right to 'lots' of land was by means of a completely new reallocation of land.

To be sure, some *chernye peredely* occurred because of the traditional rule that such redivisions were permissible if favoured by two-thirds of all the community. As there is evidence that such regulations were not adhered to in the late nineteenth century – when a simple majority and even a significant minority could push through a full redivision – it comes as no surprise to discover similar occurrences under far more unstable conditions, especially when the significant minorities were young, aggressive and armed.[14] Finally, communities in the CBE were in a far better position to implement general redivisions than in areas which had ceased division before the Revolution: they had more recent redivisional experience and could quickly elect communal officers with responsibility for the redivision (such as measurers and dividers) and this doubtless contributed to the speed of repartition.[15]

Clearly this situation in the spring of 1918 reduced the area available to the agricultural peasants of the CBE. Overall, the area of land under direct peasant control in the region did increase after the Revolution, but the average increases per capita were small. Although we should not place too much reliability on the commonly cited figures from Narkomzem (People's Commissariat for Agriculture) for the average 'additions' per capita for each province, even adjusted figures are still low.[16] In four CBE provinces, land use per household in 1918 had risen from its pre-1917 level by 32.9 per cent in Kursk, 30.9 per cent in Orel, 19.5 per cent in Tambov and 18.8 per cent in Voronezh.[17] Furthermore, the problem with any land reform determined locally was the enormous differentials that would arise in the distribution of land between volosts and between communities and villages within a volost. A sample of 11 volost norms in Ryazan province revealed a variation of 0.25 to 1.4 desyatins. In Zadonsk district of Voronezh province, the variation in village norms was not so great, though still considerable: 0.62 to 1.4 desyatins.[18] According to plans worked out by the district land authorities in 1918, land distribution between volosts should have been more equitable via transfers and so on, though few of these plans were realised. Even so, this related to land and did nothing to improve peasant ability to use it.[19]

But quantitative changes were not the only problems to arise from the land revolution. More qualitative aspects, such as the difficulties concerning peasant arrangement and use of land, were just as significant. In non-black earth regions, *chernye peredely* had often been employed to enable a more rational distribution of land among the peasantry within the mir or village. In the CBE, black repartitions were resorted to so as to satisfy all those demanding a share of land. Radical redivisions here were rarely to allow improvements in the arrangement of peasant land. The emphasis on localism – with each village or mir frequently demanding allocations from land belonging to its 'own' *pomeshchik* – often meant in practice that land additions were unusable, being situated in another volost and intermingled with the land of other communities and villages, or located at a great distance from the peasant place of residence. Thus land was increasingly divided into yet more and narrower strips, often inconveniently situated. These difficulties were further complicated by annual redivisions of land in subsequent years – usually minor adjustments to the general redistributions of 1917 or 1918.[20]

By the mid-1920s the land situation in the CBE was once again desperate. The increase in rural population, together with an upsurge in the number of peasant households (through splitting), had virtually eliminated any increases in land use per household that had arisen from the Revolution. While the percentage of the population listed as urban in the CBE was less than one third of the figure for the entire European USSR, in two provinces (Voronezh and Orel), the percentage was even lower than that recorded in 1897. By 1924 average land use per household in Kursk and Orel had decreased to *below* the 1917 level, while it remained at the same level in Tambov and exceeded that level (by some 13 per cent) only in Voronezh.[21] The CBE was the only region to show an increase between 1918 and 1922 in the percentage of villages allocated land in accordance with the eater (per capita) criterion, the basic subsistence allocative unit.[22] In the overcrowded CBE, rural population density increased significantly by the year, and many areas were land short, especially in Kursk and Orel, by 1924.[23] Even if we accept that data on land use are imprecise, land reorganisation was clearly necessary, as were initiatives to promote *promysli*, migration to urban areas and resettlement in other regions. Certainly land redistribution in much of the CBE had to be considered complete – or near complete – by 1924, since any future apportionment would have to come from the state land fund and in two provinces (Orel and Kursk) this fund was already exhausted by then.[24]

This situation is doubtless one reason why the presence of some former *pomeshchiki*, though small in absolute terms, was a source of conflict in the CBE countryside by the mid 1920s. Any further encroachment on peasants' land in a situation of acute land shortage was perceived by them as a threat to their security. There were reports of former *pomeshchiki* who had received parts of their former estates either after 1917 or during the early 1920s, creating an impediment to peasant farming. Clearly they reduced the area available to the local peasantry, but it was also alleged that they interfered with peasant production by, for example, grazing their cattle on land sown by peasants.[25]

A less fettered peasant agriculture emerged in the CBE after the Revolution, but improvements in its agricultural efficiency required land reform that would enable rearrangement of land now used by peasants. This was begun in 1919, though limited in its effect during the next two years, because of ideological design – the intention of promoting collectives – and the food crisis of the civil war, the two factors being not unconnected. The focus in the following sections of this paper will be on these reorganisation measures and their impact on peasant land use in the CBE between 1919 and 1924; that is, until official views on the role of land reorganisation began to change in the new political and economic climate.

LAND REFORM AND LAND REORGANISATION

Land reorganisation (*zemleustroistvo*) refers to changes in land use, primarily through the physical reorganisation of land, to facilitate the practising of agriculture on a more rational basis. Clearly this could include better arrangements for land use within a communal structure, including the division of large communities into a number of new, smaller settlements, as well as the consolidation and enclosure of land either for individual peasant use or for use by collective and state farms. Reorganisation of peasant land use was a central concern of the last tsarist land reform (see below), though its attempt to abolish communal land tenure and communal arrangements for land use and replace them with individually consolidated land areas and private farms stood in contradiction to peasant aspirations throughout much of European Russia and the CBE in particular.

After 1917, the situation was more fluid. On the one hand, peasants desired both more land and the freedom to create more efficient use of the land which was now under their control. Thus, the peasant demand for *chernyi peredel* contained both quantitative and qualitative notions, which might be differentiated by agrarian specialists into land revolution and land reform. Without the elimination of non-peasant owners who retained intermixing and ownership of meadows, forests and water resources etc., qualitative change was impossible. On the other hand, government, the various national, regional and local commissariats of agriculture, and the agricultural specialists (chiefly agronomists, surveyors and land reorganisers), all possessed their own notion of land reform 'from above'. Thus one may speak of at least three strands of land reform emerging during 1918–20: that of the peasants; that of the Bolsheviks with their orthodox Marxist notions of the creation of state and collective farms (the 'big is beautiful' ideology); and that of the Left SRs and the agrarian specialists (the two often overlapping) who worked in the provincial and district (and even occasionally, the volost) land departments preparing norms and plans for land redistribution.[26] The specialists frequently acted independently of government with their own ideas of what best constituted land reform for the peasants, while different types of specialist did not necessarily share a uniform view of land reform. And all presented their views to (or wished to impose them on) the peasantry, some corresponding more closely to peasant notions than others.

Before proceeding to discuss the land reorganisation that occurred during 1917–24, a word is required on the sources used and most importantly, perhaps, the question of what the statistics and maps actually reveal. Do the statistics show what the specialists intended to achieve (that is, what was on paper) rather than what was actually realised? Did policy-makers and specialists have a 'model' of land reform with which they worked and were the maps really an attempt to realise such a model? How all this related to what was happening to peasant land is the question that concerns us here. While accepting that the statistics need to be treated with caution (especially for the Civil War years) and that the land maps are probably more accurately described as land plans, that is, representations of what was intended rather than accurate geographical reconstructions of what was achieved in the countryside, much of the reorganisation discussed here does seem to have been in line with peasant aspirations. Certainly the data for the early 1920s provide an indication of the trends that were beginning to emerge, while the land maps give an idea of how improvements in peasant land use were developing. It is with such caveats in mind, however, that land reorganisation will be discussed.

1919–21: The Period of Socialist Land Reorganisation

The period known in Bolshevik parlance as 'socialist land reorganisation' (*sotsialisticheskoe zemleustroistvo*) commenced from February 1919 with the issuing of the 'Basic Law', marking the point at which legislation was to emphasise the consolidation of large land areas for use by collective and state farms. Only from this time did initiatives emanate from the centre to assist peasants, albeit in a limited way, with a more convenient arrangement of land. The Narkomzem initiated a programme of land reform (socialist land reorganisation), to be implemented via 'Instructions' of March and through land organs set up in May. Although a key part of the programme was clearly devoted to the promotion of collective forms of agriculture (the majority of articles in the edict of February are concerned with these and most of the literature, both western and Soviet, emphasise them), measures were also included which enabled improvements in the organisation and arrangement of land now under peasant use. It is on these latter measures that attention will be focused here.[27]

For the whole of European Russia the best estimate to date suggests that socialist land reorganisation during 1919–21 was planned to cover just under 126 million desyatins and was executed over 70.7 million. How much of that supposedly 'executed' remained on paper is open to surmise, and this caveat applies equally to work on individual regions such as the CBE. The figures cover all types of measures, although the emphasis on the various types differed according to province. Such measures varied from 'preparations' for land reform – calculating land areas, taking new population censuses and producing land maps – and the drawing up of biennial work plans for each province (dividing the work into two categories, 'special' and 'ordinary'), to the establishment of boundaries of land actually in the use of volosts, villages and communities (often to resolve disputes which had prevented the land from being used) and work on so-called group land reorganisation. Most attention here will be concentrated on the latter, which comprised two basic types of work: the allocation of land to volosts (after sorting out boundaries); and the allocation of land within volosts, to villages and communities. In this latter case, work could comprise sorting out boundaries, apportioning land to individual communities and villages in one integral or consolidated area, and dividing up the larger villages and communities so that new settlements (*poselki* or *vyselki*) were created, usually still using communal tenure. Allocations of land to collectives were included in both of these categories. This group of measures constituted a minority in the area where reorganisation took place, but receives disproportionate coverage in Soviet works which discuss socialist land reorganisation.[28]

Unfortunately the data on reorganisation work for 1919–21 provide no indication of how the work was divided by region although most provinces fared badly in completing work planned for 1920 and 1921. Out of 38 provinces on which information was available, three CBE ones came within the top third or so, as can be seen from Table 10.5. A table covering the period 1919–26 provides an indication of the CBE's share of just two types of reorganisation work, though admittedly the main types in our period. (see Table 10.6) This reveals that work on reorganisation between villages in the CBE comprised 15.8 per cent of all such work in the RSFSR (excluding autonomous republics) but covering 53.6 per cent of the CBE's agricultural area, while the respective figures for work within villages was 9.7 and 16.9 per cent.

Much of the reorganisation work in the CBE during 1919–21 comprised allocations of land anew within a volost. Excluding collectives, this largely involved communities and villages. Advances in the farming of individual peasant households in the CBE were largely dependent on the initial consolidation of land by entire communities and villages. Communities often held

TABLE 10.5 *Percentage of measures completed (of those planned), 1920 and 1921*

Province	*position of 38 provinces*	*% of land reorganisation measures completed by*		
	1920	*1920 (at 1 Nov)*	*1921*	*at*
Voronezh	2	55.1	70.5	1 Nov
Ryazan	13	14.1	16.0	1 Nov
Tambov	14	13.6	36.1	1 Nov
Bryansk*	15	13.0	13.0	1 Nov (1920)
Orel	24	4.6	4.2	1 Sept**
Tula	29	1.6	13.0	1 Nov
Kursk	36	0.0	19.2	1 April

SOURCE A.K. Berzin in *O zemle*, vol. I (Moscow, 1921) pp. 174–6.
* Bryansk was created from part of Orel province.
** The lower percentage completed in 1921 as against 1920 is explained by errors made in the localities when compiling the reports (in particular, showing work still being carried out, as completed) corrected when later reports were prepared, and/or the different number of volosts due to the new administrative structure.

TABLE 10.6 *Land reorganisation work in CBE as proportion of that for RSFSR, 1919–1926*

1	*2*	*3*	*4*	*5*	*6*
Region	*agricultural area (des)*	*between villages*	*3 as % of 2*	*within villages*	*5 as % of 2*
C. Agricultural	17 326 000	9 279 716	53.6	2 937 260	16.9
RSFSR (excluding autonomous republics	251 326 000	58 927 047	23.4	30 420 229	12.1
C. Agriculture as % of RSFSR	6.9	15.8		9.7	

SOURCE I. Shuleikin, 'Na RSFSR-ovskom zemleustroitel'nom fronte', *Na agrarnom fronte*, 2 (1928) p. 87.

land in several parcels (plus meadows and woodland in common) and it was necessary to unravel and divide up these lands between communities. Almost without exception, this involved the elimination of the single plan villages.[29] The objective here was to allocate to each community and village an integral area of land (or if this were not possible, two or three consolidated areas) which it could then divide between its members as it saw fit. Attention was also devoted to the splitting up of large communities and the creation of several smaller new settlements (*poselki*). Responsibility for organising these allocations of land fell to the surveyor who was attached to the volost or the one nearest. Only on very rare occasions were allocations made through commissions (*porucheniya*) created specially for the task. Hence the importance attached to surveyors, and hence an explanation of the many reports that revealed little planned work having been executed because of the dearth of surveyors.[30]

According to data from the CBE's Department of Land Reorganisation and Amelioration, new allocations of land within volosts were carried out over 23.2 per cent of the total area of the four provinces (Voronezh, Kursk, Tambov and Orel) covered in the study.[31] Of perhaps greater significance is that 77.1 per cent of this land reorganisation occurred within only one province – Voronezh – where new allocations within volosts covered half of the entire area of the province. On average that would mean only about 7.6 per cent of the measures for each of the remaining three provinces. Furthermore, the area covered by such land reorganisation measures in Voronezh province accounted for 18.4 per cent of the entire area subject to reorganisation in the Union. And one district alone – Zadonsk – was the subject of special investigation for its work on reorganisation.[32] One of the main reasons for the relatively high completion rate in Voronezh province was the success achieved in simplifying the technical work of reorganisation, which doubtless facilitated reorganisation over a much wider area. In particular, it became easier to overcome many of the inconvenient practices in land use resulting from the earlier peasant redistributions of land.[33] A factor not unconnected to this technical success, as well as to land reorganisation generally in the province, was the presence of its famous Agricultural Institute, with such leading specialists as P.N. Pershin. Even in this province, however, most of the work affected only its northern half: the extreme south-east, for example, was barely touched by such measures because of the civil war and peasant unrest.

On completion of these intra-volost allocations, each land unit (whether community, village, or collective) received its land in permanent use within defined boundaries. The 'allocations' might merely have served to confirm the boundaries once any

TABLE 10.7 *Number of land-user units* (zemlepol'zovateli) *and their* uchastki *according to the results of* zemleustroistvo *in Voronezh province*

District	*Number of land-users*	*Number of* uchastki *created*	Uchastki *per land-user*
Bobrovsk	380	392	1.03
Bogucharsk	11	11	1.00
Valuisk	293	365	1.25
Voronezhsk	645	810	1.26
Nizhnedevitsk	293	310	1.06
Novokhopersk	108	123	1.14
Ostrogozhsk	343	380	1.11
Rossoshansk	153	173	1.12
Usmansk	336	400	1.19
Total	2562	2964	1.16

SOURCE Sazonov, in Tatarchukov, p. 117 (see Table 10.8).

disputes had been resolved or they might have referred to each unit receiving a consolidated portion (or portions) of land in such use. These latter reallocations significantly reduced the great distances that formerly separated land between villages.[34] Each village in the volost undergoing reorganisation received a separate portion of land (*uchastok*) or a few portions which reduced or eliminated inter-village (or extra-village) intermingling. Table 10.7 shows how this was achieved in Voronezh province, where most such units (generally communities and villages) received land in one portion, about one-quarter of them in two portions and a few in three portions.

Much of the work on reallocation of land within volosts related to the establishment of new settlements (*poselki*). The predominance of certain types of reorganisation work in particular regions was related to the measures considered by specialists as most appropriate for improving agriculture there, though this appeared to be in keeping with peasant desires too. Before the Revolution, government attempts to resettle the peasantry on an individual basis, that is through *khutora*, occurred principally in the north-west and the west, and in the south and south-east through the creation of *otruba*.[35] The Stolypin reforms achieved little success in the CBE region. Although impoverishment was an important factor in this process, natural topographical features were important too. Poor water supplies did not favour such separation into *khutora*, while the *otrub* was not rational since, within large villages, a large area of *otrub* land would be situated at a significant distance from the farmstead and would probably impede agricultural development even more than current community practices.

Thus, during 1919–21, the emphasis was placed on community settlement anew, in other words, the splitting up of large communities and villages into smaller settlements (the process known as *poselkovoe rasselenie*). Intermingling of strips was characteristic of large villages and when reallocating such intermixed land it was necessary to consider whether the land was supplied with water and whether settlement would be possible there in future. Once a village was divided into smaller units, moreover, each was then considered an independent unit for the purposes of land reorganisation. Several benefits in land use accrued from this resettlement. The great distance between the strips themselves, and between the strips and the peasants' place of residence, were reduced while, in general, more favourable conditions for agricultural progress were created. Claims were also made that the division of larger communities into smaller settlements resulted in 'more intensive farming and a higher sown area per worker'. True, settlements usually contained more household members (both eaters and workers), and possessed more horses and a larger sown area than those households which remained in the original village.[36] Yet, virtually all the settlements which transferred to multifield crop rotation systems preferred to retain communal land tenure.[37]

During 1919–21, such a form of 'communal settlement anew' occurred in at least three provinces of the CBE – Voronezh, Orel and Tambov – according to information from the provincial land amelioration agencies (*gubmeliozemy*), and in Ryazan province from 1920. In Voronezh province the allocation of land for settlements was just one part of the overall process of allotting land anew within volosts, whereas in other provinces it usually occurred as an independent land reorganisation operation.[38] The details of this resettlement can be seen in Table 10.8. No such work seems to have occurred in Kursk province or in Bogucharsk, Rossoshansk and Usmansk districts of Voronezh province and Tambovsk district of Tambov province.[39] Nor have details for this type of work been found for Tula province.

TABLE 10.8 *Resettlement in the central black-earth* oblast′ *(1919–21) (all* uezdy *researched in four provinces)*

Provinces and districts	*No. of* poselki	*Allotted area (hectares)*	*Average size of area per* poselok *(hectares)*	*% of allotted land to area of* trud. zem.
Voronezh	(191)	(92 856)	(486)	(1.6)
1. Botrovsk	88	46 490	528	7.1
2. Bogucharsk	–	–	–	–
3. Valuisk	8	3 127	391	0.6
4. Voronezhsk	9	2 692	299	0.4
5. Nizhnedevitsk	4	981	245	0.2
6. Novokhopersk	30	22 298	743	4.6
7. Ostrogorsk	52	17 268	332	2.3
8. Rossoshansk	–	–	–	–
9. Usmansk	–	–	–	–
Kursk				
10. Belgorodsk	–	–	–	–
11. Graivoronsk	–	–	–	–
12. Kursk	–	–	–	–
13. L′govsk	–	–	–	–
14. Ryl′sk	–	–	–	–
15. Starvokol′sk	–	–	–	–
16. Shchirovsk	–	–	–	–
Orel	(580)	(70 770)	(122)	(2.9)
17. Bolkhovsk	105	11 931	113	5.5
18. Dmitrovsk	286	35 627	125	19.5
19. Eletsk	8	830	104	0.1
20. Livensk	6	968	161	0.2
21. Maloarkhangel′sk	51	6 781	133	1.6
22. Orlovsk	124	14 640	118	2.6
Tambov	(253)	(72 165)	(287)	(1.8)
23. Borisoglebsk	107	30 564	286	4.8
24. Kirsanovsk	82	25 108	306	4.0
25. Kozlovsk	4	2 206	552	0.3
26. Lipetsk	36	6 741	187	1.2
27. Morshansk	24	7 546	314	1.4
28. Tambovsk	–	–	–	–
Total for four provinces	1 024	235 791	230	1.5

SOURCE K.N. Sazonov, 'Zemlepol'zovanie i zemleustroistvo v tsentral'no-chernozemnoi oblasti posle revolyutsii', in A.N. Tatarchukov (ed.) 'Materialy po izucheniyu voprosa o vosstanovlenii khozyaistva TsChO', *Trudy Planovoi Komissii TsChO*, vol. I (Voronezh, 1926), pp. 135–6.

In the remaining CBE provinces this type of reorganisation was less widespread. More attention was devoted to *preparing* for land reform – and principally to calculating the land area – and to other measures, such as the allocation of land for collectives. In Ryazan province, for instance, the majority of work in 1919 concerned the setting up of collectives (although from 1920 work also commenced on partitioning villages and creating new settlements) while other measures to reduce and eliminate intermingling and the distance between strips had to wait until 1921.[40] (see Table 10.9) Even then little of the work planned for the winter 1920/21 – in the province's work schedule – had been achieved by the following June, the only 'basic' work of any note being

TABLE 10.9 *Land reorganisation in Ryazan province, 1919–21 (area in desyatins)*

Nature of work	*1919*		*1920*		*1921*	
	no.	*area*	*no.*	*area*	*no.*	*area*
Collective (*kommuny, arteli, obshchie zapashki*)	41	2 895	26	1 948	52	8 624
Group land reorganisation:						
(a) division of settlements *poselki, vyselki*	–	–	8	2 264	12	9 281
(b) elimination of interming., *dal'nozem*	–	–	–	–	6	38 969
Consolidation of actual land use	–	–	–	–	2	610
Other work (*sovkhozy*, state institutions, enterprises, *usad'by*, towns)	70	7 172	37	8 558	13	3 467
Total	111	10 067	71	12 770	85	60 951

SOURCE I. Bystrakov, 'Zemel'nye otnosheniya i zemleustroistvo v Ryazanskoi gubernii v period 1917–1921 gg.', in *Moskovskii Institut Inzhenerov zemleustroistva, Nauchnye trudy*, XLIII (1970) p. 82.

that on land calculations.[41] Thus work planned for completion in the summer of 1921 contained much that was left over from previous periods. In Tula province land reorganisation only commenced from the spring of 1920 and made slow progress in the next few years. In Tambov province most of the work at the beginning of 1920 was concentrated on sorting out volost boundaries and producing land surveys, the absence of which had earlier been held responsible for the lack of progress in land reorganisation.[42]

LAND REORGANISATION IN THE CBE UNDER EARLY NEP, 1922–24

The adoption of the New Economic Policy led to a reassessment of the role and nature of land reorganisation by the Bolsheviks, ushering in measures deemed more appropriate to the new economic conditions and political climate. Attempts at 'equalisation of land use', a central tenet of socialist land reorganisation, now came to an end and such tasks were excluded. General stability in the use of land demanded that the area in possession of each peasant household be affirmed on a permanent basis. By the law of 22 May 1922 (subsequently incorporated in the October land code) the area of land currently worked by volosts, villages and communities – and which had been legally allotted to them – was fixed for their permanent working use. Where there was no conflict between villages over land use, this use was confirmed via a process of state registration (*zapis'*). Once registration had occurred, it then became possible to attempt to satisfy demands for reorganisation within villages, between households, sometimes referred to as household reorganisation (*podvornoe zemleustroistvo*).[43] Thus a new programme of land reorganisation officially commenced from the summer of 1922. In practice, as far as both agrarian specialists and peasants were concerned, there was more continuity than this would suggest. For instance, reorganisation according to the edict of February 1919 was to be abolished, yet allocations of land within volosts (initiated after the edict) were to be completed in cases where the draft plans were still being worked out.[44] Other measures begun in 1919–21 also continued into the NEP, as will be shown below.

By 1922 a complex situation had developed regarding peasant

use of land. Not least of these problems were the grievances that had to be resolved. Some villages in the course of 1919–21 had actually lost land when it had been cut off from their volost and transferred to another, with the intention that another portion of land would be acquired from the latter in a future exchange. The long term aim, of course, had been to provide each volost with its own consolidated land area. The cessation of socialist land reorganisation now officially brought this to a halt, even if not in practice, as already noted. Elsewhere – particularly in the south-eastern part of the CBE, such as Bogucharsk and Kalacheevsk districts – inequalities in land use arising from the land redistributions of the revolutionary years had now been consolidated by the 1922 decree. It was for such reasons that the number of disputes over land swelled in the early 1920s while peasants in these areas still expected an equal repartition – a *chernyi peredel* – in the future.[45]

Other complications arose too. By the end of the field period (1 May–1 October 1922) land reorganisation institutions were inundated with requests for assistance from peasants, largely as a consequence of the poor harvest. Thus many of the reorganisation tasks planned for 1922 were postponed to the following year. In addition, reorganisation work required finance. The cost of resettlement could prove a considerable burden for the households involved, worsening where settlements were established on virgin lands. Although poor peasants were freed from paying for land reorganisation by a *Sovnarkom* resolution of 14 June 1923, government credit to assist such work in villages and communities began only in 1924.[46] Thus peasants had to fund such work themselves. This was the case in several volosts of Voronezh province to enable work on reallocating land within volosts to continue. It also occurred in Orel province where peasants were especially concerned to split up large villages and communities, thereby eradicating 'external' intermingling and the great distance between strips. In many cases, as during 1919–21, the surveyors relied on the hospitality of households in the community during the course of the reorganisation.[47]

In the first year of this new programme of reorganisation a sizeable proportion of the overall work related to the CBE. Of the four regions researched in a study published by the State Colonisation and Scientific Research Institute, covering the period 1 May 1922 to 1 October 1923, (the first two field seasons of the new programme), 40.2 per cent of all work was devoted to the CBE. For individual categories of measures the region accounted for between 65.5 per cent to just under 25 per cent.[48] (see Table 10.10) For all three years (1922–4), based on data taken from a study by the *gubmeliozemy*, the total area of land subject to reorganisation was increasing annually, though, as shown in Table 10.11, the pace was slowing noticeably. The work was also unevenly distributed by province (see Table 10.12), with Orel's showing being particularly poor. Both Kursk and Tambov soon caught up after their slow start during 1919–21, with the latter assuming the leading position amongst the CBE provinces in 1923 and 1924. The most important types of measures concerned inter- and intra-village work, together accounting for 78 per cent of all work during 1922–4 and even higher percentages for individual years.[49] Identifying and sorting out boundaries and the land allocations that then followed, assumed importance only in 1922, amounting to 35 per cent of all work (see Table 10.13), and this is explained by the exceptionally high percentage (71.8) of work devoted to it in Kursk that year. Inter-village work was consistently high in Tambov province while work on reorganisation within villages was highest in Orel.[50] In fact, this latter category of work was increasing annually in all provinces except Tambov (Tables 10.14 and 10.15). These variations were a reflection of the prevailing political, social and economic conditions, together with the natural and topographical features, within each province.

Further information is available on how reorganisation measures were divided by year for each district within the four provinces, revealing considerable inter-district variation. (see Figure 10.1) This is partly explained by the paucity of personnel engaged in work on land reorganisation, as well as their inequitable distribution between districts. Although some 691 specialists (including surveyors and reorganisation officers) were deemed to be at work for Narkomzem in the CBE in the autumn of 1921, this was clearly below the 1918 and pre-revolutionary levels. Specific local factors also played their part in these variations.[51]

The remainder of this section will discuss the three principal types of land reorganisation that affected the CBE during 1922–4: sorting out boundaries to enable land allocations to proceed; and reorganisation between, and then within, villages and communities.

TABLE 10.10 *Land reorganisation work in four CBE provinces, 1 May 1922–1 October 1923*

	I	*II*	*III*	*IV*	*V*	*VI*	*VII*	*VIII*	
Province	*Div. of large complex areas of land use (to eliminate interm., narrow strips, distance of strips)*	*Eliminate interm. and wedging*	*Allocate consolidated land areas to villages*	*Allocate consolidated land areas to parts of villages*	*Allocate consolidated land areas to newly established* poselki	*Boundary alterations of villages, for transfer to multifield and broad strips*	*Land reorganisation for* khutora *and* otruba	*Allocate land for collectives*	*Total area (des.)*
Orel	175 394	3 387	10 086	31 947	21 494	195	2 895	1 779	247 177
Kursk	65 775	19 619	163 062	73 224	–	13 509	11 128	1 409	347 726
Tambov	815 604	1 126	97 012	38 853	52 614	885	3 110	8 151	1 017 355
Voronezh	1 262 344	5 618	116 179	193 611	65 968	–	16 892	35 345	1 695 957
Total CBE four provinces	2 319 117	29 750	386 339	337 635	140 076	14 589	34 025	46 684	3 308 215
CBE work as % of all work in four regions*	65.5	24.0	28.1	33.1	30.2	7.2	2.4	47.1	40.3

* Four regions were researched: north-west, west, central industrial, central agricultural.

SOURCE 'Materialy po voprosu ob izbytochnom trude v sel'skom khozyaistve SSSR', *Trudy gosudarstvennogo kolonizatorskogo nauchno – issledovatel'skogo instituta*, vol. 3, Moscow, 1926, pp. 92–3.

TABLE 10.11 *Total area covered by land reorganisation in four CBE provinces (1922–24)(sq. km.)*

I Year	*II* Area Covered by Land reorganisation	*III* Total Area four provinces	*IV** Land reorganisation area as % of total area
1922	13 616.2		
1923	18 237.0		
1924	19 480.0		
1922–24	51 333.2	1 105 000	4.65

* for 1919–21 = 23.2% (IV) though distributed unevenly between provinces.

SOURCE Tatarchukov, p. 126 (see Table 10.8).

TABLE 10.12 *Percentage of all land reorganisation by province*

	1922	*1923*	*1924*	*1922–4*
Voronezh	26.5	37.0	31.8	32.3
Kursk	34.9	21.7	29.1	28.0
Orel	5.3	1.9	4.6	3.8*
Tambov	33.3	39.5	34.4	35.9
For four provinces**	100.0	100.0	100.0	100.0

* This figure apparently underestimates the degree of work undertaken in the province. An addition 2600 sq. km. was also devoted to division of land within a *volost*. (See Table 19E below)
** Not always adding up to 100% due to rounding.

SOURCE Tatarchukov, p. 126 (see Table 10.8).

Sorting out Boundaries Prior to Land Allocations

1922 saw the continuation of the work begun during the years of civil war. Most of the time was spent defining who had the rights to a certain area of land and then consolidating the area to be used. A large part of this work concerned establishing the actual boundaries of land used by peasants: sometimes it was difficult to identify the boundaries while on other occasions communities and villages disagreed over their boundaries. In 1922 such work

TABLE 10.13 *Percentage of various types of work by year*

Type of work	*1922*	*1923*	*1924*	*1922–4*
Boundary work and land allocations	35.0	6.7	9.3	15.2
Inter-village reorganisation	37.5	52.9	45.8	46.1
Intra-village reorganisation	24.3	29.7	38.7	31.7
Reorganisation of state land	3.2	10.7	6.2	7.0
Other types	0.0	0.0	0.0	0.0
	100.0	100.0	100.0	100.0

SOURCE from Tatarchukov, p. 126 (see Table 10.8).

in Kursk comprised 71.8 per cent of the total area subject to reorganisation in the province, though most of the work here concerned the allocation of land to sugar-beet factories. For Orel and Voronezh, the figures were 35.8 per cent and 29.5 per cent respectively.[52] (Table 10.14) Hardly any such work was completed in Tambov during 1922 and 1923 and none in the subsequent year. For all other provinces the percentage of work devoted to this measure fell off after 1922.

Land Reorganisation between Villages

This type of work was most developed in Tambov province, accounting for 82.1 per cent of all the province's reorganisation in 1923 and 76.2 per cent for all three years. The explanation for this lies in the worsening of the already inconvenient arrangements in land use, as a result of the 1917–18 redistribution, further complicated by events in 1919–20 (for example, occupation by White forces and peasant unrest) while relatively little work occurred in the province during socialist land reorganisation. As a consequence, land use was extremely confused and other reorganisation operations were inconceivable without first completing this inter-village work.

Such work was less significant in Kursk and Voronezh, though it still comprised about one-fifth and just over one-third respectively for the three years. Inter-village work was also more important in Orel province than indicated in Table 10.14, since a large part of the area devoted to these measures was included under other land reorganisation headings. If these data are included, total inter-village work for three years covered 6.7 per cent

TABLE 10.14 *Percentage of each type of land reorganisation, by year and province*

Province	*Boundary work & land allocations*			*Inter-village*			*Intra-village*			*Reorganisation of state property*			*Other*		
	1922	1923	1924	1922	1923	1924	1922	1923	1924	1922	1923	1924	1922	1923	1924
Voronezh	29.5	8.6	18.6	34.6	46.8	35.5	35.9	42.7	44.1	–	1.9	1.8	–	–	–
Kursk	71.8	13.8	8.5	16.3	14.7	28.7	11.9	32.2	57.7	–	39.3	5.1	0.0	0.0	0.0
Orel	35.8	23.9	18.6	1.4	2.0	1.8	62.3	69.5	74.4	–	4.5	5.1	0.4	0.1	0.1
Tambov	0.8	0.2	0.0	67.6	82.1	75.7	22.1	14.2	12.8	9.5	3.5	11.5	–	–	–

SOURCE Tatarchukov, p. 126 (see Table 10.8).

TABLE 10.15 *Distribution of various types of land reorganisation between the four provinces (1922–24)*

	Types of reorganisation as % of all land reorganisation					
Province	*boundary work and land allocations*	*inter-village*	*intra-village*	*reorganisation of state land*	*Other*	*Total*
Voronezh	16.9	39.9	41.8	1.4	–	100
Kursk	30.8	20.8	35.6	12.8	0.0	100
Orel	22.5	1.7*	69.1	3.1	0.2	100
Tambov	0.3	76.2	15.6	7.9	–	100

* Evidently not all work was included in this figure. For details see section in text concerned with inter-village. See also Table 19B.

SOURCE Tatarchukov, p. 126 (see Table 10.8).

of the area of the province covered by reorganisation, in other words, four times more than indicated in Table 10.1.[53] The examples presented here to illustrate inter-village reorganisation are taken from this province. Figures 10.1 and 10.2 show the effects of reorganisation on villages within two of its volosts, Lebedyansk and Samovsk: each village receiving its land in one consolidated area. Figure 10.3 reveals how, after inter-village reorganisation in the same province, the village of Dichnya received one integral area of land, eliminating the former inconvenient arrangements in land use. The results in these cases were clearly similar to those in the volosts of Zadonsk district (Voronezh province) where 90 per cent of villages received land in one place and 9.5 per cent two consolidated plots. The number of intermingled strips was thus reduced by one half or one third of the former number, while there was also a marked decrease in the distance between strips and between these and the peasant place of residence.[54] In Tula province most reorganisation work from spring 1920 was concerned with dividing up large areas (comprising several villages and communities) as well as large villages.[55] In both cases the objective was to eliminate intermingling and create more convenient-sized units. After a survey had been undertaken a large consolidated area was to be marked off for a particular village or for each new settlement.[56]

Figure 10.1 Land use in Lebedyansk volost of Eletsk district, Orel province (a) before, and (b) after reorganisation

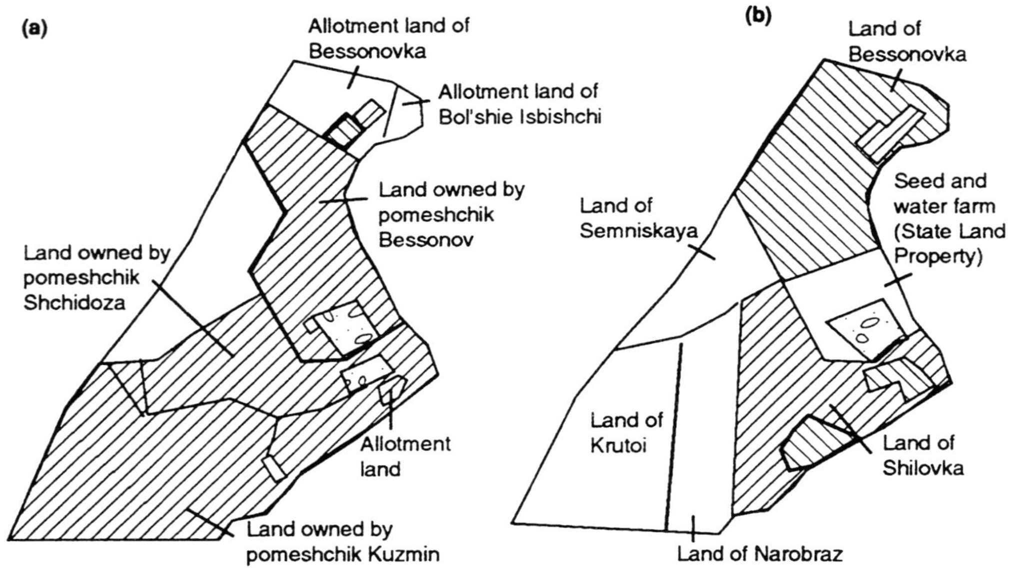

Figure 10.2 Land use of villages in Samovskaya volost, Karachevsk district, Orel province (a) before, and (b) after reorganisation

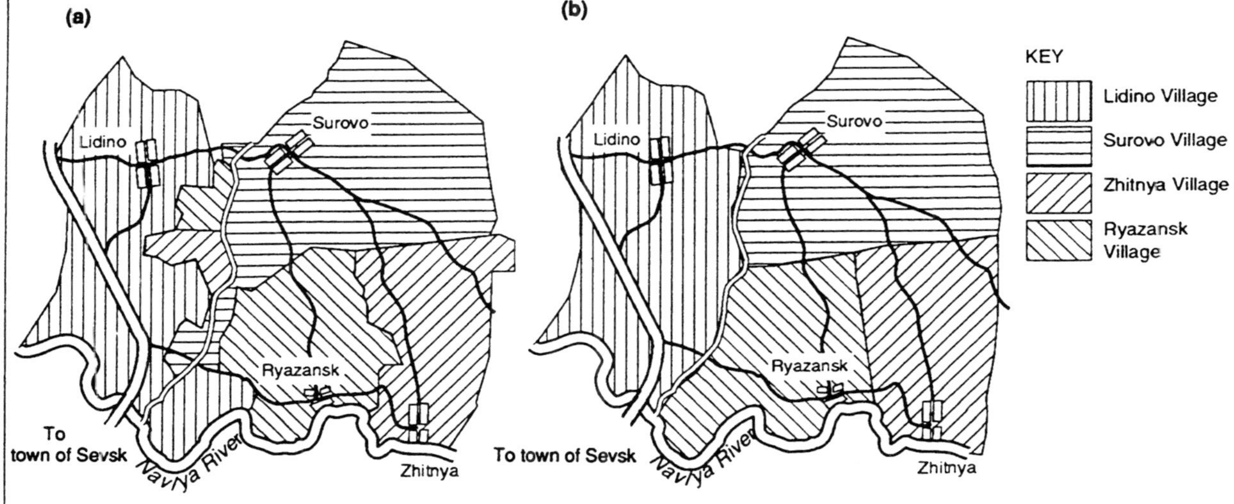

Figure 10.3 **Elimination of inconveniences in land use of the village of Dichnaya, Novosil'sk district of Orel province, before and after the Revolution**

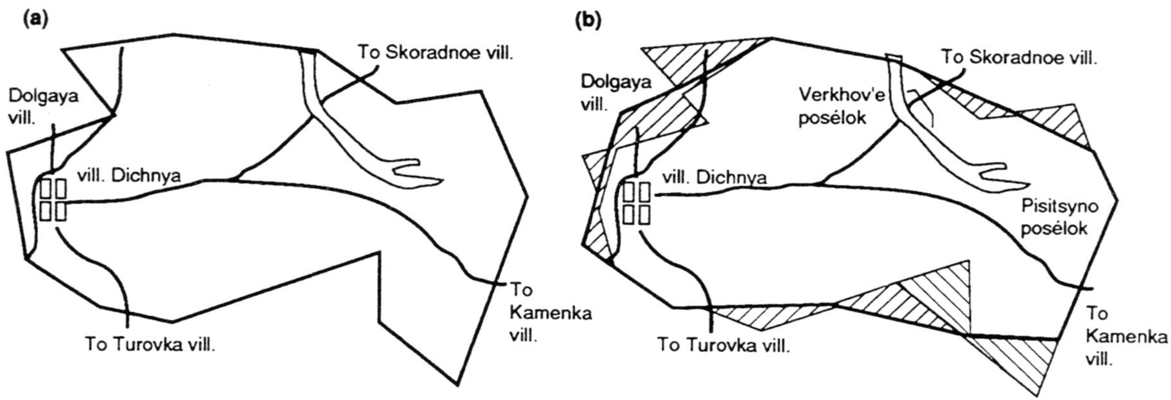

Land Reorganisation within Villages

The completion of work between villages was the principal factor which enabled work to proceed within villages. Such work accounted for 57.7 per cent of all reorganisation in Kursk province in 1924 and 35.6 per cent over all three years. Although reorganisation had been weak in Kursk during 1919–21, conditions of land use in the province – fewer large villages and less overcrowding than elsewhere in the CBE – created greater possibilities for the immediate execution of work within villages. In percentage terms such work was most widespread in Orel province (accounting for almost 70 per cent of all work there over three years) although it was not large in absolute terms. The percentage was much lower in Tambov and was falling by the year. This was the corollary of the importance attached to reorganisation between villages, which was necessary before work was possible on a greater scale within villages.[57] Such work comprised the largest area in Voronezh province (accounting for some 41.8 per cent of its area subject to reorganisation), due mainly to the earlier success here with inter-village work. Figures 10.4 and 10.5 illustrate the effects of intra-village reorganisation in two large villages of Bogucharsk district of Voronezh province, situated in the south-eastern part of the CBE. Figures 10.4a and b show peasant use of land before and after reorganisation in the village of Taly, and Figures 10.5a and b the same for the village of Seryakova.

Before land reorganisation, Taly was divided into eight units with one small village – the so-called *khutor* Solenyi (comprising twelve households) – separated from it. The land was divided into four fields and each field subdivided into smaller areas termed *stolby*. During redivision, each unit (*sotnya*) received so many *stolby* and then divided them between its constituent households.[58] As a result of reorganisation Taly was divided into seven such units (the first and eighth uniting), while the earlier established Solenyi remained and a new settlement (*poselok*), Zhelobok, set up, comprising 42 households. Table 10.6 shows that after reorganisation the maximum decrease in the number of strips was 57.1 per cent, though in several places the numbers still remained large and on occasion, as in the case of Soldatenko, even exceeded the earlier number. The results were mixed in other respects too. There was no decrease, for instance, in the average distance between strips and between them and the

Figure 10.4a Land use by four households, Taly village, Voronezh province before reorganisation

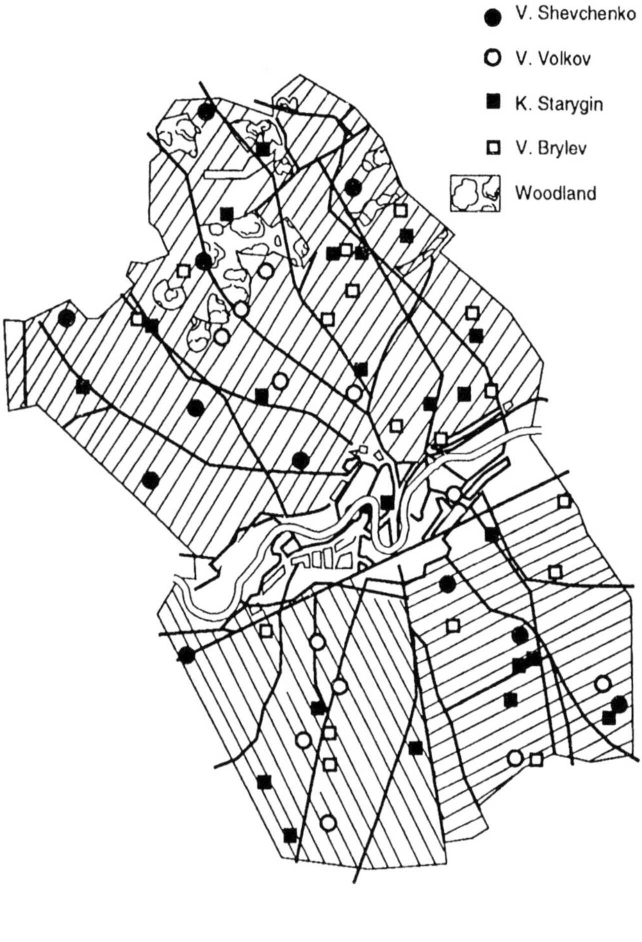

Figure 10.4b Land use by four households, Taly village, Voronezh province after reorganisation

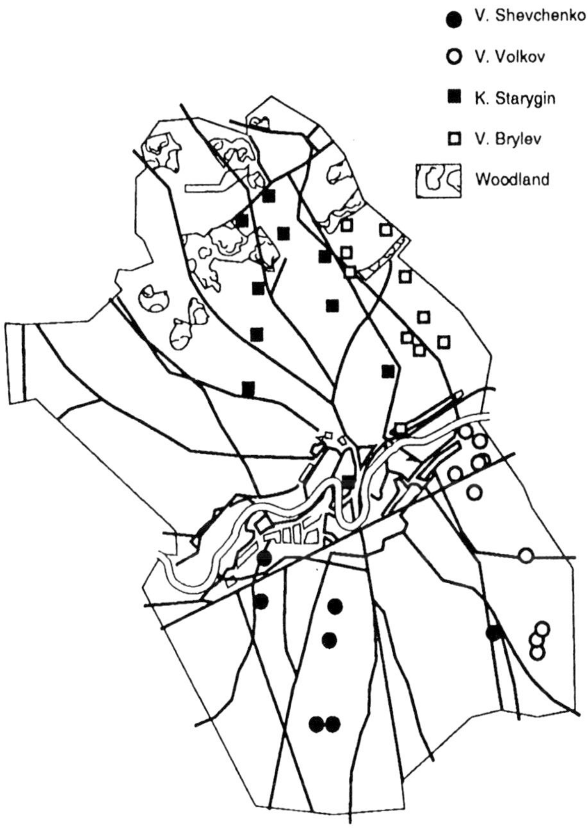

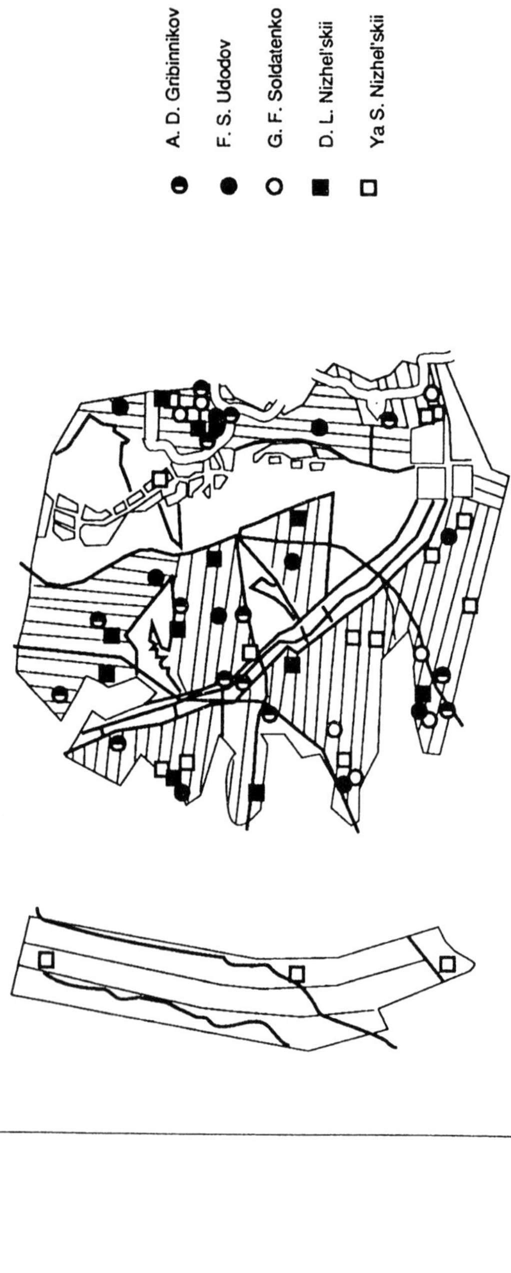

Figure 10.5a Land use by five households, Seryakova village, Voronezh province before reorganisation

Figure 10.5b Land use by five households, Seryakova village, Voronezh province after reorganisation

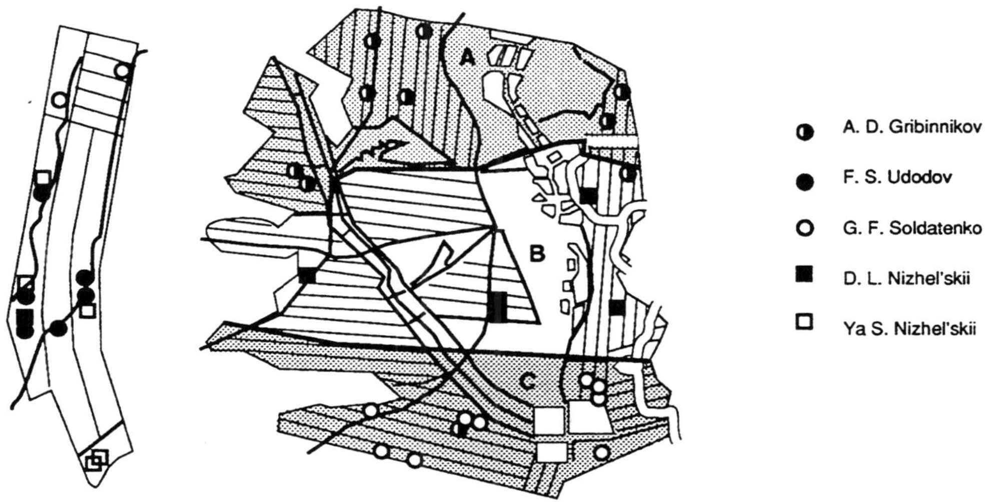

TABLE 10.16 *Land used by four households, Taly village, Voronezh province* (see Figure 10.4)

Name of householder	*Number of strips*		*Average distance of strips* (versts)	
	before reorg.	*after reorg.*	*before reorg.*	*after reorg.*
V. Shevchenko	14	6	6.24	5.12
V. Volkov	10	10	7.31	4.76
K. Starygin	21	9	5.85	4.82
V. Brylev	16	9	5.80	5.28

peasant residence. The chief reason for this was the village's central location, where all the allocations made through reorganisation were stretched out on one side of the land surrounding the peasant farms. When decreases occurred, these were due to the allocation of a smaller area and fewer strips within it.

In Seryakova, land was divided into two portions, one attached to the village, the other intermingled with that of neighbouring villages and 25 versts from the village. The community comprised two units, the large village Seryakova and the village Dolbnevka attached to it, in essence a single-plan village.[59] The land was divided into three fields and in each field there were on average four strips per household (making twelve in all); the intermingled portion was divided separately and because of its distance from Seryakova was either left unused or used for hay (*senokos*). Land reorganisation led to Seryakova being divided in three, together with the creation of a settlement (*poselok*) on the former intermingled plot, a smallish part of which was also left for Dolbnevka. From Table 10.17 it can be seen that the number of strips in Seryakova decreased less than in Taly, though the average distance between strips showed a greater fall. This was chiefly a consequence of the establishment of the settlement on the former intermingled plot. In Figure 10.5 (b) the strips per household for one field of each community are not shown since, at the time of research, the fallow field had not been divided. In Table 10.17 the number of strips shown for this field was calculated from the average number of strips in the remaining fields. The average distance of the strips was then calculated from the average distance of the field.

TABLE 10.17 *Land used by five households, Seryakova village, Voronezh province* (see Figure 10.5)

		Number of strips		*Average distance of strips* (versts)	
Name of householder	*Village*	*before* reorganisation	*after*	*before* reorganisation	*after*
A.D. Gribinnikov	1st. Seryakova	18	13	3.44	1.90
D.L. Nizhel'skii	2nd. Seryakova	17	10	3.30	2.86
G.F. Soldatenko	Dolbnevka	14	16	7.50	6.02
Ya.S. Nizhel'skii	Novo-Seryakova	16	8	4.33	2.54
F.S. Udodov	2nd. Seryakova	17	8	5.35	2.79

SOURCE Tatarchukov, pp. 132–3 (see Table 10.8).

Such results showed that reorganisation of land in this manner, especially if accompanied by resettlement on more distant land areas, could lead to improvements in the land use of individual peasant households. The setting up of *poselki* was deemed the most important measure for the CBE and the low figure for this work completed during 1922–4 (22 per cent of the peasant area devoted to reorganisation) is explained by the fact that a significant number of these settlements were created during socialist land reorganisation. Between 1919–24, 2500 settlements were established in four provinces of the CBE covering 572 868 hectares, the largest area being covered in Voronezh and the smallest in Kursk.[60] There was considerable variation between districts – the south-west and the centre of the CBE being quite weakly affected by resettlement – as well as in the average size of *poselki* and the area they covered. This variation was the result of natural economic conditions. Peasants mainly chose to resettle where drainage was good and around convenient water sources, and often these factors defined the size of the *poselok*.[61] Most of the work was initiated by peasants themselves, though executed with some specialist assistance, and only a small amount was directed by the land organs.

As the above examples indicate, success in achieving reductions in the number of strips and in the distance between strips as well as between the strips and the peasant place of residence, was not uniform and depended principally on local factors. A similar point should be made with respect to other improvements in land use. The tendency towards the creation of broad strips and multifield farming, noted during 1919–21 – and again linked to the creation of *poselki* – continued in the early twenties. Evidence from the provinces of Orel, Bryansk, Kursk, Voronezh and Tula confirms this.[62] Not only was the introduction of multifield crop rotation systems and broad strips on the increase but, more significantly, these were now occurring within a communal framework. Prior to 1917, most such improvements had been confined to enclosed holdings. Many writers on peasant agriculture stressed the importance of land reorganisation where the commune still prevailed. Within a communal framework, they argued, it was possible to transfer to improved multifield crop rotation systems and attempt to allocate to each household the smallest number of strips, in the most convenient location.[63] Yet, overall in the CBE, such work was, at best, patchy. In Orlovsk district of Orel province, there were few signs between 1913 and 1924 of improvement with regard to the number of strips per household and the distances separating them. Even in areas where most progress had been made in this direction, much work had still to be done: for instance, almost half of the communes in a volost of Voronezh province claimed to be dissatisfied with the progress of reorganisation by 1926.[64]

LAND REORGANISATION IN THE CBE: BEFORE AND AFTER THE REVOLUTION

The most noticeable feature of a comparison between the last tsarist land reform and that of the early Soviet period is the emphasis in the CBE on different kinds of land reorganisation measures. In the Stolypin period most reorganisation work in the region comprised separation of land for villages and parts of villages (54.3 per cent) and separation into *otruba* and *khutora* (42.3 per cent). During 1922–3, the largest share of reorganisation work was devoted to the allocation of integral land areas and the abolition of intermingling (especially between villages and communities), the extreme narrowness of strips and the distances between the latter as well as between them and the peasant place of residence (71 per cent) and the allocation of land to villages and parts of villages (21.9 per cent): together these comprised 94 per cent of all work in the CBE, even when

TABLE 10.18 *Land reorganisation priorities, before and after 1917*

Years	*For each 100 des. subject to reorganisation*	
	*Groups I & II**	*Group III (incl.* khutora & otruba)
1907–16	58	42
1922–3	97	3
1924	98	2
(1924–8 Perspective Plan)	(98)	(2)

SOURCE I.F. Petrov, 'Zemlepol'zovanie v tsentral'no-promyshlennom i tsentral'no-zemledel'cheskom raionakh v 1923 g.', *Trudy gosudarstvennogo kolonizatorskogo nauchno-issledovatel'skogo instituta*, vol. III (Moscow, 1926). [fn. n. 47] p. 100.
* See note 65.

settlements were increasing slowly.[65] (see Table 10.18) Clearly enclosed holdings (accounting for 42 per cent of the work before 1917) were not deemed important in this region after the Revolution, according to the land reorganisation plans, or by peasants generally – even though some private farms had been created by the peasants themselves, independent of formal land reorganisation operations – and the majority of work was devoted to improvements in the arrangement of land within a communal framework.[66]

For the Bolsheviks 1924 marked the last year of the operation of this land reorganisation policy. By 1925, a new government attitude emerged towards agriculture where land reorganisation became a 'recognised instrument of party and government policy'; a new phase in industrialisation had been approved which demanded from agriculture an increase in grain surpluses. From 1927, in yet a further turn in agricultural policy, land reorganisation found itself being used – as in 1919–21 – to promote the development of collective farming.[67] Whether very much changed at local level during 1925–7 is doubtful and even the proposals for organisation made in the 'Perspective Plan' for the next five years were modest.[68] As with the Stolypin land reforms before 1917, the period 1919–24 was too short to tell whether further progress could reasonably be expected in this same direction. What is beyond doubt, however, is that this would have required more central commitment and far more resources, both in terms of finance and trained specialist manpower and equipment.

At the same time parallels may be drawn between the Stolypin reforms and those of 1919–21. As with the pre-revolutionary reform, the policy and organisation of the reform after 1917 changed in the course of its implementation, and these changes were also a result of government (both tsarist and Soviet) responding to peasant pressures and accommodating peasant preferences on land use. In particular the reform allowed group land reorganisation, which had made headway under Stolypin, to continue. There was also sufficient flexibility in the reforms of 1919–21 to allow peasants to introduce the changes in land use they considered desirable (see the edict of February and the Tsentrozem circular of 16 May 1919) though, as with the Stolypin reforms, this flexibility was limited. For ideological reasons the emphasis of the reforms in 1919–21 was different from that before 1917 (collectives vis-à-vis enclosed holdings), yet their introduction was for similar political reasons – to maintain social stability. Neither form of tenure, however, had much appeal for a largely communal peasantry. True, in the Soviet case, part of the flexibility stemmed from the unstable political conditions of civil war; poor links between the centre and the localities meant that the ideas communicated to, interpreted by and implemented in the localities, may have been very different from those intended at the centre. The nascent Soviet regime, moreover, was still in the process of formulating its ideas. Misunderstandings arose over the aim of the legislation, while basic questions such as the best form of socialist land tenure had still to be resolved. Survival in the civil war also required a flexible response from the Bolsheviks, namely, to emphasise collectives, which would satisfy ideological purists and ideally would have resolved the food crisis, but to allow any form of peasant land use as long as it stimulated agricultural production.

CONCLUSION

Prior to 1917 the central black-earth region was the most backward in European Russia. The land revolution of 1917–18 enabled the peasantry to acquire direct control over more land, but the fact that land use was locally determined (together with the large numbers returning to the countryside) meant that it became even more complicated. By 1924, land use per household was not much better in the CBE than before the Revolution and in two provinces it was even worse. Clearly land reform was needed here. Nineteen-nineteen and the ensuing five years witnessed early attempts under the new regime to direct programmes for land reorganisation from the centre and, notwithstanding the 'official' distinction between the two periods, there was much continuity between the work initiated in 1919–21 and that in 1922–4. In the localities this was a continuation of the improvements in peasant land use within a communal structure initiated in the pre-revolutionary years. *Chernyi peredel* for the peasantry thus became a way of increasing productivity as well as output, even though it might have been better to look for improved ways of ensuring subsistence insurance rather than producing surpluses. In practice, as Sazonov noted, peasants were often responsible for initiating the work, though surveyors and land reorganisation officers seem to have been sympathetic to them, recognising that, under the conditions that prevailed in the CBE, benefits in land use could best be achieved through rearrangements of land within a communal structure.

A large proportion of the reorganisation work undertaken in the RSFSR in the early twenties was devoted to the CBE. Yet a major problem was the cost of the assistance required for reorganisation. This had to be resolved if more peasants were to be involved in the process, especially in such an impoverished region. To continue the progress made in the years to 1924 required much more investment in reorganisation, manpower and resources. It also required commitment from the centre and that needed a belief in this particular type of land reorganisation. But reorganisation was also a long and complicated business. It would take time, and in the climate of the mid 1920s this was a luxury in short supply. The pendulum of development began to swing away from slow, gradual agrarian change and land reorganisation soon followed suit.

NOTES

1. A fuller discussion of the agrarian history of the CBE may be found in J. Channon, 'Peasant Revolution and Land Reform: Land Redistribution in European Russia, 1917–21', (PhD., University of Birmingham, 1983) pp. 19–27.
2. Graeme J. Gill, *Peasants and Government in the Russian Revolution* (London, 1979) p. 192, Appendix V. By 1917 the average size of allotment per male soul in four CBE provinces (Voronezh, Kursk, Orel, Tambov) had declined since 1860 by almost 50 per cent. I.D. Balashov, (ed.) *Agrarnoe dvizhenie v TsChO v 1917 godu*, vyp. 1 (Voronezh, 1930) p. 23. See also S.G. Wheatcroft's chapter in this volume.
3. L.A. Owen, 'The Russian Agrarian Revolution of 1917–II', *Slavonic & East European Review*, XII (1934) pp. 368–86.
4. A.M. Anfimov, *Zemel'naya arenda v evropeiskoi Rossii v nachale XX veka* (Moscow, 1961). From his more recent work this is clearly a position he now finds untenable; Elvira M.W. Wilbur, 'The Peasant Economy, Landlords and Revolution in Voronezh: A Call for the Reappraisal of the Nature of the Russian Revolutionary Crisis at the Turn of the Century', (PhD. University of Michigan, 1977). Theda Skocpol, *States and Social Revolutions: A Comparative Analysis of France, Russia and China* (Cambridge, 1979) p. 132, citing Craig Jenkins, 'Agrarian Class Structure and Peasant Revolution – Russia 1917', (M.A., New York, 1974).
5. In Ryazan province, for instance, a high percentage (80–84) of peasants who separated did not receive communal resolutions (*prigovory*) to do so. Thus, it is claimed, force supported by the land captains was primarily responsible for separation in the province. *Obzor Ryazanskoi gubernii za 1911 god* (Ryazan, 1913) pp. 40–1; Yu. V. Fulin, 'Likvidatsiya pomeshchich'ego zemlevladeniya i pervye shagi po sotsialisticheskomu pereustroistvu sel's-kogo khozyaistva v Ryazanskoi gubernii (1917–18 gg.)', (cand. diss., Ryazan, 1959) pp. 82–3. For a recent view that the Stolypin reforms failed principally because of peasant poverty see J. Pallot, 'Open Fields and Individual Farms. Land Reform in Pre-Revolutionary Russia', *Tijdschrift voor economische en sociale geografie*, LXXV, 1 (1984) pp. 46–60
6. See L.A. Owen, 'The Russian Agrarian Revolution'. A more detailed discussion may be found in John Channon, 'The Bolsheviks and the Peasantry: the Land Question During the First Eight Months of Soviet Rule', *Slavonic & East European Review*, LXVI (1988) pp. 593–624 and my book, *Land to the Tillers: Peasant Revolution and Land Reform in Russia, 1917–24* (forthcoming).
7. Ben-Cion Pinchuk, *The Octobrists in the Third Duma, 1907–1912* (Seattle, 1974) pp. 55–6, 61; Eugene D Vinogradoff, 'The Russian Peasantry and the Elections to the Fourth State Duma', in Leopold H. Haimson (ed.) *The Politics of Rural Russia, 1905–1914* (Indiana, 1979) p. 226; O.H. Radkey, *The Sickle under the Hammer. The Russian Socialist Revolutionaries in the Early Months of Soviet Rule* (New York, London, 1963) pp. 319–20; for examples of *chernye peredely* see Channon, 'Peasant Revolution and Land Reform', pp. 522–3.
8. Ya. Blyakher, 'Sovremennoe zemlepol'zovanie po dannym spetsial'noi ankety TsSU 1922 g.', *Vestnik statistiki*, vol. XIII, nos. 1–3, pp. 142–3.

9. The figure was very high for the Volga region too but the extremely small sample there casts serious doubts as to its reliability. For confirmation, see O. Figes, *Peasant Russia, Civil War. The Volga Countryside in Revolution, 1917–1921* (Oxford, 1989).
10. See, for example, Sylvana Malle, *The Economic Organisation of War Communism* (Cambridge 1985); O. Kuperman, *Sotsial'no-ekonomicheskie formy promyshlennosti v SSSR* (Leningrad, 1929) p. 97; A. Okninskii, *Dva goda sredi krest'yan; videnпое, slyshannoe, perezhitoe v Tambovskoi gubernii s noyabrya 1918 goda do noyabrya 1920 goda* (Newtonville, Mass., 1986) (originally pub. 1936) pp. 175–6.
11. Excluding the Volga region. Others without such skills were less fortunate and attempted to survive by occasional work for households short of labour.
12. This phenomenon was noted from the 1870s to the 1890s. (G.T. Robinson, *Rural Russia Under the Old Regime*, reissue (Berkeley, 1972) p. 121; L. Tikhomirov, *Russia. Political and Social*, (London, 1888) pp. 286, 292; K. Kachorovskii, 'Obshchiny v revolyutsii i kontrrevolyutsii', *Volya Rossii*, (Prague) 18–19 (1924) pp. 205–6.
13. This was the case, for example, in some areas of Kursk province (see Yakov Sadovskii, 'Kak ya delil zemlyu', *Russkaya mysl'* 9–12 (1923–4).
14. Tikhomirov, *Russia*, p. 124.
15. In Kursk province, Sadovskii noted the selection of measurers and dividers in the spring of 1918 and the continuation of other redivisional practices, 'Kak ya delil zemlyu', pp. 131–2.
16. The 'additions' per capita for the six CBE provinces ranged from 0.08 to 0.50 desyatins, though provincial studies undertaken by Soviet writers, based on local materials, show the Narkomzem data to understate the increase in peasant land use. Such figures also ignore the variations between and within volosts (between villages and communities) and the effects of any inter-peasant redistribution. (see, for example, Yu. Fulin, 'Iz istorii likvidatsii pomeshchich'ego zemlevladeniya v Ryazanskoi gubernii (pereraspredelenie nadel'nykh zemel' v gubernii letom i osen'yu 1918g.', *Uchenye zapiski Ryazanskogo ped. instituta*, XXVIII (1961) pp. 128–30.
17. B.A. Tutykhin, *Tsentral'no Chernozemnaya Oblast'* (Moscow, 1929) p. 87.
18. Channon, 'Peasant Revolution and Land Reform', pp. 403–9. These figures per household would change with the increased splitting of households.
19. See the example drawn from Borisoglebsk district, Tambov province, (ibid., pp. 390–2 and Table in end pocket). The redistribution of land, of course, was not paralleled by a similar redivision of other property such as livestock, seed, and implements and so leasing of land and hiring of labour continued.
20. Further discussion of these points may be found in Channon, *Land To The Tillers*.
21. Tutykhin, *Tsentral'no Chernozemnaya oblast'*, Table, p. 87; K.N. Sazonov, 'Zemlepol'zovanie i zemleustroistvo v tsentral'no- chernozemnoi oblasti posle revolyutsii', in A.N. Tatarchukov (ed.), 'Materialy po izucheniyu voprosa o vosstanovlenii khozyaistva TsChO', *Trudy Planovoi komissii TsChO*, vol. I, (Voronezh, 1926) p. 143.
22. Blyakher, *Sovremennoe zemlepol'zovanie*, pp. 141, 145.

23. Sazonov, 'Zemlepol'zovanie', p. 143 and Map 1. The worst supplied households (in terms of average area per *dvor*) were in Graivorovsk (5.4 ha), and Ryl'sk (5.8 ha) districts of Kursk, whereas the seven districts situated principally at the centre of the *Oblast'* – Voronezh, Eletsk and Livensk – in the south-west (L'govsk, Bel'gorodsk) and the north-east (Kozlovsk and Morshansk) possessed up to 8 ha per household. In the western part of the CBE the average land area per *dvor* did not exceed 9 ha and only in the south-eastern and northern districts did the area exceed 10 ha per household.
24. Ibid., p. 156.
25. For details, see John Channon, 'Tsarist Landowners after the Revolution: Former Pomeshchiki in Rural Russia during NEP', *Soviet Studies*, XXXIX (1987) pp. 575–98.
26. This is discussed further in Channon, *Land To The Tillers.*
27. George Yaney, *The Urge to Mobilize* (Champaign, Ill., 1982) esp. ch. 12, notes these other measures but devotes most of his attention to collective forms of tenure. For the 'Polozhenie o sotsialisticheskom zemleustroistve i o merakh perekhoda k sotsialisticheskomu zemledeliyu' and the March Instructions see *Agrarnaya politika sovetskoi vlasti (1917–1918gg.) Dokumenty i materialy*, (Moscow, 1954) pp. 417–31 and 441–61 respectively.
28. For the table on land reorganisation during 1919–21 and other details, see Channon, *Land To The Tillers.*
29. At the emancipation one large allocation was sometimes made for the general use of several villages, hence the name single-plan villages (*odnoplannye seleniya*). A major problem created by this arrangement was extra-village intermingling.
30. Sazonov, 'Zemlepol'zovanie' p. 116; For a good example from Ryazan province, see Yu. I. Bystrakov, 'Zemel'nye otnosheniya i zemleustroistvo v Ryazanskoi gubernii v period 1917–1921 gg.', in *Moskovskii Institut Inzhenerov Zemleustroistva, Nauchnye Trudy*, XLIII (1970) pp. 77–83.
31. New allocations of land within volosts were carried out over 3 883 700 desyatins.
32. Sazonov, 'Zemlepol'zovanie', pp. 113–4; V Keller & I Romanenko, *Pervye itogi agrarnoi reformy* (Voronezh, 1922).
33. Sazonov, 'Zemlepol'zovanie', p. 115.
34. Ibid., p. 116.
35. *Khutora* were private farms with the arable area enclosed together with the farm and outbuildings while in the *otrub* the arable portion was enclosed but the dwelling and farm remained within the village.
36. Sazonov, 'Zemlepol'zovanie', pp. 139, 147. In this case allocations were made either per person (eater) or per worker (relating to capacity to work).
37. Ibid., pp. 133, 138. There was little difference, though, in the number of cattle possessed.
38. Ibid.; Bystrakov, 'Zemel'nye otnosheniya'.
39. The centre of peasant unrest in the CBE in the summer of 1920 was in Tambovsk district (and in the two villages of Kamenka and Khitrovo especially) but spread also to the districts of Kirsanovsk and Borisoglebsk, all in Tambov province. The *Tambovshchina* clearly prevented any work on land reorganisation from taking place.

40. Bystrakov, 'Zemel'nye otnosheniya', p. 82.
41. For the plans covering the winter period 1920–1 and the summer period 1921 see *Otchet o deyatel'nosti Ryazanskoi gubernii otdel zemledeliya* (Ryazan, 1921) pp. 42–3; for work at the time of the ninth congress of Soviets see ibid., pp. 44–5. For details of how provincial work plans were divided into 'special' and 'ordinary/basic' work, see Channon, *Land To The Tillers.*
42. *Sostoyanie sel'skogo khozyastva Tul'skoi gubernii (kak material k gubpartkonferentsii)* (Tula, 1924) pp. 37–8; Sazonov, 'Zemlepol'zovanie', pp. 113–14.
43. See P.N. Pershin, 'Zemleustroistvo i zemlepol'zovanie' in *Krest'yanskaya sel'skokhozyaistvennaya entsiklopediya*, vols. II–III, (Moscow-Leningrad, 1925) pp. 309–12. Pershin emphasises the distinction between *podvornoe zemleustroistvo* and *edinolichnoe zemleustroistvo* (principally *khutora* and *otruba*), noting that the two are sometimes confused in the literature.
44. These plans were still being worked out mainly in Voronezh province.
45. Sazonov, 'Zemlepol'zovanie', p. 126; For the increased number of disputes see K.M. Gazalova, 'Zemel'nyi sud RSFSR poryadok rassmotreniya spornykh del o semeino-imushchestvennykh razdelakh krest'yanskikh khozyaistv (1921–8gg.), *Trudy Moskovskogo Gosudarstvennogo Istoriko-Arkhivnogo Instituta*, XIX, (1965) 210; and *Sel'skokhozyaistvennaya zhizn'*, 51 (1924) p. 6.
46. For the Sovnarkom resolution of 14 June 1923 see *SU RSFSR*, 1923, no. 60, art., 567, cited in A.K. Panfilova, 'Narodnyi komissariat zemledeliya RSFSR v period vosstanovleniya narodnogo khozyaistva (1921–5gg.)', avtoreferat, (Cand. diss., University of Moscow, 1973) p. 24; for credit in 1924 see D.J. Male, *Peasant Organisation Before Collectivisation* (Cambridge, 1971) and E.H. Carr & R.W. Davies, *Foundations of a Planned Economy*, vol. I, (Harmondsworth, 1974) p. 245; by 1928 such credit had not been forthcoming in the CBE (ibid., p. 247); one calculation showed that it would cost 616 rubles (1924) for a household to set up in a *poselok* (and more if it were on virgin land). (Sazonov, 'Zemlepol'zovanie', p. 137).
47. During the civil war years they often survived like shepherds, living with a different peasant household each day, and on occasion they even set up their own households in the village. (see *O zemle*, vol. I (Moscow, 1921) pp. 169–70)
48. I.F. Petrov, 'Zemlepol'zovanie v tsentral'no-promyshlennom i tsentral'nozemledel'cheskom raionakh v 1923 g. i ego veroyatnaya evolyutsiya v blizhaishee pyatiletie' in 'Materialy po voprosu ob izbytochnom trude v sel'skom khozyaistve SSSR', *Trudy Gosudarstvennogo Kolonizatorskogo Nauchno-Issledovatel'skogo Instituta*, vol. III (Moscow, 1926) pp. 92–3 for details.
49. The percentages were as follows: 61.8 per cent in 1922, 82.6 per cent in 1923, 84.5 per cent in 1924.
50. The figures for Tambov province were from 68 per cent to 82 per cent and in Orel from 62 per cent to 74 per cent.
51. See Table in *Sel'skokhozyaistvennaya zhizn'*, 22–3, 11 November 1921, p. 8 based on the number of Narkomzem specialists engaged in work on land reorganisation in receipt of rations in the autumn of 1921. One such example of the operation of specific local factors comes from Kursk province where, in two of its districts, the emphasis was on land allocations to sugar beet factories, (Sazonov, 'Zemlepol'zovanie', p. 127).

52. Ibid.
53. Ibid., pp. 127–8.
54. Keller and Romanenko, *Pervye itogi.*
55. In the plans for land redistribution prepared during 1918, districts were frequently divided into *raiony*, each one comprising several volosts or parts of volosts, depending on the location of the land subject to division and on the land needs of the inhabitants.
56. *Sostoyanie sel'skogo khozyaistva Tul'skoi gubernii*, p. 39.
57. Sazonov, 'Zemlepol'zovanie', p. 128. The figure for Tambov during 1922–4 was 15.6 per cent.
58. *Stolby* was just one of many terms used by peasants for such areas of land.
59. See n. 30 above for single-plan villages.
60. Table 8 in Sazonov, 'Zemlepol'zovanie', p. 134.
61. Ibid., pp. 134, 136. The average size of *poselki* fell from the south-east to the north-west, in the south being larger than the north, ranging from 3–10 to over 100 households in Voronezh, and from 3 to 64 households in Orel. The area covered could vary from 20 to 100 desyatins in Tambov to 26.6 ha to 710.3 ha in Orel.
62. V.S. Kokin, 'K voprosu ob uchastii sovremennoi agronomicheskoi organizatsii v zemleustroistve', *Sel'skoe i lesnoe khozyaistvo*, 12 (1923) pp. 83–5. The information came from the Main Committee of the All-Union Agricultural Exhibition of 1923. Questionnaires were distributed to provincial exhibition committees and provincial agronomists and most of the replies came from the CBE provinces. Sazonov, 'Zemlepol'zovanie', p. 133; *Sostoyanie sel'skogo khozyaistva Tul'skoi gubernii*, p. 64. Bryansk was formerly part of Orel province.
63. Sazonov, 'Zemlepol'zovanie', p. 120; A.N. Chelintsev, *Teoreticheskie osnovy organizatsii krest'yanskogo khozyaistva* (Kharkov, 1919) p. 83.
64. Petrov, 'Zemlepol'zovanie', p. 75; Kindeev, *Voprosy zemleustroistva* (Moscow, 1925) pp. 15, 22; Male, *Peasant Organisation*; F. Zheleznov, *Voronezhskaya derevnya. Bol'she-Vereiskaya volost'*, vol. II (Voronezh, 1926), pp. 10–11. There were 28 communes in all. The volost was situated in the northern part of Voronezhsk district and was established in 1924. (p. 3) Between 1916 and 1923, progress was just as slow in the move away from the basic subsistence crops with a noticeable fall in the area sown to grass and root crops. (see table in Petrov, 'Zemlepol'zovanie', p. 102).
65. Ibid., p. 99. This was the bulk of work in groups I and II.
66. Table 20 in ibid., pp. 96–7; for weakly developed enclosed holdings during 1922–4 see Sazonov, 'Zemlepol'zovanie', pp. 131–3, Table 5; for details of peasant enclosed holdings during 1919–24 see Channon, *Land To The Tillers*; for Tula province see *Sostoyanie sel'skogo khozyaistva Tul'skoi gubernii*, p. 39.
67. Male, *Peasant Organisation*, p. 182; Carr & Davies, *Foundations of a Planned Economy* , vol. I, pp. 245–7.
68. During 1923–4, the Administration for Land Organisation, Melioration and State Land Property, attached to Narkomzem, worked out a 'perspective plan' for land reorganisation for 5 years (1924–8). The Plan was to give an accurate impression of what land reorganisation could achieve

during the next 5 years if the current policy were continued. The Plan was subject to amendment in Zemplan and then the All-Union Gosplan. The final version of the Plan appeared in *Sovetskoe zemleustroistvo i melioratsiya, (Trudy Zemplana)* (Moscow, 1925). See Petrov, 'Zemlepol'zovanie', p. 87.

11 Some Thoughts on the End of NEP

Alec Nove

'That which Lenin introduced "seriously and for a long time" did not last at all long. Stalin liquidated NEP, while pretending to follow Lenin's precepts'. This is how Anatolii Rybakov, in his *Children of the Arbat*, summarises a view also widely held by western scholars.[1] There is another view, also widely held, that on the contrary, NEP was seen all along as a temporary manoeuvre, *reculer pour mieux sauter*, and that Stalin, in ending it, was continuing Lenin's work. Then there is what could be called the 'Bukharinist-alternative' school, which speculates on what could have happened if there had been a Bukharin-Rykov leadership, that would have pursued a (slower-tempo) industrialisation strategy on the basis of a continuing NEP. One must also look to Trotskii and the 'left opposition': did they have an alternative policy and is it correct to see Stalin, in 1928, stealing their clothes? Finally there is what could be called the pragmatic view: that Stalin was driven into ending NEP by a series of unforeseen crises, which rendered its continuance increasingly difficult. This last view approximates to that of E.H. Carr.

Much hangs on the answer to the question: was there a crisis of NEP in 1927? If so, what was its cause? On this there is some disagreement. Thus it has been roundly asserted that there was none, which is going too far. One has only to look at the evidence of a goods famine (*tovarnyi golod*), of increasing market disequilibrium, which was to culminate by the end of the year in the grain procurements crisis and in emergency measures to deal with it. But if there were indeed difficulties, what were their causes? Were they inherent in NEP, or were they the consequence of the adoption of policies inconsistent with NEP? If the latter, then why and when were such policies adopted? In the pages that follow I will endeavour to discuss these questions.

Back, first, to Lenin. It is true that he spoke of NEP being intended 'seriously and for a long time'. It is also true that his last work, 'On Cooperation', far from being consistent with Stalin's policy of forcible collectivisation, was an extremely moderate and cautious document, gradualist in its approach to voluntary cooperation. In *Children of the Arbat*, Rybakov puts into Stalin's mind (he soliloquises) the following description of the contrast: 'Tactically Lenin's NEP was a correct manoeuvre, but "seriously and for a long time" was already an error. The manoeuvre was the temporary deal with the peasants to get the grain . . .' He then cites Lenin:

> . . . . To achieve through NEP the total participation of the entire population in cooperatives . . . will need a whole historical epoch . . . Without total literacy, without sufficient good sense [*tolkovosti*], without accustoming the population to the use of books, without a material basis . . . we will be unable to reach our goal.' He closed the book and put it on the shelf. This would mean inoculating the peasant with the alien philosophy of the farmer. And a farmer does not need the dictatorship of the proletariat. The farmer, the property-owner, the individualist, must be throttled in the Russian muzhik at birth. Cooperatives? Yes, but such that the peasant will be a simple labourer . . . Yes, we need books and science, and the struggle against poor harvests. All this is needed. But not prior to collectivisation; rather, on the basis of collectivisation.[2]

Yet it is not quite so straightforward. Lenin was ambiguous in his treatment of NEP. 'Seriously and for a long time' could be interpreted as his estimate of the length of time necessary before renewing the offensive. One part of him must have hated the Nepmen, regarded the forced compromise, the 'retreat', as unavoidable but to be reversed as soon as practicable. War-communism he described as an error, forced by circumstances and by 'illusions' about a direct leap into communism. NEP, then, was a return to the right road, where they should have been all along. But the right road is not a 'retreat'. Let me imagine a parallel. Lenin made treaties which recognised the independence of the so-called *limitrofy*, Estonia, Latvia and Lithuania. This too was serious, and for a long time, since there was no likelihood of their speedy re-incorporation. Yet would Lenin have disapproved of their 'joining' the USSR in 1939–40?

There is no way of settling this sort of debate. More to the point is how Lenin's views were understood by party activists. If the majority saw NEP as a hateful retreat and looked forward to the day when they would be strong enough to resume the advance, then Stalin's 'left turn' of 1928, and the measures inconsistent with NEP already taken before that year, represented a sort of consensus, with Bukharin and the 'rights' genuinely in a minority.

NEP was a market-based compromise. The destruction of market equilibrium, the refusal to accept that it is important to maintain it, all this was a gradual process, which can be dated from 1926. It was speedily noted by the then young economist, V. Novozhilov. In an article in *Vestnik finansov*, he showed that the (still modest) increase in new investment, together with the increase in personal incomes and a policy of price reductions, was bound to lead to shortages, and had already begun to do so.[3] In my economic history of the Soviet Union, I cited a decree of unique economic illiteracy; issued on 2 July 1926, it ordered a reduction by 10 per cent in the retail prices of state-manufactured goods in short supply.[4] Then there was a series of discriminatory measures aimed at limiting private activities, for example, surcharges on rail freight, higher taxes, and so on.[5] These measures were increasingly explicable by the growing gap between official and free prices: the private sector then appears to be profiteering and the supply to it (at fixed prices) of anything from state sources begins to look like an illegitimate source of enrichment. Pressure against the private sector could be seen as a natural consequence of this species of price-scissors. (See Table 11.1)

Why was such a price policy followed? I recall putting this question in Moscow to Albert L. Vainshtein, who had been deputy head of the conjuncture institute of *Narkomfin* at the time, and who survived many years of camp, prison and exile after his arrest in 1930. We spoke of political commitment to cut prices,

TABLE 11.1 *Price Index (1913 = 100) Manufactures*

	Official	*Private*
Dec. 1926	208	251
Dec. 1927	188	240
Dec. 1928	190	253

SOURCE A.N. Malafeev, *Istoriya tsenoobrazovaniya v SSSR* (Moscow, 1964) pp. 384–5.

which seemed important in the struggle against critics from the left; it will be recalled that Preobrazhenskii had advocated unequal exchange ('exploitation') to pump resources out of the predominantly private peasantry. If so, Bukharin could be partly to blame, though he should have known the importance of market equilibrium to the survival of NEP. Paradoxically, the effect of such a price policy was not to benefit the peasantry, a point well made by Novozhilov in his article: when goods are in short supply the townspeople, being nearer to the place of manufacture, are able to obtain a disproportionate share of what is officially distributed, while the peasants, last in the queue, have to rely on the higher-priced free market. No doubt this contributed to peasant unwillingness to sell to the state at official purchase prices, and so to the procurement crisis of 1927–8.

It so happens that an uncle of mine, Yu. Novakovskii, was a high official of the *Tsentrosoyuz* (cooperative) organisation at the end of the twenties. I obtained from his widow a pamphlet he wrote, which may help to establish the atmosphere of the time – the more so because he was subsequently criticised for being too moderate, and was probably lucky to die a natural death before the Great Purge. Let me quote from the pamphlet:

> Retail cooperatives, squeezing out the private trader, cooperating and organising the consumer masses, thus build a first line of trenches around the socialist fortress of Soviet state industry . . . Private commercial capital is deprived of the means of pressing upon socialist industry, increasing prices for raw materials through the fluctuations of supply and demand. Therefore, both in disposing of industrial production and in supplying raw materials to industry, consumer cooperatives create a necessary line of trenches, protecting access to socialist industry . . . Removing the mass of commodities from spontaneous market forces (*rynochnoi stikhii*), from private-trading speculation, creating inventories of food and raw materials in its shops and storehouses, consumer cooperatives build around socialist industry a third line of trenches.[6]

The year 1927 was one of growing disequilibrium, growing shortages, with private activities showing, for the first time since 1921, an absolute decline. It was also the year in which Trotskii and his comrades were exiled, and Great Britain broke off diplomatic relations, contributing to a war scare – part contrived, part genuinely felt, though in fact neither Baldwin nor Poincaré had the slightest intention of taking military action, and Japanese aggression in the Far East was yet to come. It was also the year of the fifteenth party congress. If I may cite again a conversation with Vainshtein: when I asked him whether he could put a date to a decisive change in atmosphere, without hesitation he replied, 'December 1927. Before that date I and my non-party expert colleagues were listened to, our opinions were taken seriously, whether or not our advice was accepted. After that date we were regarded as an alien and hostile element, soon to be pushed out and soon to be arrested.'

The fifteenth congress appears in Stalinist historiography as the 'congress of collectivisation'. This, of course, is misleading. The congress did indeed favour collectivisation, but it should be voluntary and on the basis of high technique. Since both these conditions were known to be absent, Bukharin and Rykov could and did vote in favour. What Bolshevik could be against? The problem with the Bukharin-Rykov position was that they had been forced to retreat from the 1925 slogan of *obogashchaites´* ('enrich yourselves') and now favoured 'limiting the exploitative tendencies of the kulak'. That ill-defined category could include every successful peasant who developed what Stalin (in the already quoted reconstruction of his thoughts by Rybakov) would call 'farmer' tendencies, that is, commercial production for the market. He could have two horses or three cows, or both, and maybe hire a labourer to help with the harvest – and he becomes a class enemy. Yet what sense is there to base agriculture on the 'middle peasant', who is *defined* as one who has only a modest amount to sell, over and above his family's subsistence? Bukharin also saw nothing wrong with the price-cutting policy, both in respect of state-produced manufactures and (in 1926) in purchase-prices for grain. It is true that subsequently he urged an increase in the latter, but the damage had been done. All this must be seen in the context of the debate on the pace of growth, the successive drafts of the first five-year plan. Even in its more moderate versions, this plan envisaged a substantial rise in investments, and a rise also in the import bill. So there were urgent reasons for a larger off-farm surplus, especially of grain. Would this be forthcoming on a voluntary basis, through the market, save at a cost which would either reduce accumulation or cut the modest living standards of the urban workers, or both at once?

Preobrazhenskii summed up the dilemmas in his unfinished work, 'Economic Equilibrium in the System of the USSR', recently republished in English by Don Filtzer.[7] He there listed the contradictions, and saw no solution other than a revolution in advanced countries. A very different observer, the Menshevik P.A. Garvi, wrote a pamphlet entitled *Bolshevizm v tupike*, Bolshevism is in a cul-de-sac.

And where in all this should one put the 'left opposition'? According to Richard Day, they had the answer: higher investment would have provided more goods and so would greater reliance on foreign trade.[8] However, a strong case can be made for a contrary view. Trotskii, in alliance with Zinov'ev and Kamenev, had many political points to make – about errors in Comintern policy, or bureaucratisation, or lack of inner-party democracy. But their *economic* policy posture was internally inconsistent. On the one hand, they criticised the leadership for too modest an investment programme, yet if it had been speeded up, the strains and shortages would have been greater. Shortages could not have been made good by imports without a sizeable increase in exports, primarily of agricultural produce, as there were no big unused sources of credits or loans.

Yet the 'left' was persistently attacking the government for being soft on kulaks. Indeed Trotskii had developed a whole theory ('Thermidor') based on the notion that the Bukharin-Rykov group were representing the petty-bourgeoisie and that Stalin was a 'centrist', vacillating between the line represented by Bukharin and the correct class line advocated by the 'left opposition'. Too late Bukharin realised that in fact he had more in common with such men as Kamenev than he had with the ruthless Stalin, when the latter suddenly changed course in 1928. Trotskii had mocked Bukharin's notion of building socialism 'at the pace of a tortoise' (*cherepash'imi shagami*) within the confines of NEP. Yet his own investment plans, which included the expansion of heavy industry, would necessarily have taken several years to complete, and meanwhile belts would have had to be tightened. The opposition also claimed that wages were too low. When, late in the day (in 1928), it was proposed that grain procurement prices be raised, the 'left' opposed this. Some members of the left, for instance, Preobrazhenskii, felt that Stalin's left turn did indeed mean that he was adopting the left's policies. Even Trotskii, who split with Preobrazhenskii when the latter sought to make peace with Stalin, insisted that Stalin's left turn was due in some part to 'our pressure'.

So while neither Trotskii nor any of his allies advocated the destruction of NEP, the policies they advocated were surely inconsistent with its continuance.

To return to the question of whether an economic crisis was developing in the second half of 1927. It could be argued that in comparison with the years that followed, especially 1931–3, the disequilibrium and shortages were mild, as indeed they were, and that they were to a considerable extent due to incorrect or wrongheaded price policies, and thus remediable. The point about prices is well taken. Thus the grain procurement crisis of the winter 1927–8 was *not* due to kulak sabotage or to a desire on the part of the peasants to combat Soviet power: simply they found the grain price too low and expected it to be raised. The violence of the government's response, which greatly upset Bukharin and his friends, was a devastating blow to the principles upon which NEP was built. Interestingly, Stalin found it politic to continue to claim that NEP would be preserved, even while he set about throttling it.

Again one has to return to the five-year plan. If even the modest rise in new investment in 1926–7 placed so great a strain on the NEP structure, how could it possibly bear the burden of the first, let alone the even higher second, version of this plan? Many previously middle-of-the-road Bolsheviks must have concluded that the 'market' strait-jacket had to be shed. Of course this did not mean that the plans had to be so over-ambitious as to take the form of what Trotskii called 'price-gallop industrialisation'. Of course Bukharin was right in his 'Notes of an Economist': one cannot build today's factories with tomorrow's bricks. There *were* fortresses the Bolsheviks could not take, the impossible remained impossible. In no way should the argument be taken as justifying the Stalinist strategy, with all its brutalities, economic waste, human suffering. This note simply discusses some of the major causes of the abandonment of NEP.

There are some more general queries. One relates to the relative role, in the Soviet situation, of fear, of the perception of military danger. In some ways this probably affected both the chosen tempi and the priority of heavy industry, and both of these were inconsistent with NEP policies. Bukharin's views in the mid-twenties logically gave priority to those industries serving the needs of the peasantry. However, the Bolsheviks also faced an internal security or political dilemma. How long could they rule in an overwhelmingly peasant country unless they undertook some version of rapid industrialisation, a revolution from above? One returns to Stalin's soliloquy, imagined by Anatolii Rybakov: it was essential to prevent the emergence of commercially-minded 'farmers'. This concern was not directly related to a sense of external danger.

Another question is raised by considering the relevance of the NEP experience in the context of recent Soviet economic reform. The whole issue of NEP, its significance, the causes and legitimacy (or illegitimacy) of its abolition, all this has come into the area of public and published discussion as part of glasnost. This has involved the rehabilitation of such political figures as Bukharin, and economists committed to peasant family production and genuine market-related cooperatives, such as Chayanov, Chelintsev, Makarov and Kondrat´ev, the latter well known in the West for his 'long-wave' theory of crises.

Opinions vary. Thus within the past few years Nikolai Shmelev has argued that the suspension of NEP was a gross error with painful consequences.[9] Andrei Nuikin has supported this, speaking of the 'catastrophe' of forcible collectivisation and citing approvingly an article in *Znanie-sila* which treated Stalin's achievement of supreme power in 1928–9 as a coup d´état (*perevorot*) and a counter-revolutionary one at that.[10] A. Nikonov, praising Chayanov, has declared that forcible collectivisation was a disastrous departure from Leninist principles.[11] In Shmelev's words, it is wrong to justify Stalin's policy of that time by reference to war danger, as Hitler and the Nazis were still insignificant. The causes of the procurement crisis of 1928 were the low prices offered to peasants.

Against this is the argument of Klyamkin.[12] On the one hand he rightly 'defends' Trotskii and the left opposition from the charge of being indirectly responsible for the 'ultra-left excesses' (*levatskie peregiby*) of collectivisation. In doing this he criticises the writer Belov, and he could also have added Mozhaev;[13] the latter even managed to attach blame to three named persons, Trotskii, Kamenev and Kaganovich, two of whom have perfect alibis, but all of whom share the characteristic of being Jews. Klyamkin has pointed out that Trotskii's extreme statements about militarisation of labour dated from 1920, at a time when Lenin too envisaged a considerable degree of militarisation ('it was war communism!'). As for Trotskii and his friends, they had presented their left-wing criticisms within the policy confines of NEP. Therefore Stalin, in launching his collectivisation drive, was 'far to the left of the left opposition'. So far so good. But then, rather surprisingly, Klyamkin takes the line that given the exigencies of the time, the crash programme of heavy-industry investment was logical and so, then, was collectivisation, though he deplores its excesses and considers the fate of the peasantry to be a major injustice – they were victims of necessity. This is not altogether unlike Gorbachev's speech on the anniversary of the October Revolution, on 2 November 1987.

In a challenging article early in 1988, G.I. Shmelev made a devastating assault on the myth that Stalin was attacking the kulaks.[14] No, he insisted, the real target was the middle peasant. So the debate has been extended. Its relevance for the present day is evident, and indeed was spelt out by Nuikin in the second of his two articles cited above. Some supporters of perestroika have stated that they have in mind something other than NEP. He asks, 'Why?'. If it is because under NEP there were some private speculators and corrupt elements, surely there is plenty of evidence of just such phenomena, with most private activity genuinely productive, whereas in the centralised planning system the private (illegal) activities were mainly redistributive.

One still awaits the formal rehabilitation of other major figures in NEP economics, such as Bazarov, Groman, Falkner and Yurovskii. One awaits Danilov's two-volume history of collectivisation, begun over twenty years ago and then suspended. The refreshingly frank rethinking of the circumstances which brought NEP to an end, linked with a deep-going critique of Stalinism, is still in full swing at the time this essay goes to press. This is in striking contrast to the situation only a few years ago and is part of the effort to fill in the 'blank spaces' in the history of the USSR. With the hope of considerably wider access to archives, there is a prospect of further discussion based on new evidence, particularly because of the importance which scholars in the former Soviet Union now attach both to NEP and to its demise. There is now every possibility of a major contribution from them to the economic and intellectual history of the period. For which we would and should be profoundly grateful. Better late than never.

NOTES

1. Part of Rybakov's novel, *Deti Arbata*, was published in *Druzhba narodov*, no. 4 (1987). This reference is on p. 107.
2. Ibid., p. 112.
3. V. Novozhilov, 'Voprosy kon´yunktury', *Vestnik finansov*, 3 (1926) pp. 335–9.
4. Alec Nove, *An Economic History of the USSR* (Harmondsworth, 1969) p. 140.
5. Ibid., pp. 136–7.
6. *Potrebitel´skaya kooperatsiya na XIII godu oktyabr´skoi revolyutsii* (Moscow, 1929) pp. 5–6.
7. See E.A. Preobrazhensky, *The Crisis of Soviet Industrialisation*, ed. and intro. D.A. Filtzer (White Plains, N.Y., 1979).
8. Richard Day, *Leon Trotskii and the Politics of Economic Isolation* (London, 1973).
9. N. Shmelev, 'Avansy i dolgi', *Novyi mir*, 6 (1987) pp. 142–58.
10. A. Nuikin, 'Idealy ili interesy? Po stranitsam gazet i zhurnalov', *Novyi mir*, 1 (1988) pp. 190–211; 2 (1988) pp. 205–28.
11. A. Nikonov, 'Razvitie kooperatsii i reshenie prodovol´stvennoi problemy', *Voprosy ekonomiki*, 2 (1988) pp. 5–7.
12. Igor´ Klyamkin, 'Kakaya ulitsa vedet k khramu?' *Novyi mir*, 11 (1987) pp. 150–88.
13. *Don*, no. 3 (1987) (the postface).
14. G.I. Shmelev, 'Ne smet´ komandovat´!' *Oktyabr´*, 2 (1988) pp. 3–26. (Not to be confused with N. Shmelev).

12 Soviet Defence Industries during the First Five-Year Plan[†]

R.W. Davies

UNCERTAIN PRIORITIES 1929–30*

The claims of defence reinforced the claims of industrialisation. Tsarist Russia had developed a strong artillery, naval shipbuilding and military chemical industry, and good aircraft design and production facilities. The rapid expansion of armaments production in 1909–14 was made possible by the advance of heavy industry in the 1890s, and in turn played a major role in the industrial boom on the eve of the First World War. But in the mid-1920s the armed forces were only half their pre-war size, while armaments production was probably lower than in 1913.[1] The technical level of Soviet armaments generally lagged far behind those of the major capitalist powers. Artillery was entirely based on pre-war designs and war-time modifications. The Soviet Union had as yet no tank industry, though it had benefitted from German technical assistance in establishing design facilities. Even at the end of 1928 the Red Army possessed only 350 lorries and 700 motor cars.[2] The aircraft industry alone challenged the advanced countries with Tupolev's designs of metal aircraft; but its batch production consisted almost entirely of simple aircraft of foreign design, and aeroengines were largely imported.[3]

In the spring of 1927 the defeat of the Chinese communists and the rupture of diplomatic relations by Britain dramatically demonstrated that the Soviet Union was a weak and isolated power in a hostile world. The subsequent war scare in the

* The author wishes to express his gratitude to Professor D. Holloway and Dr. J.M. Cooper for their comments, and to Dr. Cooper for supplying valuable material.

† Sections of this Chapter are included in R.W. Davies, *The Industrialisation of Soviet Russia*, vol. III, *The Soviet Economy in Turmoil, 1929–1930* (London, 1990) and vol. IV, *Crisis and Progress in the Soviet Economy, 1931–1933* (forthcoming).

summer of 1927 was promoted by the party leaders to strengthen their hand against the Left Opposition.[4] But the international events of 1927 undoubtedly strengthened the resolve of the leadership to accelerate the development of the capital goods industries as a basis for a modern defence industry. In December 1927, the fifteenth party congress explicitly resolved:

> Bearing in mind the possibility of a military attack . . . it is essential in elaborating the five-year plan to devote maximum attention to a most rapid development of those branches of the economy in general and industry in particular on which the main role will fall in securing the defence and economic stability of the country in war-time.[5]

In 1927–9 the plans to develop a large-scale vehicle and tractor industry, and to establish major iron and steel and chemical facilities in the Urals and beyond, were strongly influenced by the need to establish an industrial capacity which would sustain a large modern armaments industry.[6]

But the production of modern armaments could not await these long-term industrial developments. Even before the international events of 1927, the Soviet authorities had already sought to revive and strengthen armaments production, following the deterioration of Soviet relations with Britain, France and Poland in 1926. Henceforth the short-term needs of defence competed with the claims of industrialisation, as well as reinforcing them. Simultaneously, greater attention was devoted to the integration of military and civil production by using armaments factories to produce civilian goods, and by adapting civilian factories so that they were ready for war-time conversion to military needs.[7]

In the course of 1928 and 1929, as the rising ambitions of every sector of the economy were recorded in successive drafts of the five-year plan, influential military leaders stressed the immediate claims of the armaments industries.[8] Early in 1928 a report by Tukhachevskii, chief of staff since November 1925, pointed out that the Soviet armed forces lagged technically behind the rest of Europe, and called for immediate and comprehensive technical rearmament, including the establishment of a powerful air force and of tank units with fast-moving tanks armed with guns.[9] According to a Soviet historian, Tukhachevskii's proposed figures were 'really grandiose for that time', and were condemned by Voroshilov and Stalin as unrealistic.[10] In May 1928, following this incident – though not entirely because of it – Tukhachevskii resigned from the post of chief of staff and was relegated to the command of the Leningrad military region.[11] Tukhachevskii, who had commanded the Warsaw offensive in 1920, combined his call for increased armaments with strong advocacy of the use of the Red Army as a spearhead of world revolution. He was replaced by the cautious non-party professional soldier, Shaposhnikov, and this temporarily restrained plans for massive rearmament.[12] The plan approved by the government on 30 July 1928, envisaged that the stock of tanks would reach a mere 1075 by the end of 1932.[13]

In the debate on the five-year plan at the sixteenth party conference in April 1929, Krzhizhanovskii, speaking on behalf of Gosplan, acknowledged, in response to complaints from the military, that military needs were insufficiently elaborated and 'possibly underestimated' in the plan, while Unshlikht, deputy people's commissar for war, was extremely critical of the military aspects of the plan.[14] This marked the beginning of a major shift in armaments policy. Shortly after the conference, even though the first Soviet tanks were only just being completed, the five-year plan for tank production was greatly expanded: 5000 tanks were to be manufactured in the course of the plan.[15] Two months later, on 10 July, Chinese troops acting on instructions from Chiang Kai-shek seized the Chinese Eastern Railway in Manchuria, which was jointly owned and managed by the Soviet and Chinese governments, and expelled its Soviet employees.[16] This was certainly the most serious direct challenge of a foreign power to the authority of the Soviet government since the years of civil war. Five days later, on 15 July 1929, the politburo adopted an important resolution 'On the Conditions of the Defence of the USSR'. While the resolution must have been in preparation for some time, it was presumably hurried through as a result of the Chinese attack. The resolution noted with satisfaction that the past five years had seen 'the creation of a strong army prepared for battle, fully reliable *in a political respect*, and corresponding *in a technical respect* to the level of development of the productive forces of the country.' According to the resolution, the adoption of the five-year plan created 'favourable conditions for the considerable qualitative and quantitative improvement of the defence of the USSR'; the next stage must be that in the course of the plan 'a modern military-technical basis for defence must be established'. As well as the modernisation of existing armaments, this would involve 'in the course of the next two years the acquisition of prototypes of modern artillery and of all modern types of tanks, armoured cars, etc., followed by their introduction into the army'. In the case of the air force, which was more advanced, the resolution called for 'the rapid development of its quality to the level of advanced bourgeois countries' and the 'inculcation, cultivation and development of Soviet research and design capacity, especially for aircraft engines'.[17] A few days later, the Revolutionary Military Council (RVS) of the USSR undertook to revise its five-year plan in the light of the politburo resolution.[18] The increased importance attached to the rapid development of the defence industries was marked by the establishment of the very senior post of Chief of Armaments to which Uborevich was appointed, and by the creation of a new Administration for Motorising and Mechanising the Red Army under Khalepskii.[19]

In response to the seizure of the Chinese Eastern Railway, the Soviet authorities established a Far Eastern Army under Blyukher and broke off relations with the Chiang Kai-shek government.[20] In the next two months strenuous but unsuccessful efforts were made by the Soviet side to reach agreement with Chiang Kai-shek; until November the Far Eastern Army undertook only minor military operations.[21] Behind the scenes the appropriate response to Chinese aggression was hotly debated. At the Moscow party conference in September 1929 Korostelev, from the Moscow party control commission, criticised 'a certain – I would call it – delicacy' on the part of the Soviet authorities in dealing with the Chinese attack:

> It seems to me that we have not displayed enough force or sufficiently rebuffed these rash adventurers. The more law-abiding restraint there is on our part, it seems to me, the more insolence and attacks on our territory there would be; and it is probable that the more rebuff we give to these attacks the less inclination there will be to seize our territory.[22]

Another delegate even more bluntly declared that 'the central committee is following an insufficiently harsh line'.[23] In a confused reply, Molotov argued that the object of the Chinese attack was to '*unwind the offensive against the USSR* by the imperialists', with the implication that the Soviet Union should avoid becoming the victim of provocation through hasty response; but he also admitted that the aim of the attack was 'to discredit the Soviet Union as a powerless country eaten up by economic difficulties and internal political complications'.[24] In November the Red Army acted more forcefully, and successfully routed the Chinese forces, using some of its new aeroplanes as well as troops; and Soviet rights on the railway were fully restored.[25]

This alarming incident strengthened the argument for an immediate effort to increase military strength, reinforcing the claim for expanding the military five-year plan at a time when all sectors of the economy were pressing for higher targets. On 11 January 1930, Tukhachevskii sent a report from Leningrad to Voroshilov arguing that 'the successes of our socialist construction . . . pose the urgent task of reconstructing the armed forces, taking into account all the latest technical factors, the possibilities of military-technical production and the developments in the countryside'; he called for an increase in the number of divisions and an expansion of artillery, aviation and tank armies.[26] This report was not published; but in a public lecture to the newly-established military section of the Communist Academy, later printed in the Academy journal, Tukhachevskii took the same line. He urged that the new mass production facilities in Soviet industry should be utilised, and criticised conservative fears that the mass use of motor vehicles was ruled out in the USSR by the state of the roads. Military thought, according to Tukhachevskii, also lagged behind the advance of industrialisation, and in contrast to other military experts he strongly advocated the use of large-scale offensive operations, condemned the strategy of defence in depth modelled on the Napoleonic war of 1812, and rejected the view that the proletarian state did not have the right to overthrow the bourgeoisie of another country by force.[27] Elsewhere he repudiated the claim of another expert that it was 'better to give up Minsk and Kiev than take Belostok and Brest' rejecting such views as 'the influence of bourgeois ideology on the theory of military art'.[28]

Tukhachevskii's report of January 1930 remained unanswered for several months; he wrote to Stalin in April requesting a reply, but Stalin bluntly responded that the adoption of this programme would lead to the elimination of socialist construction and its replacement by some kind of system of 'Red militarism'.[29] According to a Soviet historian, Stalin also observed that 'he could not understand how a Marxist can have such unrealistic ideas – to adopt such a project would mean to militarise the whole country and this was worse than any wrecking'.[30] To Tukhachevskii's humiliation, Stalin's reply was read out by Voroshilov to the RVS, nevertheless Tukhachevskii returned unsuccessfully to the argument on several occasions in the course of 1930.[31] Tukhachevskii was not alone in pressing for a rapid improvement in Soviet military strength, though others did not associate themselves with Tukhachevskii's offensive strategy. Military and planning officials concerned with the defence industries insistently urged both the immediate expansion of armaments production and the reorientation of the whole of industry to defence needs (see below). How far this new campaign had the active support rather than the mere acquiescence of Stalin and his supporters in the politburo is not known. It was soon followed by a further substantial shift in defence policy. According to the official Soviet history of the Second World War:

> In the period of preparation for the sixteenth congress of the party the CC CPSU (b) and the Soviet government required the RVS USSR to examine again the plan of military construction on the following principles:
> (a) numerically – not to lag behind our probable adversaries in the most important theatre of war;
> (b) in technology – to be stronger than our adversary in the three decisive types of armament, i.e. air force, artillery and tanks.[32]

This campaign for the strengthening of the defence industries reached its climax at the time of the sixteenth party congress, though without any public reference to the new guidelines. On 2 June Unshlikht was transferred from his post as deputy people's commissar for war to a deputy chairmanship of Vesenkha.[33] Unshlikht was a vigorous protagonist of the development of modern armaments,[34] and his appointment was evidently intended to augment the priority afforded to military orders within industry. Two weeks later, a striking article by Mekhonoshin, the head of the defence section of Gosplan, called for the forced development of the production of high quality alloys, non-ferrous metals and machine-building, including precision engineering, so that industry was ready for war-time military needs: tanks and tractors, civilian and military aircraft, armoured cars and automobiles, field and civil communications and electricals, and merchant and military shipping, must all be adapted so as to enable a rapid shift from civilian to defence production in time of war. Mekhonoshin insisted that developments so far were too slow; 'the whole attention of industrial and planning agencies, party and trade-union agencies' must be concentrated on this issue.[35] On the day on which the congress opened, *Izvestiya* published a full-page article on 'Military Development for the Sixteenth Congress', in which Ventsov, the head of the Mobilisation Section of the Staff of the Red Army, insisted, implicitly contradicting the politburo resolution of July 1929, that 'until recently the utilisation of technology for defence purposes and saturation of the army with technology have lagged behind the general technical development of industry'.[36]

At the congress itself Voroshilov, after discussing in some detail the substantial rearmament recently undertaken by the Western powers, including Poland and Romania, also claimed that industrial officials 'do not yet take the question seriously enough':

> Our war industry, and industry as a whole, both in the quantity and in the quality of its supplies of everything required for defence, is still hobbling quite badly.[37]

He added that he would return to this question in the debate on Kuibyshev's report, and would 'have to say something not entirely pleasant for our industry', but in the event he did not speak again at the congress. Instead Muklevich, from the Political Administration of the Red Army, resumed the attack on industry, complaining that 'often under the cover of secrecy nothing at all is done'. Civilian and military output were not yet interchangeable, the plans of armaments factories were vague and general and 'with many military orders there are delays, high costs and poor quality'. Shipbuilding was a case in point; with the development of a merchant fleet, the officials of the industry had neglected military orders, and endeavoured to push military shipbuilding out of their factories altogether.[38] Unshlikht, from his new vantage point within industry, also complained that orders from the Commissariat for War were frequently 'considered to be second-priority orders of secondary importance, with which there is no need to hurry', and insisted that an immediate improvement was essential:

> In the year 1930–31 the break-through must certainly take place. *It is absolutely essential to obtain a sharp reduction in prices, a considerable improvement in the quality of production; orders must not be left incomplete, and the period in which they are carried out must be shortened*, both for prototypes and for batch production.[39]

The major reports at the congress by Stalin and Kuibyshev had little to say about the defence industries, and the congress resolutions merely insisted on their importance in general terms. But soon after the congress Smilga, a prominent old Bolshevik and former oppositionist with considerable experience both in the Red Army and in planning, was appointed head of the Mobilisation-Planning Administration of Vesenkha, and both he and Budnyak, a prominent official concerned with the armaments industries, were appointed to the presidium of Vesenkha: Unshlikht, Smilga and Budnyak now constituted a formidable pressure group within the industrial administration.[40] The needs of the defence industries gradually received greater emphasis. In an article in the economic newspaper on 13 August 1930, Zarzar, in charge of 'aerofication and automobilisation' in Gosplan, called for major improvements in the aircraft industry. He pointed out that the design and production of engines was lagging behind airframes; and complained that Soviet civil aviation received less of its income in subsidies than its European equivalents and must be developed rapidly.[41] In a further article he proposed more attention to airships, and more generally complained that the 1928 and 1930 variants of the five-year plan for 'aerofication' were inadequate; Dirazhblestroi, responsible for constructing airship factories, and Aviastroi, responsible for constructing aircraft factories, must be developed on a par with Dneprostroi.[42]

The issues continued to be hotly disputed behind the scenes, and the higher party authorities intervened on several occasions in favour of the needs of defence. On 16 August 1930, three days after the publication of Zarzar's first article, Stalin and Voroshilov, on holiday in Sochi, wrote to the politburo objecting to the dilatoriness of the commission on civil aviation headed by Rudzutak:

> The military air force of the largest imperialist countries is mainly based on the might of the civil air force . . . In view of our almost complete lack of a civil air force and the related absolute weakness of the military air force, we consider it necessary to make up for lost time . . . In connection with this it is necessary to construct a number of factories (east of the Volga) for engines, aircraft and airships, so as to raise the Civil Air Force to 10–15 thousand tons within a short period of time. Of course this will involve setting up a special agency.

Such developments would cost 'hundreds of millions' of rubles.[43]

The party leaders also intervened in support of aeroengine development at this time. While Stalin and Voroshilov were still in Sochi, Baranov, head of the Air Force, and Uborevich sent them a telegram complaining that aircraft engine design was hampered by lack of facilities. After talking to the designer Charomskii, Voroshilov sent a telegram of support to the party central committee headquarters, and a subsequent meeting attended by politburo members agreed to the formation of an Aero-Engine Institute.[44]

As in other industries these efforts to strengthen the defence industries were undermined by the large number of arrests of specialists in the course of 1929 and 1930. In October 1929, for example, five former generals working in war industry were found guilty of spying and sentenced to death; their associates were imprisoned in concentration camps.[45] In the aircraft industry, the leading designers Polikarpov and Grigorovich were arrested in September 1929, but from 1930 were employed in a Central Design Bureau (TsKB) established at the 'Aviarabotnik' factory No. 39 in Moscow, under the supervision of the Technical Section of the OGPU. The TsKB, formed in the spring of 1930 combined a number of separate design bureaus, and employed both imprisoned and free staff.[46]

The TsKB had a staff of 300 by the end of 1930, and 500 by the autumn of 1931.[47] According to the aircraft designer Yakovlev, who worked there with other free engineers, 'the organisation was overstaffed and senseless, the expenditure great and the results small; only Polikarpov worked brilliantly'.[48] Polikarpov and Grigorovich were eventually released in 1933.[49]

Firm evidence is lacking on the extent to which the mounting attention devoted to the defence industries in 1929 and 1930 resulted in practice in an increase in their share of industrial resources: only scrappy statistics are available on investment and production in 1928–30. In 1929, after long delays, Tupolev's first military aircraft, the all-metal reconnaissance bi-plane ANT-3, went into production.[50] In the summer and autumn of that year Soviet aviation undertook a series of remarkable and well-publicised flights, including a flight from Moscow to London and back on the nine-seater three-engined passenger aircraft ANT-9 and from Moscow to New York via Siberia on the ANT-4; this was the heavy two-engined bomber monoplane TB-1 with its armour removed. Both of these aircraft went into batch production at this time.[51] In 1930 aircraft production was substantially higher than in 1928 and 1929 (see Table 12.1) and under the peculiar conditions of GPU control, research and design facilities expanded.[52] Investment in civil aviation, presumably in the infrastructure, expanded from the minute figure of 5 million rubles in 1929 to 30 million rubles in 1930.[53] In 1930, with the batch production of the MS-1 based on the Renault light tank, tanks were manufactured in substantial numbers for the first time.[54]

After the sixteenth party congress, production in the defence industries evidently accelerated. In October–December 1930, the production of 'other machine-building', the main item of which was the defence industries, was 25.6 per cent higher than in the previous quarter, while the production of machine-building and metal-working as a whole increased by only 18.1 per cent (see Table 12.3). But the increase of capital investment in 'other machine-building' was slightly less rapid than in the sector as a whole.[55]

In spite of this progress, the defence industries were often less successful in fulfilling their plans than the other sectors of heavy industry. The production of tanks amounted to only 20 per cent of the plan in 1929, 65 per cent in January–March 1930, and 20 per cent in April–June and July–September 1930.[56] In 1930, passengers and freight carried by civil aviation also lagged far behind the five-year plan approved in the spring of 1929;[57] and in October–December 1930, in spite of Politburo support, invest-

TABLE 12.1 *Armaments production 1926–34*

	1926	*1927*	*1928*	*1929*	*1929/30*[b]	*1 Oct 1930–31 Dec 1931*[b]	*1932*	*1933*	*1934*
Tanks and tankettes	–	–	–	1[a]	170[3b]	740[3b]	3 038[3]	3 509[3]	3 565[3]
Aircraft	469[1]	575[1]	870[1]	785[2]	899[3b]	860[3b]	1 734[3]	2 952[3]	3 109[3]
of which, fighters	–	–	–	106[2]	–	120	74	336	570
bombers	–	–	–	88[2]	–	100	72	291	392
all military	309[1]	495[1c]	610[1]	–	–	–	–	–	–
Artillery pieces	–	–	–	–	952	1 966	3 574	4 638	4 123
of which, small guns	–	–	–	–	344	1 040	972	2 884	2 521
machine guns	–	–	–	–	600	870	1 576	1 703	1 527
large guns	–	–	–	–	(8)	(56)	(26)	(51)	(75)
Machine-guns (thousand)	–	–	–	–	9.7	41.0	45.0	32.7	29.2
Rifles and carbines (thousand)	–	–	–	–	126	174	224	241	303

Notes

[a] Derived by subtracting figures for 1929/30, 1930/31, and 1932 from total production in first five-year plan, given as 3949 in *Istoriya vtoroi mirovoi voiny*, vol. I, 260.

[b] These figures are given as for 1930 and 1931 in the source; but some of the figures in the column for 1931 appear as for '1930–1931' in *50 let*, p. 193, and in VIZh, 2 (1971) 7. The figures for tank production cannot, however, be for 1930–1 (average), because in that case the total for 1930–2 would be 740 + 740 + 3038, higher than the total output of 3949 in the first five-year plan. It seems impossible that the production of aircraft, for example, in the two years 1930 and 1931 was only 860, when production was already over 600 in 1928, and in any case this would make the column for 1930 in the Table above inexplicable. It therefore seems plausible that '1930–1' in the original table in the archives was for the special quarter of 1930 (Oct.–Dec.) plus the calendar year 1931; in this case the figure for 1930 presumably refers to the economic year 1929/30.

[c] Production of Aviatrest is given as 200 in VIZh, 12 (1964) 7, but its figures for 1929 onwards coincide with Shumikhin's figures for total production.

[d] Excluding naval guns.

[e] Residual.

SOURCES *Istoriya vtoroi mirovoi voiny*, vol. 1 (Moscow, 1973), 214, except where otherwise stated.

[1] V.S. Shumikhin, *Sovetskaya voennaya aviatsiya, 1917–1941* (Moscow, 1986) p. 103.

[2] Ibid., p. 157.

[3] VIZh, 12 (1964) 7 (given as the production of Aviatrest).

This Table is a revised version of part of Tables II–VII in Cooper, 'Defence Production'.

ment in civil aviation amounted to only 50 per cent of the quarterly plan.[58] While defence factories and military orders were supposed to be afforded top priority, the urgent claims of the key civilian projects, such as the Ural-Kuzbass combine and the tractor and lorry factories – which themselves had considerable military potential – frequently overrode the claims of the directly military projects.[59] High priority civilian research sometimes drove out military research. In 1930, when the automobile-engine research institute NAMI was transferred to the administrative control of the vehicle and tractor corporation, its aviation department (with its equipment) was ejected from NAMI premises and transferred physically as well as administratively to the aviation research institute TsAGI, even though the latter was so short of space that it was partly accommodated in an old church.[60] And urgent civilian production sometimes drove out military production. In October 1930 Vesenkha ruled that the maximum use should be made of defence industry factories for civilian production for the heavy machine-building industry, as part of the drive to reduce imports.[61] In December, Voroshilov complained to Ordzhonikidze that a mere 29.6 per cent of the quarterly allocation of 24 000 tons of pig-iron to artillery factories had been received by December 14;[62] in contrast total production of pig-iron in October–December 1930 amounted to as much as 79.8 per cent of the quarterly plan of 1 546 000 tons.[63] The problems of affording priority to the defence industries partly reflected the inherent difficulties of the task of assimilating what in many respects required a more complex technology, and was more demanding in terms of materials, workmanship and quality standards than anything previously produced in Russia. But at the end of 1930 the defence industries were evidently still of lower priority in practice than the tractor or iron and steel industries. The authorities proceeded on the assumption that there was no immediate threat of a major war, and the delicate balance between longer-term and immediate military strength was still tilted towards the construction of a powerful heavy industry as a basis for future defence.

DEFENCE IMPERATIVES, 1931–33

The shift of resources towards immediate defence needs, which already began in 1930, was taken much further in the remaining years of the five-year plan. On 10 January 1931, a 'calendar plan' for the development of the Red Army in 1931–3 was approved by RVS. This plan was described by Soviet military historians as having 'completed the elaboration of an integrated scientifically-based first five-year plan of military development'.[64] Simultaneously in January 1931 a revision to the previous guidelines for the Red Army five-year plan, approved by the politburo, significantly declared that the army should be numerically not equal to but 'superior to our probable adversaries in the most important theatre of war.'[65]

A larger army obviously presupposed that industry must supply a greater quantity of weapons. And in the course of 1931 international developments impelled the authorities to attach even greater urgency to the fulfilment of these objectives. In March the Japanese military attaché in Moscow sent a telegram to the General Staff in Tokyo, which was intercepted by Soviet intelligence, denigrating Soviet military capacity and calling for 'a speedy war with the Soviet Union'.[66] In September, Japan invaded Manchuria, where powerful émigré organisations formed a 'Russian National Union of the Far East', supported by the Japanese; a memorandum from General Sobolevskii called for 'the overthrow by force of the communist dictatorship ruling over the Russian people' and the establishment of an independent Russian national buffer state on Siberian territory with the assistance of a dissident Red Army; to this end it would be 'indispensable to enter into friendly cooperation with any outside power, which is interested in striking a blow upon the Soviet government'[67] (an obvious reference to Japan).

The Soviet authorities reacted sharply to these alarming developments. On 11 June 1931, Uborevich, deputy people's commissar for military and naval affairs and head of armaments in the Red Army, was transferred to the Belorussian military district and was replaced by Tukhachevskii,[68] and Baranov, head of the Red Army air forces since 1924, was transferred to the presidium of Vesenkha, where he was placed in charge of the aircraft industry.[69] In view of the disputes about armaments policy in which Tukhachevskii had been involved in the previous three years, his appointment was a startling move; and it was soon followed by changes in armaments policy.[70] In August 1931, STO approved a new programme for tank production in 1931–3; this became known as the 'big tank programme' and accepted the proposal to establish mechanised army units which could engage in deep operations. For industry, this involved the large-scale production of tanks not previously manufactured in the USSR, including the T-26 medium tank (based on the Vickers 6-ton model), the T-27 machine-gun carrier (based on the Vickers Carden-Lloyd model), and the track-wheeled BT (based on the 10-ton United States Christie).[71]

The production of armaments in 1931 was very much higher than in 1930, increasing by an estimated 74 per cent, as compared with an increase of 39 per cent for the rest of the machine-building and metal-working industries (see Table 12.3). In 1931 the production of tanks, artillery and small arms all increased substantially (see Table 12.1). Production by the Shipbuilding Corporation Soyuzverf′, which is believed to have included naval vessels, also increased (see Table 12.3, General Note). Capital investment in the armaments industry increased by 76 per cent, in the rest of machine-building by 67 per cent. In support of this expansion, the defence industries received 67 per cent of their claim for rolled steel, as compared with the 56 per cent received by the rest of the economy: no other sector received so high a proportion.[72] Investment in the aircraft industry expanded particularly rapidly; in 1931 it was greater than in the whole period 1927–30.[73] By 1931, six aircraft factories in Moscow and Moscow region employed 21 000 persons as compared with a mere 2 900 in 1925/26.[74] Investment in shipbuilding in 1931 was also much higher than in previous years.[75]

Production of explosives, poison-gas and other chemicals for defence purposes increased by an estimated 46 per cent. Although this increase was less rapid than the expansion of armaments, it outpaced the rest of the chemical industry, which grew by 27 per cent. But investment increased somewhat more slowly in the military chemical industry than in the rest of the chemical industry. (See Tables 12.3 and 12.4.) Investment in civil aviation rose sharply[76]; this sector was frankly described by Kuibyshev earlier in the year as the '*base of defence in the event of the emergence of military action*'.[77] But all these substantial increases appear to have resulted not so much from the Japanese crisis as

TABLE 12.2 *Stock of military equipment 1928, 1932 and 1933*

	1 Jan 1928[a]	*1 Jan 1932*[a]	*1 Jan 1933*	*1 Jan 1934*	*1 Jan 1935*[a]
Tanks and tankettes	92	1 401	(4 439[b])	(7 948[b])	10 180
of which, tankettes	–	348	–	–	2 547
Aircraft in Air Force	1 394	3 285	–[c]	–[c]	6 672
Artillery pieces	7 000[1d]	14 000[2]	–[c]	17 000[1]	–
of which, 76mm and over	6 645	10 684	–[c]	–[c]	13 867
Machine guns : light	8 811	22 553	–	–	83 922
heavy	24 230	33 118	–	–	53 492
TOTAL	33 041	55 671	–[c]	–[c]	137 414
Rifles and carbines (th)	1 596	2 292	(2 516[b])	(2 757[b])	3 050

Notes

[a] The source simply gives the calendar year, but the figures are compatible with production figures only on assumption that it really refers to January 1.

[b] Estimated by adding production figures for year concerned to stock at beginning of year; figure is therefore too high because it does not allow for scrapping.

[c] Scrapping rate evidently too high for estimate as in Note[b] to be feasible.

[d] Jan 1. 1929.

SOURCES *Istoriya vtoroi mirovoi voiny*, vol. I (1973), 270, unless otherwise stated.

[1] G.S. Kravchenko, *Ekonomika SSR v gody Velikoi Otechestvennoi Voiny*, 2nd edn (Moscow, 1970) p. 80.

[2] V.P. Kazakov, *Vsegda s pekhotoi, vsegda s tankami* (Moscow, 1969) p. 8.

This Table is a revised version of part of Table X in Cooper, 'Defence production'.

TABLE 12.3 *The defence production residual 1930–1931 (gross production, million rubles at 1926/27 prices)*

	1930	*1931*	*Increase in %*
Total machine-building and metalworking	4 089.2[1]	5 723.8[1]	40.0
Less listed combines	2 826.5[1]	3 920.6[1]	38.7
Less Republican industry: metal industry	707.3[2]	837.0[2]	18.3
Residual machine-building and metalworking	(555.4)	(966.2)	74.0
Total chemical Group 'A'	1 002.4[3]	1 317.6[3]	31.4
Less listed combines	762.9[4a]	955.9[4a]	25.3
Less Republican industry: chemical Group 'A'	119.7[2]	141.3[2]	18.0
Residual chemical	(119.8)	(220.4)	84.0
Total machine-building and metalworking residual plus chemical residual	(675.2)	(1 186.6)	75.7

Notes

General note The residual items may include non-defence production which has not been separately listed, but no major missing civilian items have been detected. The rate of growth is in any case too rapid for miscellaneous items of civilian production.

The defence combines and factories included in the residual items produced some civilian production (perhaps a substantial amount); this probably appears as part of the residual. Non-defence combines and factories produced some defence production, which probably appears as part of their production. The most important items here are:

(1) shipbuilding – apparently ships for the Red Navy were produced by the combines Soyuzverf′ (the production of which was 210.7 million rubles in 1930, 251.6 in 1931) and Rechsoyuzverf′ (54.3 in 1930, 61.3 in 1931). Alternative figures for Soyuzverf′ production are given in *Desyat′let* (1932), 8 (million rubles): 1928/29 93; 1929/30 159; Oct.1–Dec. 31, 1930 51; 1931 218.

(2) tanks and tankettes, armoured cars, which were produced in civilian factories.

[a] The production of the following is given on p. 41 of *Itogi* : lacquers and dyes; rubber; and on p. 175: basic chemistry (including chemical mining, which does not appear elsewhere); plastics; cooking-chemical; anilyne dyes (artificial fibre and chemical-pharmaceutical, listed with Chemicals Industry on p. 175, appear elsewhere in the series on pp. 36–44).

SOURCES all from *Itogi* (1932),[1] pp. 39–40;[2] pp. 63–5;[3] p. 41;[4] pp. 41, 175.

from the decisions after the sixteenth party congress to devote more attention to the defence industries. According to a Soviet source, tank production began to increase in July-December 1931,[78] but other slender evidence available in the quarterly industrial production figures does not indicate that defence production increased more rapidly in the second half of the year.

From the beginning of 1932, however, following the Japanese invasion of Manchuria, much greater attention was devoted to the defence industries. At the session of TsIK in December 1931 Molotov spoke in strong terms of the 'growing danger of military intervention against the USSR'. The state budget for 1932 presented to TsIK by the people's commissar for finance, Grin'ko, incongruously proposed that defence expenditure should decline as a proportion of the total budget.[79] Defence expenditure in 1931, while increasing by 23 per cent as compared with 1929/30, was also reported to have declined as a proportion of the budget. These figures obviously concealed the true picture: according to data presented by Litvinov to the League of Nations, the budget allocation for 1931 did not contain any allowance for the cost of armaments.[80] At the TsIK session, in an unprecedented episode, one of the delegates, taking these modest defence proposals at their face value, or possibly acting on behalf of those in high places who wished to increase defence expenditure further, criticised Grin'ko's silence about expenditure on the Red Army, asking rhetorically 'Are not our expenditures too modest?' In response to Molotov's reference in his report to the squeeze which must be imposed on the economy in the interests of the iron and steel industry, the delegate insisted that 'if, in the interests of defence of our frontiers from all kinds of provocative actions, we have to squeeze very many sectors of the economy and other requirements, we must do this'.[81] In support of this argument, another delegate, Gorbachev by name, drew attention to the extent of Polish, French, United States and Japanese rearmament.[82] Grin'ko merely replied rather lamely that the strength of our defence lies mainly in the development of socialist industry, together with agriculture and culture. The budget proposals were for the moment approved without alteration.[83]

In the meantime, however, action was taken at a higher level. On 23 December 1931, while the TsIK session was in progress, the politburo established a 'commission to develop measures to reduce the military danger in the Far East'; its members

TABLE 12.4 *Capital investment in the defence industries*

(a) Capital investment residual 1930–1931
(million rubles, 'at the value of work actually carried out')

	1930	*1931*	*Increase in %*
Machine-building and metalworking[a]	858.2	1 404.2	63.6
Less listed items	671.7	1 076.6	60.3
Residual machine-building and metalworking (including republican machine-building)	186.5	327.6[b]	75.7
Chemical Group 'A'	391.8	787.6	101.0
Less listed items	260.4	596.5	129.1
Residual chemical 'A' including republican	131.4	191.1	45.4
TOTAL residual machine-building and metalworking plus chemical, including republican	317.9	518.7	63.2

Notes
General note The comments to Table 3 probably also apply here, except that specific allocations for the construction of armaments shops in existing factories may have been financed as part of the residual item.
The residuals in the Table are too large, for the following reasons:

(1) *Machinery and metal-working*. The residual includes:
  (i) the combines or trusts for pumps and compressors, machinery repair, welding (VAT), castings (Soyuzformolit'e), Orgametall and the research institute TsNIIMash. Financial allocation for these organisations amounted to 25.7 million rubles in 1931 (see pp. 198–9); financial allocations are somewhat larger than 'the value of work actually carried out'.
  (ii) probably republican machine-building, investment in which was planned to amount to 79.9 million rubles in 1932 (pp. 198–9).

(2) *Chemicals*. The residual includes the combines or trusts for plastics, artificial rubber, and rubber-growing (Kauchkonos), and republican industry. Financial allocations for these organisations amounted to 90.2 million rubles in 1931, including 39.7 for republican industry and 35.0 for artificial rubber (see pp. 196–7). The allocation to republican industry was planned to fall to 26.6 in 1932, while that to artificial rubber was planned to rise to 63.0.

[a] Covers 98 per cent of all investment; excludes some local machine-building and metalworking, and chemical industry (see *Itogi* (1932), 115), but includes metalworking and electrical engineering, given separately in the original table.

[b] Investment in reconstruction of aircraft factories in 1932 amounting to 75 million rubles (see above) is evidently part of this total.

SOURCE all from *Itogi* (1932) pp. 117–9.

(*b*) *'Other industry' state budget allocation, 1928/29–1932 (million rubles)*

1928/29[1]		*1929/30*[2]		*1931*[3]		*1932*[4]	
Plan	*Actual*	*Plan*	*Actual*	*Plan*	*Actual*	*Plan*	*Actual*
80.0	76.0	124.0	129.7	455.0	587.5	700.0	714.4

Note This is the total allocation to 'other industry' under the National Economy heading of the state budget; this no doubt includes net allocations to working capital, including subsidies, and excludes allocations to investment from defence industry profits etc.

SOURCES [1] *Otchet Narodnogo komissariata Finansov Soyuza SSR ob ispolnenii edinogo gosudarstvennogo byudzheta za 1928–1929* (1930) p. 86.
[2] *Otchet . . . za 1929–1930* (1931) p. 84.
[3] *Otchet . . . za 1931* (1932) p. 5.
[4] *Otchet . . . za 1932* (1932 (*sic*) [1933]) p. 5.

included Stalin, Voroshilov and Ordzhonikidze.[84] Then, on 28 December (the day on which the TsIK session closed) the importance of the defence industries was symbolised by the establishment of a *glavk* (Chief Administration) for the aviation industry GUAP, with Baranov at its head, on the basis of the aviation corporation VAO.[85] The urgent necessity of strengthening Soviet military power in the Far East was confirmed early in January 1932, when Japanese officials responded to a Soviet offer of a non-aggression pact by open talk about annexing the Soviet Far-Eastern coastline and Kamchatka.[86] The dangers were publicly recognised – perhaps even exaggerated – by the Soviet authorities. Molotov told the seventeenth party conference at the end of January that 'the danger of imperialist attack has considerably increased',[87] while on the occasion of Red Army Day an editorial in the industrial newspaper went so far as to refer to the 'extremely alarming international situation, clearly recalling 1914', resulting from Japanese imperialism's policy of 'blood and war'.[88]

All the evidence points to a further substantial increase in the armaments effort from the beginning of 1932. A year later, at the plenum of the party central committee in January 1933, Kirov dated the switch to defence production as having taken place on the initiative of Stalin 'in the past eighteen months [i.e. since approximately July 1931] and especially in 1932'.[89] On the same occasion Stalin referred to 'the refusal of neighbouring countries to sign non-aggression pacts with us' and 'the complications in the Far East', as the factors which had made it necessary to 'reorient a number of factories to the production of modern defence weapons', leading them to be closed for four months in 1932.[90] Our knowledge of what happened is fragmentary. In January 1932, the politburo indicated the enhanced importance attached to armaments by deciding to appoint party organisers directly responsible to the central committee at large military factories.[91] In February the politburo ordered that the huge Putilov works in Leningrad should participate in the production of the medium T-26 tank by producing 3000 sets of running gears. The works ceased turbine production for five months; a special steel-casting shop was built at the factory, and afforded 'super-priority' by the central authorities; the factory was allocated 156 million rubles for the cost of conversion.[92] The huge 'Bolshevik' factory in Leningrad was also involved in production of new tank models, possibly the T-26 and T-27.[93] In Kharkov, the vast locomotive works developed the production of the BT tank in association with the Kharkov tractor factory.[94] Similar conversions took place in other industries. In April 1932 the British embassy in Moscow reported that factories in Rostov and Mytishchi (near Moscow) had recently been partly converted to military production, and that other defence factories were working at high pressure.[95] Nor were longer-term needs neglected. In February 1932, Tukhachevskii stressed the importance of the 'strong design cadres in all spheres of armament' which had already been established, and announced that the basis for a completely new system of communications had been laid by the radio industry.[96] In the following month he convened a meeting of rocket engineers with military specialists, stressing the importance of new types of weapons and calling for the strengthening of research and development in rocketry.[97]

The greater attention to military needs had wider economic repercussions than those directly resulting from the transfer of men and materials away from civilian production at the factories concerned. Major civilian factories had to supply skilled manpower for new and expanded defence factories which were rarely mentioned in the press. Thus the Putilov works sent some of its best party members to key posts in tank factories;[98] the AMO automobile works in Moscow sent its production manager to the aircraft industry so that the latter could acquire the experience of the automobile industry.[99] Civilian planning staffs were increasingly diverted to military projects. On 1 June 1932, the Stalingrad tractor factory and the research institute NATI were instructed to design a diesel-powered universal tractor/transporter based on the Carden-Lloyd tankette, under technical conditions approved by the military.[100] More or less simultaneously, the tractor industry began to prepare for the conversion of most or all of its production during the course of the second five-year plan to caterpillar tractors: military needs dictated the proposed pace and scale of the conversion.[101]

Following the extensive visit of Voroshilov to the Far East in the summer of 1931,[102] and the establishment of the integrated Far Eastern construction organisation Dal'stroi directly responsible to STO in November 1931,[103] a commission under Gamarnik, head of the political administration of the Red Army, decided in February 1932 to establish a base for military production in the interior 400 kilometres from Khabarovsk, at the small village of Permskoe on the Amur, which at that time could be reached only by plane or by a river open to goods traffic only in summer.[104] The Amur base was planned to include a ship-building and aircraft factory. The politburo despatched Kosarev, general secretary of the Komsomol, to the Far East in March 1932, and following his visit 5586 young communists were sent to Permskoe in the spring from all parts of the Soviet Union.[105] While work was only in its preliminary stages in 1932 – an extravagant plan to complete the military factories by the end of the year got nowhere – the new project drew heavily on the scarce enthusiastic manpower of major civilian factories and construction sites, including Dneproges and the new automobile plant in Nizhnii Novgorod, as well as on senior managers and engineers.[106]

Tension in the Far East abated only momentarily in the course of 1932. While some prominent Japanese politicians sought to overcome the breach with the Soviet Union, the influential war minister Araki remained in post, and told a journalist in June 1932 that war with the Soviet Union was 'sooner or later inevitable'.[107] The Soviet ambassador in Japan reported in August that the Japanese army was preparing for war, and military factories were working day and night.[108] The Soviet authorities were no doubt further alarmed by a report from their chargé d'affaires in London that the Japanese government had asked Britain and France whether it could have their direct support in the event of war with the USSR.[109]

It has not been possible to assess the extent to which such additional defence projects drew upon manpower and materials in the course of 1932. Stalin's claim that this was the sole factor leading to underfulfilment of the five-year plan for industry cannot of course be taken seriously. Nor should the abruptness of the shift to defence investment and production be exaggerated: the major expansion of the defence industries had already begun in 1931. But the additional claims of defence in the course of 1932 certainly exacerbated all other economic difficulties.

Following the substantial investments of 1931 and 1932, armaments production expanded rapidly in 1933, when several other major industries were stagnating. The production of tanks and guns rose substantially; and 1933 saw the mass production of modern military aircraft for the first time, with the quadrupling of fighter and bomber production in a single year (see Table 12.1). Between 1928 and 1933 the Soviet armed forces increased in size from 630 000 to 885 000 men:[110] and the military equipment of the Soviet armed forces was transformed. The approximate increase in stock is indicated in Table 12.2; the number of aircraft, tanks and automobiles expanded enormously (from a very low level) the stock of guns more than doubled, and the number of rifles increased from 1.5 to 2.5 million. In general, by the end of 1933, the quantity of Soviet armaments far exceeded that of its major rivals France and Japan, and Germany had hardly begun to rearm.[111] A vast improvement had also taken place in the level of military technology. Voroshilov, in his report to the seventeenth party congress in January 1934, was able to claim with some justice that since 1930 the army 'has become as it were a different army in principle, in relation to the quantity and quality of its armament, its organisational structure and the military preparedness of its cadres'. According to Voroshilov, though the poor state of the railways and the decline in the number of horses presented the army with considerable transport problems, in the defence industry mechanical horse-power per soldier had increased from 2.6 in 1929 to 7.74 in 1933, and was 'considerably higher than in the French and American armies and even higher than in the British army, which is the most mechanised'.[112] Voroshilov was unable to anticipate that the precipitate rearmament of Nazi Germany, together with the disorder in the armed forces resulting from the purges, would gravely damage the relative defence capacity of the USSR before the end of the second five-year plan in 1937.

CONCLUSIONS

Bolshevik economic policy was strongly influenced by the pressing needs of defence. In the mid-1920s the economic gap between the USSR and the other great powers was wider than in 1913, particularly in technology; and the armaments industries lagged to an even greater extent. All the Soviet leaders were convinced that sooner or later their country would be attacked by hostile capitalist powers; and from 1927 onwards, with the defeat of the Chinese communists and the breaking-off by Britain of diplomatic relations with the USSR, the Soviet sense of international isolation was acute. To 'overtake the advanced countries in an economic and technical respect' was essential if the Soviet Union was to become militarily strong enough to rebuff the eventual attack.

Soviet long-term planning was strongly influenced by military considerations. The military argument in favour of the expensive Ural-Kuznetsk iron and steel combine – and the associated tractor and heavy engineering factories at Chelyabinsk and Sverdlovsk – was decisive: the USSR must establish a modern heavy industry remote from the frontiers.[113] Much effort was devoted to the design of civilian factories so that they could be readily transferred in emergency to military needs.

It proved extremely difficult, within this general context, to determine the importance to be attached to the immediate strengthening of the Soviet defence industries in case of a sudden attack. Investment in armaments factories and the allocation of increased resources to armaments production meant that less was available for non-military industry. Many military men accepted that the modernisation of the armed services must be a lengthy process; but others, notably Tukhachevskii, pressed for the allocation of greatly increased resources to direct military needs. In 1928 and 1929 the Soviet authorities assumed that major military attacks on the Soviet Union would not occur immediately. But in the course of 1930–2 resources were increasingly switched to directly military needs, under the impact first of the increased tension in Europe in 1930 and then of Japanese hostility and the Japanese invasion of Manchuria in 1931. During 1931–3 a major effort was undertaken to develop a modern armaments industry; and by the end of 1933 the Soviet Union was militarily one of the strongest great powers.

But these developments took place at a time when the other great powers – with the exception of Japan – were not substantially increasing the resources devoted to armaments. The seizure of power by the Nazis in January 1933 transformed the situation. In spite of the industrial development of the USSR in 1929–33, Germany remained industrially and technically much more advanced than the USSR, and the Soviet military developments described in this Chapter soon proved inadequate in face of German rearmament.[114]

NOTES

1. The armed services numbered 630 000 in December 1926 as compared with 1 200 000 in the Army alone in April 1914. S.G. Wheatcroft, 'Changes in the Pattern of Employment in the USSR, 1926–1939', unpublished paper presented to Social Science Research Council Conference on Soviet Economic Development in the 1930s (CREES, University of Birmingham, 1982), p. 7; P. Kenez, 'A Profile of the Pre-Revolutionary Officer Corps', *Californian Slavic Studies*, 7 (1973) 133; for armaments production in 1913, 1926/27 and 1927/28, see P. Gatrell and R.W. Davies, 'The Industrial Economy', in R.W. Davies (ed.) *From Tsarism to the New Economic Policy* (London, 1990).
2. *Voenno-istoricheskii zhurnal*, 12 (1964) 9 (hereafter VIZh).
3. See J.M. Cooper and R.A. Lewis, 'Research and Technology', in Davies (ed.), *From Tsarism.* . . . For Voroshilov's assessment of the backwardness of the Soviet defence industry in 1927, see *Pyatnadtsatyi s"ezd VKP (b): dekabr' 1927 goda: stenograficheskii otchet*, vol. II (Moscow, 1962) p. 988.
4. See A.G. Meyer, 'The War Scare of 1927', *Soviet Union/Union Sovietique*, V, 1 (1978) 1–25; the author underplays the leaders' sense of danger by underestimating the significance of the party central committee resolution of 1 June 1927.
5. *Kommunisticheskaya partiya Sovetskogo Soyuza v rezolyutsiakh*, 2nd edn, vol. II *1924–1930* (Moscow, 1954) p. 452.
6. See E.H. Carr and R.W. Davies, *Foundations of a Planned Economy, 1926–1929*, vol. I (London, 1969), pp. 426–31, 439 and R.W. Davies, 'A Note on

the Ural-Kuznetsk Combine', *Soviet Studies*, XXVI (1974), pp. 272–4.

7. See Carr and Davies, *Foundations*, pp. 426–31.
8. In his careful study of Soviet military literature, M.V. Boetticher, *Industrielisierungspolitik und Verteidigungskonzeption der UdSSR, 1926–1930* (Düsseldorf, 1979) argues that the military stressed the importance for defence both of heavy industry and of the supply of food, fodder and horses from a stable agriculture. He claims that there was no 'rational justification, from the point of view of security', for the rapid industrialisation policies of the party leadership at the end of the 1920s (M.V. Boetticher, 'Soviet Defence Policy and the First Five-Year Plan', unpublished working paper, West European Conference on Soviet Industry and the Working Class in the Inter-War Years, University of Birmingham, 1981 (CREES, University of Birmingham, 1981) p. 17. But this does not refute the view that increasing pressure from the military for the expansion of heavy industry was one of the factors influencing the party leadership in 1927–30; moreover, Boetticher underestimates the significance of the campaign by Tukhachevskii and his colleagues.
9. A further unpublished report, 'Future War', prepared in the IV Administration of the Red Army in 1928 by Tukhachevskii, Ya.K. Berzin and others, called for the establishment of (1) motorised rifle and machine-gun units (*chasti*), supported by fast moving tanks, (2) large cavalry units supported by armoured cars and fast-moving tanks, and (3) large air-attack units (VIZh, 5 (1983) pp. 79, 82–3 – R. Savushkin).
10. VIZh, 4 (1963) p. 66 (G. Isserson); Tukhachevskii's figures have not been available.
11. Ibid.; M.N. Tukhachevskii, *Izbrannye proizvedeniya*, vol. I (Moscow, 1964) p. 11.
12. On the replacement of Tukhachevskii, see E.H. Carr, *Foundations of a Planned Economy, 1926–1929*, vol. II (London, 1971) pp. 319–20.
13. VIZh, 8 (1968) p. 105; for the production of tanks in 1928–32, see Table 12.1.
14. See Carr and Davies, *Foundations*, p. 431.
15. VIZh, 8 (1968) p. 106; the plan was approved on 6 May.
16. See E.H. Carr, *Foundations of a Planned Economy, 1926–1929*, vol. III (London, 1978) pp. 898–900.
17. *KPSS o vooruzhennykh silakh Sovetskogo Soyuza* (Moscow, 1969) pp. 264–6; the resolution is published with some omissions.
18. *50 let Vooruzhennykh sil SSSR* (Moscow, 1968) p. 569 (dated 17 July); the previous five-year plan, of which details have not been available, was approved in 1928.
19. Ibid. p. 569 (decisions of 18 July; on the same day RVS approved decrees on the tank-tractor-armoured car and artillery equipment of the army).
20. See J. Degras (ed.), *Soviet Documents on Foreign Policy*, vol. II (London, 1952), pp. 391–2.
21. Ibid. pp. 393–7; Carr, *Foundations*, vol. III, pp. 908–9.
22. *Pervaya Moskovskaya oblastnaya konferentsiya Vsesoyuznoi kommunisticheskoi partii (bol'shevikov): stenograficheskii otchet*, vol. I (Moscow, 1929) p. 110.
23. Ibid. p. 143; the delegate, Fomin, was described as an ordinary worker.
24. Ibid. pp. 150–1.

25. See Carr, *Foundations*, vol. III, p. 909; the protocol signed between the Chinese and Soviet sides was published in *Pravda*, 23 Dec. 1929.
26. Tukhachevskii, *Izbrannye*, vol. I, p. 12.
27. *Vestnik kommunisticheskoi akademii*, 39 (1930) pp. 202–10.
28. Tukhachevskii, *Izbrannye*, vol. II (1964), pp. 144–6; this attack on A. Verkhovskii, the expert concerned, A. Svechin and V. Melikov was originally published in 1930 as a preface to a translation of the German military historian Delbruck's history of military art.
29. Tukhachevskii, *Izbrannye*, vol. I, p. 12.
30. VIZh, 4 (1967) p. 67; only brief extracts have been made available both of Tukhachevskii's report and of Stalin's reply. In his commentary Marshal S. Birezov approves the spirit of Tukhachevskii's report, but remarks that 'the specific figures need further refinement', frustratingly failing to cite any figures (Tukhachevskii, *Izbrannye*, vol. I, p. 12).
31. Ibid., p. 12; in a letter to Stalin dated 30 Dec. 1930, Tukhachevskii complained that the terms of Stalin's reply had made it impossible for him to raise for discussion various matters concerned with the development of defensive capacity; he had been removed from his responsibilities for the teaching of military strategy in the Military Academy.
32. *Istoriya vtoroi mirovoi voiny*, vol. I (Moscow, 1973) p. 258; no date is given for these guidelines. On 13 June 1930 'RVS USSR approved a corrected plan for the construction of the Red Army' (*50 let*, p. 569); *Istoriya vtoroi mirovoi voiny*, vol. I, p. 258, implies that this plan was based on the new guidelines, but according to V. Kardashov, *Voroshilov* (Moscow, 1976), p. 242, it was based on the more circumspect guidelines of 15 July 1929.
33. *Sbornik postanovlenii i prikazov po promyshlennosti* (VSNKh USSR) (hereafter SP), 1929/30, art. 1478 (dated 6 June) reporting TsIK decree of 2 June.
34. See Carr and Davies, *Foundations*, p. 431 and above.
35. *Izvestiya*, 16 June 1930 (K. Mekhonoshin).
36. *Izvestiya*, 26 June 1930 (S. Ventsov and I. Petukhov).
37. *XVI s"ezd Vsesoyuznoi Kommunisticheskoi partii (b)* (Moscow, 1931) p. 285.
38. Ibid., pp. 506–7; Muklevich was former head of the navy (see Carr, *Foundations*, vol. III, pp. 630–1).
39. *XVI s"ezd*, p. 538.
40. SP, 1929/30, arts. 1673 (dated 17 July), 1734a and 1735 (both dated 28 July); *Sobranie zakonov i rasporyazhenii SSSR* (hereafter SZ) 1930, ii, arts. 160 (dated 16 July), 212 (dated 21 July).
41. *Ekonomicheskaya zhizn'*, 13 Aug. 1930; Zarzar was apparently transferred from the air force to the presidium of Gosplan in 1930 (*Za industrializatsiyu*, 6 Sept. 1933).
42. *Pravda*, 10 Sept. 1930.
43. Cited from the archives in Kardashov, *Voroshilov*, pp. 250–1. The five-year plan adopted in the spring of 1929 allocated 100 million rubles to civil aviation, presumably for aerodromes and other infrastructure (*Pyatiletnii plan narodno-khozyaistvennogo stroitel'stva SSSR*, 3rd. ed., vol. I (Moscow, 1930), p. 68.
44. *Byli industrial'nye: ocherki i vospominaniya* (Moscow, 1970), pp. 109–15 (A.D. Charomskii); for the circumstances leading to Baranov's and Uborevich's telegram, see below. The Aero-Engine Institute was established by a

decision of RVS on 3 Dec. 1930; it was later renamed Central Institute for Aviation Engine Construction (TsIAM) (Ya. Yakovlev, *Sovetskie samolety: kratkii ocherki*, 4th ed. (Moscow, 1982), p. 315.

45. *Pravda*, 20 Oct. 1929; Krzhizhanovskii later reported that ten former generals and 19 former colonels had been found guilty of wrecking in war industry (*Pravda*, 12 Feb. 1930).
46. Ya. Yakovlev, *Tsel´zhizni* (Moscow, 1967) p. 96; B. Gunston, *Aircraft of the Soviet Union* (London, 1983) pp. 89, 238, who claims to have discussed the matter with Tupolev. The Aviarabotnik factory was renamed the 'Menzhinskii' factory after the head of the OGPU.
47. R.A. Lewis, *Science and Industrialisation in the USSR: Industrial Research and Development, 1917–1940* (London, 1979) p. 135; V. Shavrov, *Istoriya konstruktsii samoletov v SSSR do 1938g.*, 2nd ed. (Moscow, 1978) p. 408.
48. Yakovlev, *Tsel´ zhizni*, p. 96.
49. Gunston, *Aircraft*, pp. 89, 238.
50. Yakovlev, *Tsel´ zhizni*, p. 58; it had passed its state tests in 1926.
51. Yakovlev, *Sovetskie samolety*, pp. 20–1, 265, 359–60.
52. See Lewis, *Science and Industrialisation*, p. 135.
53. *Pravda*, 9 Feb. 1933 (A. Gol´tsman).
54. See Table 12.1, and also VIZh, 8 (1968) p. 106.
55. Estimated from data in *Itogi raboty promyshlennosti VSNKh za 1931g. i perspektivy tyazheloi promyshlennosti na 1932g.: materialy k dokladu tov. Ordzhonikidze XVII vsesoyuznoi konferentsii VKP (b)* (Moscow, 1932) pp. 117–9.
56. *Istoriya vtoroi mirovoi voiny*, vol. I, p. 260.

57.

	1927 (Actual)	1928 (Actual)	1928/29 (Plan)	1929 (Actual)	1929/30 (Plan)	1930 (Actual)	1930/31 (Plan)	1931 (Actual)
Passengers (thousand)	7.9	9.5	12.8	12.0	30.0	14.9	51.7	22.6
Freight & posts (tons)	190.0	248.0	340.7	287.6	827.9	339.5	1560.0	669.1
Distance flown (thousand/km)	2044.9	2497.8	4399.9	3561.9	9252.6	4879.4	12 766.5	6144.3

(Plan figures from M. Kokorin, *Oborona SSSR i pyatiletka* (Moscow, 1930), p. 28; actual figures from *SSSR za 15 let* (Moscow, 1932), p. 187; the actual figures are higher than those in *Sotsialisticheskoe stroitel´stvo SSSR: statisticheskii ezhegodnik* (Moscow, 1935) p. 455, which exclude airlines of local significance and flights by the Derulyuft company.)

58. *Za industrializatsiyu*, 21 Feb. 1931 (Kuibyshev).
59. See Tsentral´nyi Gosudarstvennyi Arkhiv Narodnogo Khozyaistva SSSR (hereafter TsGANKh) f. 3429, op. 1, d. 5197, l. 20 (materials to Vesenkha presidium decree of 30 Oct. 1930, on the geological survey of the raw material basis for industry).
60. *Byli industrial´nye*, p. 111; for the Politburo intervention in this matter see above.
61. TsGANKh, f. 3429, op. 1, d. 5195, l. 146 (decree of Vesenkha presidium

dated 29 Oct., no. 1537). The importance of this was stressed by Orzhonikidze at the XVI party congress in June 1930 (*XVI s'ezd*), pp. 309–10.

62. V. Akshinskii, *Kliment Efremovich Voroshilov: biograficheskii ocherk* (Moscow, 1974), pp. 156–7; 2900 tons were received in October, 2900 in November, and 1300 from 1–14 Dec.
63. For the plan, see SZ, 1930, art. 575; for actual production, see *Chernaya metallurgiya, zhelezorudnaya, marganetsevaya i koksovaya promyshlennost' SSSR: statisticheskii sbornik* (Moscow, 1935) p. 62. Artillery works also received iron and steel from their own metallurgical facilities.
64. *50 let*, p. 197.
65. *Istoriya vtoroi mirovoi voiny*, vol. I, p. 258; for the previous guidelines of June 1930 see above.
66. J. Haslam, *Soviet Foreign Policy, 1930–33: the Impact of the Depression* (London, 1983) p. 73; the Japanese ambassador in Moscow sympathised with this approach.
67. US National Archives, State Department files, 861.0/11500, Haslam, *Soviet Foreign Policy*, p. 77.
68. *50 let*, p. 196; Egorov, an old crony of Stalin's on the south-western front at the time of the advance on Warsaw in 1920, replaced Shaposhnikov as Chief of Staff, perhaps in order to act as a counterweight to Tukhachevskii.
69. SP, 1931, art. 416 (dated 3 July); *Za industrializatsiyu*, 6 Sept. 1933; according to a recent Soviet account, this appointment was made after Baranov, following a trip abroad, successfully proposed to the politburo that the Soviet Union should acquire foreign licences and technical assistance for the development of aircraft engines (*Byli industrial'nye*, p. 112; this chapter was written by the aircraft-engine designer A.G. Charomskii).
70. Tukhachevskii's appointment has not been explicitly associated with a change in armaments policy by Soviet military historians; in *Marshal Tukhachevskii: vospominaniya druzei i soratnikov* (Moscow, 1965) pp. 207–8, it is linked to the decision to expand the training of commanders and military engineers.
71. See J.M. Cooper, 'Defence Production and the Soviet Economy, 1929–1941', unpublished *Discussion Papers*, SIPS no. 3 (CREES, University of Birmingham, 1976) p. 13; S.M. Tupper, 'The Red Army and the Soviet Defence Industry, 1934–41' (unpublished PhD, University of Birmingham, 1982), pp. 13–5, 359–60; VIZh, 6 (1968) pp. 106–7. According to J. Milson, *Russian Tanks, 1900–1970* (Harrisburg, Pa., 1971) p. 37, the RVS decided to produce the Vickers and Christie models on 13 Feb. 1931. A special commission headed by Khalepskii, and including Budnyak, which visited the US and UK at the end of 1929 to purchase tank designs, secured permission from the British Board of Trade for the USSR to purchase 15 medium tanks, 26 Carden-Lloyd Mark VI machine-gun carriers, eight Carden-Lloyd amphibious tanks and 15 Vickers-Armstrong six-ton tanks; permission for production on licence was granted for most models (ibid. p. 34).
72. Estimated from data in *Sovetskaya metallurgiya*, 5–6 (1932) pp. 307–8, 310, 312 (I.I. Spivak); defence is listed as 'special requirements'.
73. E.I. Soldatenko, *Ukreplenie oboronosposobnosti SSSR v pervoi pyatiletke* (Khar-

kov, 1957) p. 25; this figure (75 million rubles in 1931) is said to refer to capital investment in the reconstruction of aircraft factories.

74. Soldatenko, *Ukreplenie*, p. 25.
75. Investment in Soyuzverf′ amounted to 30 million rubles against 17.5 million rubles in the whole period before 1931. (*Desyat′ let Sovetskogo sudostroeniya* (Moscow, 1932) p. 40.
76. According to the head of civil aviation, A. Gol′tsman, it increased from 30 million rubles in 1930 to 130 million rubles in 1931 (*Pravda*, 9 Feb. 1933); according to later figures it increased from 35 to 81 million rubles (*Sotsialisticheskoe stroitel′stvo SSSR: statisticheskii ezhegodnik* (Moscow, 1935), pp. 494–7). The plan for 1931 was 150 million rubles (*Za industrializatsiyu*, 21 Feb. 1931).
77. *Za industrializatsiyu*, 21 Feb. 1931 (address to first USSR Conference on Civil Aviation).
78. VIZh, 8 (1968) p. 106.
79. SZ, 1931, art. 501 (dated 28 Dec.); for the 1931 figures, see note below.
80. *Dokumenty vneshnei politiki SSSR*, vol. XIV (Moscow, 1968) p. 281; Litvinov's table included the following headings: pay; maintenance of personnel; animals, harness and fodder; fuel, transport, etc.; construction of barracks, etc.; defence construction; military property.
81. *2 sessiya Tsentral′nogo Ispolnitel′nogo Komiteta Soyuza SSR, 6 sozyva* (1931), Bull. 12, pp. 4–5 (Balakhnin).
82. Ibid., pp. 26–9.
83. Ibid., Bull. 15, pp. 10–11. At the session the expected expenditure figure for 1931 was given as 1131.9 million rubles, and Grin′ko was therefore able to claim that expenditure in 1932, at 1278.5 million rubles, was budgeted to increase by 13 per cent (*ibid.*, Bull. 10, p. 33, Bull. 15, p. 10). But the final figure for 1931 was 1288.4 million rubles (SZ, 1933, art. 40, dated 31 Jan. 1933).
84. *Istoriya vtoroi mirovoi voiny*, vol. I, pp. 277–8.
85. Yakovlev, *Sovetskie samolety*, p. 315.
86. See Haslam, *Soviet Foreign Policy*, p. 80.
87. *XVII konferentsiya VKP (b): stenograficheskii otchet* (1932) p. 156.
88. *Za industrializatsiyu*, 23 Feb. 1932.
89. *Pravda*, 22 Jan. 1933; a few months later Ordzhonikidze spoke of the urgent production of larger quantities of aircraft, and of large-capacity aero-engines and tanks, which had taken place in 1932 (G.K. Ordzhonikidze, *Stat′i i rechi*, vol. II (Moscow, 1957) pp. 498–9).
90. I.V. Stalin, *Sochineniya*, vol. XII (Moscow, 1951) p. 1980 (report of 7 Jan.).
91. *Industrializatsiya SSSR, 1929–1932 gg.: dokumenty i materialy* (Moscow, 1971) p. 608 (decision of 12 Jan.).
92. S. Kostyuchenko et. al. *Istoriya Kirovskogo zavoda, 1917–1945* (Moscow, 1966) pp. 388–92. The new shop was built following a Narkomtyazhprom order of 7 March 1932: the factory asked for 700 million rubles for the conversion, but Ordzhonikidze pointed out that a new tank factory could be built for the same amount of money. The Putilov factory was later responsible for producing the KV heavy tank.
93. See Cooper, 'Defence Production', p. 13; A.C. Sutton, *Western Technology*

and Soviet Economic Development, 1930–1945 (Stanford, 1971) p. 241.

94. *Skvoz'ognennye gody* (Kharkov, 1966) pp. 107–29; *Istoriya Khar'kovskogo traktornogo zavoda im. Ordzhonikidze*, vol. I (Kharkov, 1960), p. 173. The factory became a major centre of the tank industry, and its design team was responsible for the T-34, a major Soviet tank in the Second World War.
95. Haslam, *Soviet Foreign Policy*, p. 84, citing Strang's despatch to Simon (Foreign Secretary).
96. *Pravda*, 23 Feb. 1932.
97. A.P. Romanov, *Raketom pokoryaetsya prostranstvo* (Moscow, 1976) pp. 35–6, 39; the unified rocket research institute was established in October 1933. For account of rocket research in 1931–3, see P.T. Astashenkov, *Akademik S.P. Korolev* (Moscow, 1969) pp. 42–67.
98. Kostiuchenko *et al.*, *Istoriya Kirovskogo*, pp. 391–2.
99. *Direktor I.A. Likhachev* (Moscow, 1971) p. 10.
100. TsGANKh f. 7622, op. l, d. 1076, 11. 276–7; this was followed by a decree of STO (see TsGANKh f. 7620, op. l, d. 133, 1.83, not precisely dated). The report (see G. Hilger, *The Incompatible Allies* (New York, 1953) p. 246) that a special shop for manufacturing tanks was already under construction at the Stalingrad factory in 1932 does not seem to be correct.
101. See the discussion reported in TsGANKh, f. 7620, op. l, d. 133, *passim*.
102. See Haslam, *Soviet Foreign Policy*, pp. 72–3.
103. Unpelev, *Zavershenie sotsialisticheskoi rekonstruktsii promyshlennosti Dal'nego Vostoka (1933–1937gg)* (Vladivostok, 1975) p. 197.
104. Yu. [G.A.] Zhukov, *Lyudi 30-kh godov* (Moscow, 1966) p. 228; 'the devil himself couldn't get here', Gamarnik remarked.
105. Zhukov, *Lyudi*, p. 228; only a minority withstood the harsh conditions – the number working there fell to 1300 by October 1932 (*Pozyvnye istorii*, vol. II (Moscow, 1970) p. 331 (E. Dorodnov). For a dramatic description of the first settlers' seven-day journey from Khabarovsk to the site through river and storm, see *Stroiteli trekh gorodov* (Khabarovsk, 1967) pp. 23–7.
106. *Voprosy istorii*, 8 (1982) pp. 8, 85–8; *Stroiteli trekh gorodov*, p. 39. In May 1932, Narkomtyazhprom appointed Ivanov, former head of the Stalingrad tractor factory, as its plenipotentiary and Kattel' as head of the project (ibid. 36).
107. *Dokumenty vneshnei politiki SSSR*, vol XV (Moscow, 1969) pp. 447–8 (despatch of 2 Aug.).
108. Ibid. xv, p. 464 (despatch of 11 Aug.).
109. Ibid., xv, p. 791 (despatch from Bogomolov of August 19); Anthony Eden's alleged reply, 'not at the present stage', could hardly have been lukewarm comfort to the Soviet authorities.
110. For the 1933 figure, see *Voprosy istorii KPSS*, no. 11, 1978, p. 82.
111. See Tupper 'The Red Army', ch. 2, which concludes that in 1934 'no other army could match these stock figures'.
112. *XVII s'ezd VKP (b): stenograficheskii otchet* (Moscow, 1934) pp. 224–32.
113. See Davies, 'A Note on the Ural-kuznetsk Combine', pp. 272–4.
114. On the deterioration of the comparative Soviet position by 1937, see Tupper, 'The Red Army', ch. 5.

Bibliography of Olga Crisp's Publications

We have endeavoured to list all Olga Crisp's publications, with the exception of the short reviews.

I BOOKS

Studies in the Russian Economy Before 1914 (London, Macmillan, 1976).

Civil Rights in Imperial Russia, co-edited with Linda Edmondson (Oxford, Oxford University Press, 1989).

II CONTRIBUTIONS TO BOOKS

'Russia, 1860–1914', in Rondo Cameron (ed.) *Banking in the Early Stages of Industrialization* (Oxford, Oxford University Press, 1967) pp. 183–249.

'Tugan-Baranovskii, Mikhail (1865–1919)', in David L. Sills (ed.) *International Encyclopedia of Social Sciences*, vol. XVI (New York and London, Macmillan and The Free Press, 1968) pp. 164–7.

'The Pattern of Russia's Industrialization up to 1914', in P. Léon, F. Crouzet, and R. Gascon (eds) *L'Industrialisation en Europe au XIXe siècle* (Paris, Centre National de la Recherche Scientifique, 1972) pp. 435–70.

'Sergei Witte, 1849–1915', in F. Crouzet (ed.) *Les Hommes d'Etat Célèbres*, vol. V (Paris, Editions d'Art, Lucien Mazenod, 1975).

'Russian Public Funds in France', in Maurice Lévy-Leboyer (ed.) *International Capital in France* (Paris, Ecole des Hautes Etudes en Sciences Sociales, 1978) pp. 263–74.

'Labour and Industrialization in Russia', in P. Mathias and M.M. Postan (eds) *The Cambridge Economic History of Europe*, vol. VII, part 2, (Cambridge, Cambridge University Press, 1978) pp. 308–415.

'Horses and Management of a Large Agricultural Estate in Russia at the End of the Nineteenth Century', in F.M.L. Thompson (ed.) *Horses in European Economic History: A Preliminary Canter* (Reading, British Agricultural Society, University of Reading, 1983) pp. 156–76.

'L'industrializzazione europea. Rivalutazione del caso russo', in D.S. Landes, Peter Mathias, Giorgio Mori, D.C. North et al. (eds) *Rivoluzione industriale tra il settecento e l'ottocento* (Milan, Arnoldo Mondadori Editore, 1984). This was also published in Spanish as P. Mathias et al. (eds) *La revolucion industrial* (Barcelona, Editorial Critica, 1988.

'Peasant Land Tenure and Civil Rights Implications before 1906', in Olga Crisp and Linda Edmondson (eds) *Civil Rights in Imperial Russia* (Oxford, Oxford University Press, 1989) pp. 33–64.

'French Investment in Russian Joint-Stock Companies, 1894–1914', reprinted in R.P.T. Davenport-Heines (ed.) *Capital, Entrepreneurs and Profits* (London, Frank Cass, 1990).

'Russia', in Richard Sylla and Gianni Toniolo (eds.) *Patterns of European Industrialization. The Nineteenth Century* (London and New York, Routledge, 1991).

III ARTICLES

These do not include those which were later selected for publication in the volume *Studies in the Russian Economy.*

'The Russian Liberals and the 1906 Anglo-French Loan to Russia', *Slavonic and East European Review*, XXXIX (1961) pp. 497–511.

'Making Karl Marx a Farmer's Son', *The Statist*, 27 March 1964.

'The Russo-Chinese Bank. An Episode in Franco-Russian Relations', *Slavonic and East European Review*, LII (1974) pp. 197–212.

IV LONG REVIEWS

Roger Portal, *L'Oural au XVIIIe siècle. Etude d'histoire économique* (Paris, 1950). Reviewed in *Slavonic and East European Review*, XXX (1952) pp. 304–11.

Jerome Blum, *Lord and Peasant in Russia from the Ninth to the Nineteenth Century* (Princeton and London, 1962). Reviewed in *Slavonic and East European Review*, XLI (1962–3) pp. 559–61.

Theodore von Laue, *Sergei Witte and the Industrialization of Russia* (New York, 1963). Reviewed in *Soviet Studies*, XVI (1964–5) pp. 90–4.

Michael Confino, *Domaines et seigneurs en Russie vers la fin du XVIIIe siècle* (Paris, 1963). Reviewed in *Slavic Review*, XXV, 4 (1966) pp. 692–6.

J.P. McKay, *Pioneers for Profit: Foreign Entrepreneurship and Russian Industrialization, 1885–1914* (Chicago, 1970). Reviewed in *Soviet Studies*, XXIV (1972–3) pp. 152–8.

Daniel Field, *The End of Serfdom. Nobility and Bureaucracy in Russia, 1855–1861* (Cambridge, Mass., 1976) and *Rebels in the Name of the Tsar* (Boston, 1976). Reviewed in *English Historical Review*, XCIII (1978) pp. 413–17.

Index

Entries are arranged in letter-by-letter order. Location references to figures and tables are given in italics.